ESSENTIALS OF
CANADIAN LAW

THE *CHARTER* *OF RIGHTS* *AND FREEDOMS*

ROBERT J. SHARPE
and
KATHERINE E. SWINTON

IRWIN
LAW

THE *CHARTER OF RIGHTS AND FREEDOMS*
© Robert J. Sharpe and Katherine E. Swinton

Published in 1998 by
Irwin Law
325 Humber College Blvd.
Toronto, Ontario
M9W 7C3

ISBN: 1-55221-015-4

Canadian Cataloguing in Publication Data

Sharpe, Robert J.
    The Charter of Rights and Freedoms

(Essentials of Canadian law)
Includes bibliographical references and index.
ISBN 1-55221-015-4

1. Canada. Canadian Charter of Rights and Freedoms.   2. Civil rights — Canada.
I. Swinton, Katherine.   II. Title.   III. Series.

KE4381.5.S52 1998   342.71′085   C98-930582-1
KF4483.C519S52 1998

Printed and bound in Canada.

1   2   3   4   5   02   01   00   99   98

To The Right Honourable Brian Dickson

SUMMARY
TABLE OF CONTENTS

DETAILED
TABLE OF CONTENTS

CHAPTER 14:
CHARTER RIGHTS IN THE CRIMINAL PROCESS   *152*

FOREWORD

Because only some sixteen years have passed since the introduction of the *Charter of Rights and Freedoms*, it is impossible to measure its full impact on Canadian society. But even with such a short history, one can confidently say that it is difficult to find anything of comparable importance to the administration of law and justice in Canada since the beginning of our country. Consequently, a book dedicated to furthering the understanding of the *Charter* is welcome; one that is of the nature and quality of this volume is especially so.

In this connection, the book reflects the impressive experience, scholarship, and talents of the authors. Both Madame Justice Swinton and Mr. Justice Sharpe are distinguished former academics who taught *Charter*-related subjects for many years. Both wrote extensively in the areas covered by the book and were widely sought for their opinions on *Charter* topics. Their involvement with constitutional issues from a practical as well as an academic viewpoint resulted in their gaining a unique perspective — teacher, scholar, practitioner — on a variety of these issues. That they now can add their experience as judges to this perspective enhances even more an otherwise outstanding set of credentials, all of which combine to create a high expectation for their book. In my view, the reader will indeed not be disappointed because Justices Swinton and Sharpe have made an excellent contribution to the field.

To elaborate, their writing is incisive yet lucid, comprehensive yet succinct, expository yet analytical. Their references to other readings are a helpful tool for the non-specialist to whom the authors aim their explanations of the *Charter*, its interpretation by the courts, and its practical application. An additional tool for the non-specialist is the glossary provided at the end of the book. However, I must say that I believe the authors are too modest when they state their goals for readership of their book. There is no doubt that non-specialists will find the book most useful, but I am sure specialists will as well.

I congratulate Justices Sharpe and Swinton for a most successful book; and, because the *Charter* is something of a moving target, I look forward to future editions.

THE HONOURABLE MR. JUSTICE FRANK IACOBUCCI
SUPREME COURT OF CANADA

PREFACE

This project began when the authors were both professors of Constitutional Law at the Faculty of Law, University of Toronto. We are grateful for the excellent research assistance provided by three students at the Faculty of Law: Jacqueline Code, Marie Irvine, and Marko Vesely.

David Schneiderman, Director of the Centre for Constitutional Studies at the Faculty of Law, University of Alberta, was an anonymous reviewer of the manuscript, whose identity we have since learned. We are grateful for his careful reading of the manuscript and his many thoughtful suggestions.

We also express our appreciation to the editors at Irwin Law for their assistance in the final stages of preparation. Finally, we thank William Kaplan for his ongoing patience and faith in our ability to complete the project.

INTRODUCTION

The amendment of the Canadian constitution in 1982 to include the *Charter of Rights and Freedoms* brought about a fundamental change in Canadian law and politics.[1] The *Charter* significantly increased the law-making power of Canadian courts. Decisions on many important public issues, formerly within the exclusive authority of Parliament and the provincial legislatures, are now subject to judicial review. *Charter* litigation has become an important tool used by interest groups to advance their political ends. Canadian courts now play a central role in deciding how the law should deal with such intractable issues as abortion,[2] mandatory retirement,[3] the legitimacy of laws restricting pornography[4] and hate propaganda,[5] and the definition of what may properly constitute a criminal offence.[6]

The *Charter* has unquestionably had a profound impact upon the role of the judiciary. The courts are now empowered to deal with issues that range far beyond what was seen as appropriate to the judicial function before 1982. In the pre-1982 era, to most Canadians the Supreme Court of Canada was a remote institution that had little, if any, real impact

---

1   *Canadian Charter of Rights and Freedoms*, Part I of the *Constitution Act, 1982*, being Schedule B to the *Canada Act 1982*, (U.K.), 1982, c. 11 [*Charter*].
2   *R. v. Morgentaler*, [1988] 1 S.C.R. 30, 44 D.L.R. (4th) 385.
3   *McKinney v. University of Guelph*, [1990] 3 S.C.R. 229, 76 D.L.R. (4th) 545; *Stoffman v. Vancouver General Hospital*, [1990] 3 S.C.R. 483, 76 D.L.R. (4th) 700.
4   *R. v. Butler*, [1992] 1 S.C.R. 452, 70 C.C.C. (3d) 129.
5   *R. v. Keegstra*, [1990] 3 S.C.R. 697, 61 C.C.C. (3d) 1.
6   *R. v. Vaillancourt*, [1987] 2 S.C.R. 636, 47 D.L.R. (4th) 399.

upon their lives. Since entrenchment, however, the Supreme Court has been recognized by the Canadian public as a seat of great power and influence. It has become the institution to which citizens may turn for protection of their fundamental rights and freedoms.

Media attention to legal issues has increased significantly, which is undoubtedly attributable in large part to the *Charter*. Decisions of the courts are routinely front-page news. The Supreme Court of Canada has developed a media-relations policy to ensure that its judgments are adequately reported, and the Canadian Judicial Council has suggested that provincial superior and appellate courts do the same.[7] Some judges have taken the view that they should become more visible and vocal. Interviews and profiles of judges in the daily news media are not uncommon as reporters try to demystify the judicial process and explain it in terms the ordinary citizen can understand. Judges contribute to scholarly journals, discussing their changed role under the *Charter*.[8]

This book attempts to explain the *Charter of Rights and Freedoms* to non-specialist readers interested in acquiring a basic understanding of the Canadian legal system and the Canadian constitution. We will survey the manner in which the Canadian courts have come to terms with a constitutionally entrenched bill of rights, focusing on the decisions of the Supreme Court of Canada. The purpose is to explain the *Charter*, its interpretation by the courts, and its practical application, rather than to present anything approaching a theoretical or philosophical account of *Charter* rights. It is, however, almost impossible to discuss the *Charter* without a theoretical framework. As will become apparent, we are believers in the *Charter* and in the important role it confers upon the courts. In our view, the courts are properly charged with the task of defining and protecting fundamental rights and freedoms in a modern liberal democracy. Furthermore, the Canadian experience to date suggests that an entrenched bill of rights enhances rather than detracts from fundamental democratic values.[9]

---

7   See R.J. Sharpe, "The Role of a Media Spokesperson for the Courts — The Supreme Court of Canada Experience" (1991) 1 Media & Comm. L. Rev. 271.

8   Justice Beverley McLachlin, a former academic, has been particularly active in this regard. See the following by B.M. McLachlin: "The Role of the Court in the Post-*Charter* Era: Policy-Maker or Adjudicator?" (1990) 39 U.N.B.L.J. 43; "The *Charter* of Rights and Freedoms: A Judicial Perspective" (1989) 23 U.B.C. L. Rev. 579; "The *Charter*: A New Role for the Judiciary" (1991) 29 Alta. L. Rev. 540; "The Canadian *Charter* and the Democratic Process" (1991) 18 Melb. U. L. Rev. 350.

9   Further discussion is found in R.J. Sharpe, "Judicial Development of Principles in Applying the *Charter*" in N.R. Finkelstein & B.M. Rogers, eds., *Charter Issues in Civil Cases* (Toronto: Carswell, 1988) c. 1; R.J. Sharpe, "A Comment on David Beatty's 'A Conservative's Court: The Politicization of Law'" (1991) 41 U.T.L.J. 469.

CHAPTER 1

HISTORICAL CONTEXT

A. THE PRE-1982 CANADIAN CONSTITUTION

The *Charter of Rights and Freedoms* should be seen as one element in Canada's evolving constitution. While the *Charter* now occupies centre stage and has become the focus of public attention, its enactment in 1982 did not mark the beginning of rights protection in Canadian law. This introductory chapter will attempt to place the *Charter* in its proper constitutional context and will provide a brief survey of the protection of fundamental rights and freedoms in Canadian law before 1982.

Canada's primary constitutional document, the *British North America Act, 1867* (renamed the *Constitution Act, 1867* in 1982) contained two major features: a parliamentary system of government and federalism.

1) Parliamentary Supremacy

The first feature of our pre-1982 constitution was a parliamentary system of government modelled upon the principles of British parliamentary democracy. The preamble to the *Constitution Act, 1867*, states that Canada is to have "a Constitution similar in Principle to that of the United Kingdom." Apart from this very general reference, the basic principles of British constitutionalism are not spelled out in the written constitution. They are to be found in conventions, traditions, and practices that evolved over time and that continue to govern the structure of Canadian government.

The central concept of the British constitution is the supremacy of Parliament. The elected representatives of the people, assembled in

Parliament, have unlimited power to make the law. The role of the courts is limited to deciding cases by interpreting the law as laid down by Parliament or as defined by the common law. In particular, judges do not have the authority to invalidate laws that have been duly enacted through the democratic process of Parliament. The one thing — perhaps the only thing — Parliament cannot do is to bind its successors. Whatever one Parliament has laid down as the law can be changed by the next.

The fundamental rights and freedoms of a liberal democracy (that is, freedom of expression, religion, association, and assembly) as well as basic legal rights (fair trial, freedom from arbitrary arrest, the presumption of innocence, and right to a jury trial) are, however, very much a part of our British parliamentary heritage. That tradition clearly recognizes and respects the importance of fundamental rights and freedoms but holds that Parliament is the proper institution to decide upon their meaning and scope. Courts are entitled to take these principles into account when deciding cases and interpreting statutes, particularly where there is any ambiguity in the law, but the primary and final responsibility for achieving an appropriate balance between the rights of the individual and the general public interest remains with the elected representatives of the people sitting in Parliament.

Until 1982, the Canadian approach to the protection of fundamental rights and freedoms was strongly influenced by the principle of the supremacy of Parliament. As will be seen shortly, Canadian courts did exercise the power of judicial review in some cases to protect fundamental rights, but these cases were really exceptions rather than the rule. Canada's written constitution offered relatively little by way of rights protection until 1982.

2) Federalism

The second fundamental element of the Canadian constitution is federalism, that is, the division of legislative powers between the Parliament of Canada and the ten provincial legislatures. This division of powers is contained in Canada's original constitution, the *Constitution Act, 1867*. Canada is geographically, culturally, and linguistically diverse. The division of legislative power between a central national Parliament and ten provincial legislatures, defining the areas in which each level of government is entitled to act, represents an attempt to accommodate that diversity.

The federal structure itself contains a form of rights protection. When an ethnic or religious minority is concentrated in a geographical area, the grant of state or provincial status ensures a measure of self-government for that minority, especially if it constitutes a majority within that unit. Self-government allows the group to adopt laws that are informed by its distinctive culture or language. One of the reasons for adopting a federal state in Canada was to provide a measure of self-government for French Canadians who were and continue to be a majority in the province of Quebec.

While Canada's pre-1982 written constitution was silent on the power of judicial review, from the early years of Confederation, Canadian courts routinely acted as the referee in deciding whether legislative matters fell within federal or provincial jurisdiction, and they have invalidated those laws enacted without a proper constitutional basis. In this respect, the Canadian constitution has, almost from the very beginning, departed in one respect from the fundamental principle of parliamentary supremacy. Canadian judges have exercised the power of judicial review for over one hundred years, striking down a significant number of statutes, both federal and provincial, on the ground that the law fell outside the authority assigned to the enacting body by the constitution.

The division of powers between the federal Parliament and the provincial legislatures and the role played by the courts in resolving jurisdictional conflicts is a complex subject that is dealt with in another volume in this series. It is, however, appropriate here briefly to consider the manner in which the pre-*Charter* constitution protected certain fundamental rights.

B. RIGHTS PROTECTION THROUGH COMMON LAW AND STATUTORY INTERPRETATION

The legal protection of fundamental rights and freedoms does not rest entirely upon the explicit provisions of the constitution nor upon the *Charter of Rights and Freedoms*. Concern for civil liberties has always been an important feature of Canadian law. Throughout our history, judicial decisions have played an important role in the protection of fundamental rights,[1] and while Parliament may be supreme, our political culture has demanded that it pay heed to the basic rights of all citizens.

Most of our most important civil rights, such as *habeas corpus*, trial by jury, and the presumption of innocence, were creations of the common law. These rights are founded upon judicial decisions extending far

---

1 See B. Laskin, "An Inquiry into the Diefenbaker *Bill of Rights*" (1959) 37 Can. Bar Rev. 77.

back in the Anglo-American legal tradition. They are judge-made rights, often supplemented or bolstered by statutes, which formed an essential aspect of our legal system long before 1982 and the *Charter*.

Another important part of our legal tradition has been judicial review of administrative action. Judicial commitment to the rule of law has resulted in the nullification of decisions by officials or administrative tribunals when they have acted without jurisdiction, while the rules of natural justice have ensured fairness in administrative procedures.[2]

In addition, in the interest of protecting liberal values, courts have imported certain presumptions when interpreting statutes.[3] For example, it is presumed that the state would not expropriate property without compensation. If property is taken, compensation must be given absent a clear signal from a legislature that it does not intend to provide it.

Other rights and freedoms now enshrined in the *Charter* never crystallized as specific rights in the common law but did have force as basic principles that underlay the whole structure of the law, informing both political debate in Parliament and legal decision making in the courts. As the Supreme Court of Canada has said, rights and freedoms did not spring from a vacuum in 1982.[4] Freedom of expression and religion, for example, were well-known and well-respected principles of the Canadian constitution. These values were sometimes embodied in statutes to extend protection in specified circumstances.[5] They were vitally important principles that the courts drew upon when interpreting and applying statutes or developing the common law. A leading example is the decision of the 1951 Supreme Court of Canada in *Boucher* v. *R.*,[6] where a Jehovah's Witness was charged with seditious libel because of a pamphlet that he distributed. The Supreme Court of Canada ordered a new trial because the trial judge had virtually ignored a defence of speaking in good faith.

---

2   See, for example, *Roncarelli* v. *Duplessis* (1958), [1959] S.C.R. 121, 16 D.L.R. (2d) 689.

3   See J. Willis, "Statutory Interpretation in a Nutshell" (1938) 16 Can. Bar Rev. 1.

4   See, for example, *R.* v. *Big M Drug Mart Ltd.*, [1985] 1 S.C.R. 295, 18 D.L.R. (4th) 321; *Reference Re Provincial Electoral Boundaries (Saskatchewan)*, [1991] 2 S.C.R. 158, 81 D.L.R. (4th) 16.

5   *Freedom of Worship Act*, (1850–51), 14 & 15 Vict., c. 175; *Constitution Act, 1867*, s. 93.

6   *Boucher* v. *R.*, [1951] S.C.R. 265, [1951] 2 D.L.R. 369.

C. THE *CONSTITUTION ACT, 1867*, AND THE PROTECTION OF FUNDAMENTAL RIGHTS

While the scope for judicial review under the 1867 constitution was essentially limited to questions of legislative jurisdiction as between the provinces and the federal Parliament, the courts did establish an element of rights protection through judicial review.

First, the *Constitution Act, 1867*, contains certain specific minority rights enforceable through the courts. The right to use English and French in Parliament, in the legislature of Quebec, and in the courts established by the federal Parliament (that is, the Supreme Court of Canada, the Federal Court, and the Tax Court) and by the province of Quebec is guaranteed by section 133.[7] Minority-religion education rights were secured for the Roman Catholic minority in Ontario and the Protestant minority in Quebec by section 93, and similar rights were accorded by the terms admitting some new provinces after 1867. Provisions relating to the appointment and tenure of judges (sections 96–100) have been interpreted to guarantee an independent judiciary and to secure the role of the courts as overseers of the legality of administrative and executive action. Although probably not judicially enforceable, the 1867 constitution also secures certain democratic rights relating to the length (section 50) and regularity (section 20) of sessions of Parliament.[8] As noted above, federalism itself may be seen as a form of minority-rights protection, particularly in the case of Quebec and the preservation of French language and culture and the civil law tradition.

Second, despite the limited nature of explicit rights protection under the 1867 constitution, civil liberties were protected in a number of cases through federalism review. The Supreme Court of Canada found that certain laws that limited fundamental rights could be attacked in the courts on the ground that authority to enact the law fell outside the scope of the powers accorded the enacting provincial legislature by the *Constitution Act, 1867*.

Perhaps the most notable example was the 1938 decision, *Reference Re Alberta Legislation*,[9] striking down Alberta legislation that interfered with the right of newspapers to report freely on the economic policies

---

7   Similar rights with respect to the legislature and courts of Manitoba were specified in the *Manitoba Act, 1870*, and language rights have been expanded under the *Charter*: see below, chapter 16.

8   Section 20 was repealed by the *Charter* in 1982. For further discussion of democratic rights, see chapter 8, "Freedom of Conscience and Religion."

9   [1938] S.C.R. 100, [1938] 2 D.L.R. 81 [*Alberta Press*].

of the government. The law at issue was part of the package of measures put forth by the newly elected Social Credit government, which asserted that its economic and monetary policies would be effective only if media coverage was "accurate." While provinces normally have extensive authority to regulate businesses operating within the province, the Supreme Court of Canada held that the Alberta legislature lacked the legislative authority to enact a law that struck at the very foundation of our parliamentary democracy. Although freedom of expression and freedom of the press were not specifically protected by the constitution, the Court found that the right of every citizen to criticize government was a necessary and inherent element of Canada's constitution, and beyond the reach of a provincial legislature. Cannon J. reasoned as follows:

> Freedom of discussion is essential to enlighten public opinion in a democratic State; it cannot be curtailed without affecting the right of the people to be informed through sources independent of the Government concerning matters of public interest. There must be an untrammelled publication of the news and political opinions of the political parties contending for ascendancy. As stated in the preamble of the *British North America Act* [now the *Constitution Act, 1867*], our constitution is and will remain, unless radically changed, "similar in principle to that of the United Kingdom." At the time of Confederation, the United Kingdom was a democracy. Democracy cannot be maintained without its foundation: free public opinion and free discussion throughout the nation of all matters affecting the State within the limits set by the Criminal Code and the common law.[10]

Fifteen years later, in *Saumur* v. *Quebec (City)*,[11] the Supreme Court of Canada returned to the theme of the inherent rights of citizenship in a democracy, striking down a municipal bylaw that forbade the distribution of pamphlets without the permission of the chief of police. The action challenging the validity of the bylaw was brought by a member of the Jehovah's Witnesses. By a majority, the Court held that the bylaw was invalid. While the judges offered various reasons, Rand J., one of the majority of the Court which found in Saumur's favour, held that the effect of this measure was to confer on the police an unacceptably open-ended discretion amounting to a power of censorship. Like Cannon J. in the *Alberta Press* case, Rand J. drew upon the rights of citizenship inherent in democratic government to determine that the action was beyond the power of the provinces or the municipalities. He stated:

---

10   *Ibid.* at 145–46 (S.C.R.).
11   [1953] 2 S.C.R. 299, [1953] 4 D.L.R. 641.

[F]reedom of speech, religion and the inviolability of the person, are original freedoms which are at once the necessary attributes and modes of self-expression of human beings and the primary conditions of their community life within a legal order . . . The Confederation Act recites the desire of the three Provinces to be federally united in one Dominion "with a constitution similar in principle to that of the United Kingdom." Under that constitution, Government is by parliamentary institutions, including popular assemblies elected by the people at large in both Provinces and Dominion: Government resting ultimately on public opinion reached by discussion and the interplay of ideas. If that discussion is placed under licence, its basic condition is destroyed: the Government, as licensor, becomes disjoined from the citizenry.[12]

Four years later, in *Switzman* v. *Elbling*,[13] another case from Quebec, the Supreme Court again adverted to the inherent rights of the citizen and the necessary conditions fundamental to democracy. At issue was the provincial "Padlock Act" which made it illegal for anyone to make use of a house for the propagation of communism or bolshevism. Rand J. again made an eloquent appeal to the fundamental rights of citizens in a democracy in finding the law beyond the powers of the provincial legislature:

Parliamentary Government postulates a capacity in men, acting freely and under self-restraints, to govern themselves; and that advance is best served in the degree achieved of individual liberation from subjective as well as objective shackles. Under that Government, the freedom of discussion in Canada, as a subject-matter of legislation, has a unity of interest and significance extending equally to every part of the Dominion . . . This constitutional fact is the political expression of the primary condition of social life, thought and its communication by language. Liberty in this is little less vital to man's mind and spirit than breathing is to his physical existence. As such an inherence in the individual is embodied in his status of citizenship.[14]

These judicial pronouncements are significant. They identify a rationale for judicial review grounded in the principles of democracy so powerful that it can be exercised in the absence of an explicit bill of rights. Thus, even before the *Charter of Rights,* the courts were able to justify interference with legislative choices that were themselves inimical to the principles of democratic government.

---

12   *Ibid.* at 329–30 (S.C.R.).
13   [1957] S.C.R. 285, 7 D.L.R. (2d) 337.
14   *Ibid.* at 358 (D.L.R.).

It has to be recognized, however, that the success of pre-*Charter* rights protection was limited. As noted, the cases and individual opinions referred to stand out as exceptions to the norm. More often, judges were unwilling to challenge the traditional conception of a strictly limited judicial role. Moreover, the cases cited all dealt with challenges to provincial authority, and the suggestion that there was an "unwritten bill of rights" in the 1867 constitution protecting fundamental freedoms from both levels of government garnered little support.[15] Constitutional protection of rights and freedoms based upon the division of powers between the federal and provincial governments, while significant in certain specific instances, was necessarily limited and subordinate to the basic rule of the pre-1982 approach to the protection of rights, namely, parliamentary supremacy. While the courts were prepared to protect fundamental democratic rights from provincial invasion, the general rule was that if the elected representatives of the people decided that the public interest required a law curtailing an individual right, there was little the courts could do.

D. THE *CONSTITUTION ACT, 1867,* AND PROTECTION AGAINST DISCRIMINATION

Another significant limitation of pre-*Charter* rights protection was the failure of the courts (and indeed, until the advent of human rights codes, discussed below, of the entire legal system) to protect minorities from discrimination. A series of cases coming before the Supreme Court and the Judicial Committee of the Privy Council (then Canada's court of last resort) dealt with challenges to overtly racist legislation.[16] It was argued that the federal power with respect to "naturalization and

---

15   See the opinion of Abbott J. in *Switzman* v. *Elbling*, above note 13 at 371 (D.L.R.). For a post-*Charter* affirmation of this principle, see *O.P.S.E.U.* v. *Ontario (A.G.)*, [1987] 2 S.C.R. 2, 41 D.L.R. (4th) 1, Beetz J.; *Reference Re Public Sector Pay Reduction Act (P.E.I.), s. 10* (1997), 150 D.L.R. (4th) 577 at 623–28 (S.C.C.).

16   The discussion that follows is an abbreviated version of the first part of R.J. Sharpe, "Citizenship, the *Constitution Act, 1867,* and the *Charter*" in W. Kaplan, ed., *Belonging: The Meaning and Future of Canadian Citizenship* (Montreal: McGill-Queen's University Press, 1993) at 221. For further discussion, see B. Ryder, "Racism and the Constitution: The Constitutional Fate of British Columbia Anti-Asian Legislation, 1884–1909" (1991) 29 Osgoode Hall L.J. 619; J. St-G. Walker, "*Race*," *Rights and the Law of the Supreme Court of Canada* (Waterloo, ON: Wilfrid Laurier University Press, 1997).

aliens" in section 91(25) and Parliament's residual power to ensure "peace, order and good government" under section 91 included authority to ensure the enjoyment of ordinary legal rights without discrimination on the basis of race and national origin. These challenges proved unsuccessful.

Union Colliery Co. of British Columbia Ltd. v. *Bryden*,[17] the first case to raise these issues at the highest level, involved a challenge to British Columbia legislation forbidding the employment of "Chinamen" below ground in a coal mine. The prohibition was but one of a shockingly long list of legislative measures introduced in British Columbia attempting to prevent or restrict the settlement of Chinese immigrants in the province. The province asserted that the law was designed to ensure safety in the mines. The Privy Council rejected this characterization of the law and found that the law was unconstitutional: "[T]he whole pith and substance of the enactments . . . consists in establishing a statutory prohibition which affects aliens or naturalized subjects, and therefore trench upon the exclusive authority of the Parliament of Canada."[18] Although written in a formalistic style, with virtually no explicit appeal to the concept of equality, the Privy Council's opinion in *Bryden* gave some hope that despite the absence of any explicit anti-discrimination provision in the constitution, the courts might be prepared to protect racial minorities on the basis of the division of powers. The opinion provided a possible ground for the elaboration of an important branch of federal legislative power to ensure the rights and privileges attached to Canadian citizenship.

That hope proved short-lived. Shortly after *Bryden*, a naturalized Japanese resident of British Columbia challenged the constitutional validity of the province's electoral law, which denied the vote to all those of Japanese descent, whether naturalized or not. The plaintiff, Tomey Homma, relied upon the expansive definition of the Dominion's power over naturalization in *Bryden* and upon the specific terms of the *Naturalization Act* of Canada, which provided that a naturalized alien was entitled to all political and other rights, powers, and privileges to which a natural-born British subject is entitled in Canada.[19] The province contended that section 92(1) of the *Constitution Act, 1867,* granting the power to legislate with respect to the constitution of the province, authorized it to decide which British subjects residing in the province should enjoy the franchise. The franchise was considered a privilege

17 [1899] A.C. 580, 68 L.J.P.C. 118, 81 L.T. 277 (P.C.) [*Bryden*].
18 *Ibid.* at 587.
19 R.S.C. 1886, c. 113, s. 15.

conferred by legislation rather than a right. Many subjects — women, those under the voting age, and certain office holders — did not have the vote. Tomey Homma succeeded in the British Columbia courts but the case was appealed to the Privy Council.[20] There, *Bryden* was abandoned and in its place was adopted an analysis which emphasized, to the exclusion of other values, the protection of provincial legislative authority. The franchise was seen as a privilege the province was entitled to grant or withhold as it saw fit. The constitution's grant of federal power was said to be too narrow to preclude discrimination on racial grounds. Race, like gender, was simply a category the province was entitled to adopt in determining who should have the "privilege" of the franchise.

For a time, the courts continued to follow *Bryden* with respect to legislative barriers to employment on racial lines. But even this suffered a setback with the decision of the Supreme Court of Canada in *Quong-Wing* v. *R.* in 1914.[21] At issue was the constitutional validity of a Saskatchewan law that created the following offence:

> No person shall employ in any capacity any white woman or girl or permit any white woman or girl to reside or lodge in or to work in or, save as a *bona fide* customer in a public apartment thereof only, to frequent any restaurant, laundry or other place of business or amusement owned, kept or managed by any Chinaman.

Quong-Wing, described in the decision of the Supreme Court of Canada as "a Chinaman and a naturalized Canadian citizen,"[22] was convicted of employing a white woman. He challenged the law, relying on *Bryden*. However, a majority of the Supreme Court of Canada saw the legislation as a valid exercise of the provincial legislative capacity to establish proper conditions of employment for women and thought that "[t]he difference between the restrictions imposed on all Canadians by such legislation and those resulting from the Act in question is one of degree, not of kind."[23]

The overt racism of the legislation challenged in these cases is shocking to the modern reader. Equally disturbing is the implicit acceptance of the racist assumptions underlying the legislation by many of the judges. Yet the failure of the courts to develop an expansive conception of basic rights of citizenship as implicit in the federal power with respect to "naturalization and aliens" is perhaps not surprising. The language of the constitution hardly led inexorably to that conclusion. It

---

20   *Cunningham* v. *Tomey Homma*, [1903] A.C. 151.
21   (1914), 49 S.C.R. 440.
22   *Ibid.* at 443, Fitzpatrick C.J.
23   *Ibid.* at 445.

would have taken an exercise of judicial creativity and imagination of considerable magnitude to articulate a conception of citizenship which would embody at the federal level the authority to define and protect the essential attributes of citizenship, while at the same time respecting the legitimate claims of provincial power.

E. HUMAN RIGHTS CHARTERS

The failure of the Canadian legal system to respond to the issue of racial and other forms of discrimination was not an isolated phenomenon. In the period immediately following the Second World War, there was an international trend towards the elaboration of human rights charters of various kinds. The horrors of war, the Holocaust, and the rise of totalitarianism created a climate in which it was increasingly felt that human rights values deserved enhanced recognition and protection. No nation was blameless — the fears of war had prompted Canada to perpetuate shameful discrimination against Japanese Canadians. There was an awakening to the evils of racism and a widespread feeling that new laws and legal techniques were required.

The adoption of formal charters proclaiming fundamental rights and freedoms occurred at both the national and international levels. The United Nations adopted the *Universal Declaration of Human Rights* in 1948. A large number of European states signed the *European Convention for the Protection of Human Rights and Fundamental Freedoms* in 1953. Other instruments came into being over the next two decades, to which Canada was a signatory — for example, the *International Covenant on Civil and Political Rights* in 1966.

As colonialism collapsed, the constitutions of newly independent states almost invariably contained entrenched charters of rights and freedoms. Even in nations with established constitutional regimes, the protection of human rights and the struggle against discrimination and racism attracted unprecedented attention. The decision of the Supreme Court of the United States in its 1954 ruling, *Brown* v. *Board of Education*,[24] was a watershed. The Court found that racially segregated schools violated the guarantee of equal protection of the laws, and it overruled a late-nineteenth-century precedent that had implicitly sanctioned racial segregation by allowing states to establish "separate but equal" facilities.[25] In *Brown*, the Supreme Court proclaimed that separate

24   347 U.S. 483 (1954) [*Brown*].
25   *Plessy v. Ferguson*, 163 U.S. 537 (1895).

schools were inherently unequal and thereby created an impetus for the dismantling of racial segregation in all areas. The focus of rights protection in American constitutional law shifted from property and traditional democratic rights to the struggle for equality, and the courts assumed an overtly activist role.

Both the *Canadian Bill of Rights,* enacted in 1960, and the Canadian *Charter* of 1982 were certainly influenced by these international developments and may be seen as a product of the same general trend.

F. HUMAN RIGHTS CODES

In domestic Canadian law, human rights codes emerged in the post-war period as an important tool in the legal protection of the basic right to be free from discrimination. These codes, first enacted at the provincial level, initially provided protection against racial and religious discrimination. As awareness of other forms of discrimination has grown, so too has the list of forbidden grounds of discrimination. Age and gender followed race and religion, and eventually disability was added. Other grounds found in different codes and applying to various activities include place of origin, marital status, receipt of public assistance, record of offence, and, most recently, sexual orientation.

A significant feature of human rights legislation is that, with the exception of Quebec, anti-discrimination protection is achieved through an administrative process rather than through judges and courts. Typically, legislation creates a commission which is mandated to deal with individual complaints and to take appropriate educative and related remedial measures. Individual complaints are investigated by the commission at no cost to the complainant, and an attempt is made to resolve the matter by agreement or through mediation. Cases that cannot be resolved informally are referred to a judicial-style board of inquiry which decides disputed questions of fact and law and which exercises broad remedial powers.

Detailed consideration of human rights legislation is to be found in another volume in this series. It is important to note here, however, that human rights codes played an important role in the struggle against racism, sexism, and other forms of discrimination before the *Charter* and will continue to do so in light of the *Charter*'s limited application to private action.[26] Moreover, when interpreting and applying the equality

---

26   See chapter 5. For further discussion of human rights codes, see W.S. Tarnopolsky and W.F. Pentney, *Discrimination and the Law* (Toronto: DeBoo, 1990).

guarantee of the *Charter*, the courts have paid close heed to the provisions of human rights codes and to the jurisprudence developed by human rights commissions.

G. THE *CANADIAN BILL OF RIGHTS*, 1960

While human rights legislation has been a success, another post-war, pre-*Charter* experiment in the statutory protection of fundamental freedoms was a disappointment. The 1960 *Canadian Bill of Rights*, an ordinary act of Parliament, declared a list of important civil rights to be fundamental and provided that all laws should "be so construed and applied so as not to abrogate, abridge or infringe" any of the rights or freedoms so declared.[27] The list of rights and freedoms protected is similar, although not identical, to that found in the *Charter*. Although it has been superseded in importance, it remains on the books and, as will be explained, should not be ignored, for it contains certain guarantees not found in the *Charter*.

The *Bill of Rights* suffered from two fundamental defects. First, it applied only to federal laws and thus did not reach the laws of the provinces. This meant that the actions of provincial legislatures and those acting under provincial authority were immune from its application. This feature of the *Bill of Rights* was seen by the future chief justice of Canada, Bora Laskin, then a law professor, as an inexcusable abdication of federal authority.[28]

Second, as the *Bill of Rights* was an ordinary Act of Parliament and did not form part of the constitution, the mandate it conferred upon the courts was suspect. Judges were reluctant to find that Parliament had, with one stroke of the legislative pen, authorized them to invalidate other duly enacted laws. The very notion seemed to run counter to the basic precepts of parliamentary supremacy.

While the *Bill of Rights* acquired "*quasi*-constitutional" status in the view of Laskin C.J.C.,[29] with the notable exception of *R. v. Drybones*,[30] the courts did not consider that this enactment of the Parliament of Canada conferred upon the judiciary the authority to invalidate duly enacted laws. *Drybones* involved a provision of the federal *Indian Act* which made it an offence for an Indian to be intoxicated off a reserve, a

---

27   R.S.C. 1985, App. III, s. 2.
28   Above note 1.
29   *Hogan v. R.*, [1975] 2 S.C.R. 574 at 597, 48 D.L.R. (3d) 427.
30   (1969), [1970] S.C.R. 282, 9 D.L.R. (3d) 473 [*Drybones*].

harsher regime than that applied to others in the Northwest Territories, who were guilty of an offence only if found intoxicated in a public place. The Supreme Court of Canada struck down the offence on the ground that it violated the *Bill*'s guarantee of "equality before the law and the protection of the law." The ruling in *Drybones* suggested that the Court was prepared to give some weight to the *Bill of Rights*, but that promise proved short-lived. Instead, the Supreme Court made a hasty retreat. Although *Drybones* was never repudiated or overruled, its motivating spirit was abandoned. The rights and freedoms the *Bill* declared were almost invariably interpreted in a disappointingly formal and narrow fashion. In *Canada (A.G.)* v. *Lavell*,[31] the Court refused to apply *Drybones* in the suit of an Aboriginal woman who lost her *Indian Act* status upon marrying a non-Aboriginal man. The same result did not apply where a man with *Indian Act* status married a non-status woman. Thus, the law created what seems to be an obvious form of sex discrimination. The Court adopted a purely formal definition of equality and dismissed the challenge on the ground that the law was applied equally to all women in Lavell's situation. This is but one of a long list of cases in which the courts adopted a narrow and restrictive interpretation of the *Bill of Rights*, thereby rendering much of its authority nugatory.

Despite its limited success, there are two provisions of the *Bill of Rights* that have to be kept in mind since they have no counterpart in the *Charter*. The right of property is protected by section 1(a), and section 2(e) guarantees everyone "the right to a fair hearing in accordance with the principles of fundamental justice for the determination of his rights and obligations." The *Charter* does not protect property rights, and the guarantee of a fair hearing is arguably narrower, applying only in the criminal process under section 11(d) or, under section 7, where one's "life, liberty and security of the person" are implicated.

The *Bill of Rights* experience was very much in the minds of the political actors who enacted the *Charter*. The courts were given a deliberate push away from the cautious and highly deferential posture they exhibited in the *Bill of Rights* case law. As the Supreme Court of Canada has observed,[32] the judges of Canada did not seek a mandate for judicial review: that choice was consciously and deliberately made by the political leaders of the day.

---

31   (1973), [1974] S.C.R. 1349, 38 D.L.R. (3d) 481.
32   *Reference Re s. 94(2) of the Motor Vehicle Act (B.C.)*, [1985] 2 S.C.R. 486 at 497, 24 D.L.R. (4th) 536.

FURTHER READINGS

HOGG, P.W., *Constitutional Law of Canada*, 4th ed. (Toronto: Carswell, 1996) cc. 31 and 32

LYSYK, K.M., "The Canadian Charter of Rights and Freedoms: General Principles" (1994) 16 Advocates' Q. 1

McLACHLIN, B.M.,"The Charter: A New Role for the Judiciary" (1991) 29 Alta. L. Rev. 540

RUSSELL, P.H.,"The Political Purposes of the Canadian Charter of Rights and Freedoms" (1983) 61 Can. Bar Rev. 30

TARNOPOLSKY,W., *The Canadian Bill of Rights*, 2d rev. ed. (Toronto: McClelland and Stewart, 1975)

TARNOPOLSKY, W.S., & W.F. PENTNEY, *Discrimination and the Law* (Toronto: DeBoo, 1990)

CHAPTER 2

THE LEGITIMACY OF JUDICIAL REVIEW

There has been a lively debate in Canada, particularly since the enactment of the *Charter of Rights and Freedoms* in 1982, regarding the legitimacy of judicial review. Although judicial review on federalism
grounds has been a feature of the Canadian constitution since the early
days of Confederation, the tradition of parliamentary supremacy
remained strong until the advent of the *Charter*. In that tradition, there
are no constraints upon what Parliament can do, and it is thought that
Parliament is the best place to achieve an appropriate balance between
individual rights and freedoms and the broader public interest. This
principle had always been qualified in Canada by the practice of judicial
review on federalism grounds, but the *Charter of Rights and Freedoms*
added significantly to the judiciary's power.

Under the *Charter*, the questions put to judges involve issues of
value and moral choice, which are not only more open-ended and
apparently less constrained by strict legal principles but also of greater
significance to the average citizen than those relating to federalism. For
example, does the right to life, liberty, and security of the person in section 7 include a woman's right to choose whether to have an abortion?
Does the right to freedom of expression include the right to spread
hatred against particular racial or religious groups?

The result of a *Charter* decision is also more significant than one
made on federalism grounds. Because the Canadian constitution exhaus-
tively grants legislative power to either the federal Parliament or the provincial legislatures, the result of a decision holding that, say, a province

cannot enact a certain law will almost inevitably be that the federal government can. On the other hand, the result of a *Charter* decision striking down a law is that, unless resort is had to the "override" clause, neither level of government can enact the law. Hence, a *Charter* decision has a much more telling impact upon the scope for legislative choice.

The debate over the legitimacy of judicial review is fuelled by the fact that the Canadian judicial system in general, and the adjudication of constitutional cases in particular, is premised on the assumption that questions coming before the courts are legal rather than political and as such are to be decided strictly upon legal grounds. As will be noted later in chapter 7, the procedure for a constitutional case is more or less the same as that used for a property or contracts dispute between two private parties. The same judges decide the constitutional issue as decide the private dispute, and in theory they decide the constitutional issue on grounds similar to those that apply to the private dispute. It has become increasingly obvious, however, that many, if not most, *Charter* issues involve matters of value and public policy quite different in nature from the questions formerly posed to the courts. It is not surprising to find many observers asking whether it is legitimate to give unelected and unaccountable judges a definitive say on these vitally important and highly controversial matters.

From a formal perspective, there is a clear answer. As the Supreme Court itself has pointed out, the judges did not ask for the *Charter of Rights and Freedoms* nor for the powers it confers upon them.[1] The enactment of the *Charter* and the decision to confer a broader mandate upon the courts was the conscious choice of the elected representatives of the people. In 1982 the constitution was amended to include an explicit supremacy clause,[2] and individuals were expressly given the right, under section 24(1) of the *Charter*, "to obtain such remedy as the

---

1   In *Reference Re s. 94(2) of the Motor Vehicle Act (B.C.)*, [1985] 2 S.C.R. 486, 24 D.L.R. (4th) 536, Lamer J. states at 497 (S.C.R.):

> It ought not to be forgotten that the historic decision to entrench the *Charter* in our Constitution was taken not by the courts but by the elected representatives of the people of Canada. It was those representatives who extended the scope of constitutional adjudication and entrusted the courts with this new and onerous responsibility. Adjudication under the *Charter* must be approached free of any lingering doubts as to its legitimacy.

See also *Vriend* v. *Alberta*, [1998] S.C.J. No. 29 at para. 131–32, Iacobucci J. [*Vriend*].

2   Section 52(1) of the *Constitution Act, 1982*, states: "The Constitution of Canada is the supreme law of Canada, and any law that is inconsistent is, to the extent of the inconsistency, of no force or effect."

court considers appropriate and just in the circumstances." Accordingly, the text of the constitution reflects the conscious political choice to grant judges extensive power to interfere with decisions of the democratically elected representatives of the people.

While it is clear that the power of judicial review is legally legitimate, one may still ask whether this power is legitimate in a more fundamental sense. Is it consistent with the most fundamental values of the constitution — the principles of democracy and the right of the citizens of Canada to elect and remove those who exercise political power?

A. JUSTIFICATION FOR JUDICIAL REVIEW — FEDERALISM

The legitimacy of judicial review on federalism grounds has been challenged, but this practice is perhaps more readily justified than is judicial review under the *Charter*. A federal system needs a referee to resolve jurisdictional disputes that cannot be sorted out through the ordinary political process. The federal structure of government represents a conscious decision to allocate functions between national and regional governments and to divide responsibility for certain legislative subject matters accordingly. Situations are bound to arise where the political actors will not be able to resolve their differences about jurisdiction — hence the need for some specified body to settle the matter according to the principles established by the constitution. Canadian courts have not hesitated to wield the power of judicial review on federalism grounds, striking down many laws, both federal and provincial. While some scholars have argued that the resolution of jurisdictional disputes could be the responsibility of a non-judicial political authority,[3] their arguments have been unpersuasive.[4] Controversy may surround particular decisions of the courts on the division of powers between the federal and provincial authorities, but the appropriateness of the courts exercising the power of judicial review is generally well accepted.[5]

An important factor contributing to the acceptance of judicial review in the area of federalism has been the development of interpre-

---

3   P. Weiler, *In the Last Resort: A Critical Study of the Supreme Court of Canada* (Toronto: Carswell Methuen, 1974).

4   K.E. Swinton, *The Supreme Court and Canadian Federalism: The Laskin-Dickson Years* (Toronto: Carswell, 1990), c. 2, refutes the arguments made by Weiler, above.

5   Compare, however, H. Brun & G. Tremblay, *Droit constitutionnel*, 2e ed. (Montreal: Yvon Blais, 1990) at 453–54 and 490–92.

tative doctrines designed to minimize intrusion into legislative decision making. The emphasis upon purpose over effects limits judicial review significantly, avoiding a situation where the courts would be called upon to review the impact of all manner of legislation. It reflects the modern judicial tolerance for overlapping powers, and this deferential judicial stance has produced many areas where both levels of government act concurrently. The courts have not insisted upon excessively sharp distinctions being drawn or upon jurisdictional categories being viewed as watertight compartments.

Another element of judicial deference has been the adoption of a traditionally narrow view of paramountcy. While the rule is that, in the event of conflict, federal law prevails, the courts have, in the past, defined conflict narrowly, as being a situation where one law requires one thing and the other law requires precisely the opposite.[6] Recent cases suggest the acceptance of a broader test in some circumstances, which leads to a finding of paramountcy when the provincial law seriously interferes with the underlying policy objectives of the federal legislation.[7] However, there are still many policy areas in which federal and provincial laws overlap and in which federal paramountcy does not lead to dismantling of the provincial scheme in the absence of conflict in the strict sense.

B. JUSTIFICATION FOR JUDICIAL REVIEW — *CHARTER OF RIGHTS AND FREEDOMS*

More controversial is judicial review under the *Charter*, which clearly puts the courts in the position of overruling the democratically elected representatives of the people on value-laden questions of public policy. Many critics argue that an entrenched bill of rights undermines democratic debate and decision making. In Peter Russell's words, "The principal impact of a charter on the process of government can be neatly summarized as a tendency to judicialize politics and politicize the judiciary."[8] He goes on to say:

> The danger here is not so much that non-elected judges will impose their will on a democratic majority, but that questions of social and

---

6   *Multiple Access Ltd.* v. *McCutcheon*, [1982] 2 S.C.R. 161, 138 D.L.R. (3d) 1.

7   *Bank of Montreal* v. *Hall*, [1990] 1 S.C.R. 121, 65 D.L.R. (4th) 361; *Husky Oil Operations Ltd.* v. *M.N.R.* (1995), 128 D.L.R. (4th) 1 (S.C.C.).

8   P. Russell, "The Political Purposes of the *Canadian Charter of Rights and Freedoms*" (1983) 61 Can. Bar Rev. 30 at 51–52.

political justice will be transformed into technical legal questions and the great bulk of the citizenry who are not judges and lawyers will abdicate their responsibility for working out reasonable and mutually acceptable resolutions of the issues which divide them.[9]

The fear is that litigation in the courts will replace open public debate on important issues of public policy.

Other critics add to this a concern about the lack of judicial expertise in many of the areas litigated. In view of the relative resources and expertise of judges vis-à-vis legislatures and bureaucracies in making decisions on complex issues, these critics denounce the use of *Charter* litigation to make determinations affecting important policy matters involving difficult tradeoffs between competing interests.

Still other commentators point to the vagueness and indeterminacy of constitutional language as a reason for concern about judicial review. Words such as "liberty" and "equality" are so open-ended, it is argued, that judges cannot help but infuse the constitution with their own values. Why, it is asked, should we trust nine Supreme Court judges with the task of delineating the meaning of those phrases for a diverse society, rather than leave such issues to be resolved through open legislative debate?

This criticism of judicial review is shared by those from the left, who worry that judicial decisions will tend to favour liberal values hostile to an interventionist state, especially where the state intervenes to promote greater equality among groups and classes. For example, Andrew Petter has written:

> First, we must bear in mind what has just been said about a charter of rights: it gives to citizens only insofar as it takes from government. For example, the guarantee of equality rights in the Charter does not give people a guarantee of social equality; it does not even commit the government to guaranteeing social equality. Its role is much more limited. What it does is inhibit government from implementing measures that would bring about or perpetuate inequality.[10]

In effect, the fear is that the individual-rights focus of the *Charter* will undermine a more communitarian spirit expressed through legislative action. Inevitably, those on the left invoke the ghost of the *Lochner* case

---

9   *Ibid.* at 52.

10   A.J. Petter, "The Politics of the *Charter*" (1986) 8 Supreme Court L.R. 473 at 476. Another critic from this perspective, who examines the Supreme Court's performance in some detail, is M. Mandel, *The Charter of Rights and the Legalization of Politics in Canada*, 2d ed. (Toronto: Thompson, 1994).

from the turn-of-the-century United States, where the Supreme Court struck down protective labour legislation limiting the hours of bakery workers to ten in a day and sixty in a week as an unjustifiable limitation on liberty.[11] These critics fear that powerful forces will be able to use the *Charter's* framework of individual rights to protect their own self-interest at the expense of the less advantaged.

The legitimacy of judicial review under the *Charter* has also been challenged by critics on the right.[12] These scholars argue that unelected judges have assumed an unacceptable law-making role under the *Charter* and that interest groups and others with a left-wing agenda are able to exploit this new-found judicial power to achieve left-wing policies that would not otherwise attract majority support. Abortion, equality rights for minorities, especially gays and lesbians, and rights for those accused of crime have attracted particular attention.

Other observers come to the defence of judicial review. They argue that the entrenchment of constitutional rights is consistent with the fundamental principles of democracy. There is a strong argument that democracy cannot be explained simply in terms of majority rule and that adherence to certain fundamental values and principles is necessary for democracy to flourish.[13] An obvious example would be judicial review to protect the right to vote, which is the very cornerstone of democracy. Should the majority of the day be entitled to deny that right to certain members of society, without having to justify the decision other than by the force of their numbers? Surely the power of judicial review, requiring demonstrable justification for the decision, enhances, rather than detracts from, democratic values. Similarly, free and open debate of public issues is essential to democracy, and the exercise of the power of judicial review to protect the fundamental freedoms of expression, opinion, and the press can be seen as enhancing and reinforcing democracy. Majorities of the day have a tendency to try to suppress the expression of unpopular views that threaten the status quo. Judicial review serves to bolster democratic values by requiring reasoned justification for laws that limit the rights of those who hold views diverging from the prevailing wisdom of the day.

---

11   *Lochner* v. *New York*, 198 U.S. 45 (1905).
12   See R. Knopff & F.L. Morton, *Charter Politics* (Scarborough: Nelson Canada, 1992).
13   J.H. Ely is a strong proponent of this view in *Democracy and Distrust: A Theory of Judicial Review* (Cambridge: Harvard University Press, 1980). Patrick Monahan echoes his view, with his own refinements, in *Politics and the Constitution: The Charter, Federalism and the Supreme Court of Canada* (Toronto: Carswell, 1987).

Other fundamental freedoms, less directly implicated in the democratic process, are nonetheless essential if democracy is to flourish. The values of individual dignity, autonomy, and freedom of choice, reflected in the freedom of religion and equality and in the protection of life, liberty, and security of the person, are preconditions to individuals being capable of making independent, intelligent, and informed decisions. Judicial intervention to protect these values against incursions by majoritarian actions may be seen as enhancing and protecting democracy rather than undermining it. Chief Justice Dickson made this point when striking down a law that infringed on freedom of religion: "The ability of each citizen to make free and informed decisions is the absolute prerequisite for the legitimacy, acceptability, and efficacy of our system of self-government."[14]

In a similar vein, decisions of the courts protecting minorities or other vulnerable groups may be defended on the basis of democratic principle.[15] Judicial review, from this perspective, is justified to protect those whose voices are not adequately heard in political debate because they are too few or too unpopular. It is argued that judicial review strengthens democracy by ensuring that the rights and interests of all citizens are protected. The Supreme Court of Canada has been particularly active in defending the rights of those accused of crimes, as well as minority rights. This aspect of judicial review is also reflected in the Court's generous[16] interpretation of a rather vague guarantee of Aboriginal rights in section 35 of the *Constitution Act, 1982*.[17] The minority-language education rights in the *Charter* have also been interpreted liberally by the Court.[18] Perhaps even more significant was the court's initial interpretation of the equality guarantee, section 15 of the *Charter*, namely that the focus for equality review must be upon historic patterns of discrimination and disadvantage, an interpretation that included explicit reference to the need to protect those vulnerable groups who lack an effective voice in majoritarian politics. In the leading decision, the Court held that a law prohibiting non-citizens from being admitted to the legal profession was contrary to the guarantee of equality and jus-

---

14   R. v. *Big M Drug Mart Ltd.*, [1985] 1 S.C.R. 295, 18 D.L.R. (4th) 321 at 361.

15   *Vriend*, above note 1.

16   Not all commentators agree that the interpretation has been "generous": see K. McNeil, "Envisaging Constitutional Space for Aboriginal Governments" (1993) 19 Queen's L.J. 95.

17   R. v. *Sparrow*, [1990] 1 S.C.R. 1075, 70 D.L.R. (4th) 385.

18   *Mahé v. Alberta*, [1990] 1 S.C.R. 342, 68 D.L.R. (4th) 69.

tified interfering with the majoritarian decision to exclude non-citizens by an appeal to basic democratic principles:

> Non-citizens, to take only the most obvious example, do not have the right to vote. Their vulnerability to becoming a disadvantaged group in our society is captured by John Stuart Mill's observation in Book III of *On Liberty and Considerations of Representative Government* that "in the absence of its natural defenders, the interests of the excluded is always in danger of being overlooked . . ."[19]

The Court reiterated this theme in a 1998 decision holding that Alberta's human rights legislation, which failed to protect gays and lesbians, violated the guarantee of equality:

> Democratic values and principles under the *Charter* demand that legislators and the executive take these [democratic attributes] into account; and if they fail to do so, courts should stand ready to intervene to protect these democratic values as appropriate. As others have so forcefully stated, judges are not acting undemocratically by intervening when there are indications that a legislative or executive decision was not reached in accordance with the democratic principles mandated by the *Charter*.[20]

The justification for judicial review just described is sometimes called a "process-based" approach, since the main function of the *Charter* is seen to be the checking of malfunctions in the operation of the democratic process. The underlying assumption is that Parliament and the legislatures should be left with considerable scope to make determinations about the shape of public policy, but that the *Charter* allows the courts to intervene where the political process is deficient in some way.[21]

---

19   *Andrews v. Law Society (British Columbia)*, [1989] 1 S.C.R. 143 at 152, 56 D.L.R. (4th) 1, Wilson J. This approach is further described in chapter 15, "Equality."

20   *Vriend*, above note 1 at para. 142, Iacobucci J.

21   Ely, above note 13. For a similar defence of the role of the *Charter*, from the perspective of the left, see R. Penner, "The Canadian Experience with the *Charter of Rights*: Are There Lessons for the United Kingdom?" [1996] Pub. L. 104 at 113:
> [T]hough a bill of rights cannot be, instrumentally, a *sword* in the vanguard of transformative politics as urged by some, it can be a *shield* capable of defending the disempowered, the disadvantaged, the marginalised and the discriminated-against in society in certain, albeit limited, respects; and it is capable moreover of being called upon defensively at times of political crisis when a determined government can all too easily secure a parliamentary majority for the suspension or erosion of hard-won rights — rights of speech, association, demonstration, especially of vigorous protest.

Another justification offered for judicial enforcement of a charter of rights emphasizes the central importance of rights protection to individual self-development. As with the process model, this theory is based on a perception that majoritarian politics may have deficiencies that require correction. But this model can take the courts much further in curtailing government action and, in the abstract, is based upon an unwavering and unqualified commitment to the protection of individual autonomy. Consider, for example, the following quotation from Lorraine Weinrib advocating a "constitutional rights" model of judicial review:

> This model welcomes judicial protection of individual rights and their value structure to continuously correct for the perceived inadequacies of majoritarian politics. Underlying this model is respect for the dignity, equality and autonomy of each member of the community. The individual must be able to espouse, and follow, and modify his or her own conception of the good. Whatever the sources and trajectories of these commitments, the aim of collective political life is to create and preserve a structure in which each of us, to an equal extent, may pursue and act upon these commitments, either alone or in a given or chosen community.[22]

Assessing the relative merits of the arguments for and against judicial review requires looking at what the courts do not do, as well as what they do. While the critics of the left assert that the Court will import conservative values, it is important to put in perspective the outcomes of some of the so-called "bad cases" that they decry. In some of these cases, the failure to adopt the view of the left does not automatically translate into a victory for the right. For example, when the Supreme Court of Canada refused to find that collective bargaining was a constitutional right under the guarantee of freedom of association, that did not mean an end to collective bargaining; rather, it pushed the debate about the nature and scope of labour powers into the political arena.[23] Similarly, when the courts refuse to recognize positive rights — for example, to welfare as an element of security of the person — that does not prevent political debate and action with respect to welfare policy; instead, it leaves the difficult policy choices to the political process.

---

22   L. Weinrib, "Limitations on Rights in a Constitutional Democracy" (1996) 6 Caribbean L. Rev. 428 at 439.

23   *Reference Re Public Service Employee Relations Act (Alberta)*, [1987] 1 S.C.R. 313, 38 D.L.R. (4th) 161; *P.S.A.C. v. Canada (A.G.)*, [1987] 1 S.C.R. 424, 38 D.L.R. (4th) 249; *R.W.D.S.U., Locals 544, 496, 635, 955 v. Saskatchewan*, [1987] 1 S.C.R. 460, 38 D.L.R. (4th) 277, discussed in chapter 10.

Finally, in other areas, while the result in a given case may provide a victory to a powerful economic interest, the decision often has implications throughout the legal system in ways that may also benefit the less advantaged. For instance, when a powerful corporation wins protection against unreasonable searches and seizures in the criminal process, it will not be the only beneficiary.

In the chapters that follow, we will see that Canadian courts have demonstrated a marked deference in certain areas which, it may be argued, results from their recognition of the limits of the judicial function. The Canadian Supreme Court has been unsympathetic to claims of pure economic rights and has refused to become embroiled in most distributional issues.[24] This has been manifested by the Court's refusal to imply a right of property in the constitution, its rejection of overtures to protect rights of contract, and its dismissal of the claim for constitutional protection of the right of collective bargaining. This cautious and deferential stance contrasts sharply with the Court's willingness to engage its power to protect freedom of expression and the rights of criminal accused. While the Court has expressed a commitment to vigilance in the protection of minorities from prejudice and stereotypes, it has also insisted that governments be given some leeway in making difficult social-policy decisions — for example, in the design of benefit schemes or the tax system.

The Court's refusal to intervene in the areas of property, contract, and collective bargaining reflects its view that economic and social-policy questions are best left to the legislative arenas. Similarly, the Court has respected and upheld legislative initiatives to protect vulnerable groups when these initiatives have been challenged as violating the fundamental freedoms of more powerful interests in society.[25] The Court recognizes that Parliament and the legislatures have an important role in enhancing and protecting these very same values that inform judicial review, wisely refusing to claim the exclusive authority to determine when those rights should be protected.

---

24   See, for example, *Irwin Toy Ltd.* v. *Quebec (A.G.)*, [1989] 1 S.C.R. 927, 58 D.L.R. (4th) 577, holding that commercial expression is protected by s. 2(b) of the *Charter*, but making it clear that purely economic rights are not protected.

25   See *Edwards Books & Art Ltd.* v. *R.*, [1986] 2 S.C.R. 713, 35 D.L.R. (4th) 1 at 49, Dickson C.J.C. stating that care had to be taken so that the *Charter* "does not simply become an instrument of better situated individuals to roll back legislation that has as its object the improvement of the condition of less advantaged persons."

In sum, it can be argued that the purpose of constitutionalizing rights is to facilitate, not frustrate, democracy. The *Charter* protects the values of individual dignity, autonomy, and respect which are essential for free and open democratic debate, and it gives a voice to many in our society who are effectively excluded from the political process. A true democracy is surely one in which the exercise of power by the many is conditional on respect for the rights of the few. Majorities may fail to respect individual dignity and conscience and may be inclined to shut out annoying and unpopular views. Constitutionalizing rights empowers the courts to check these unworthy inclinations by requiring those who exercise power to justify their actions through evidence and reasoned argument when the bedrock values of our democratic tradition are impinged. The Canadian experience to date indicates that the judiciary is capable of exercising the powers of judicial review to protect such fundamental rights as freedom of religion and expression and the right to equality without unduly inhibiting the capacity of the elected representatives to develop social policy.

C. CONCLUSION

Overall, we suggest that the *Charter* has had a beneficial impact upon democratic life in Canada. Fundamental human rights are now properly at the forefront of public debate, and the claims of those often drowned out in the cut and thrust of day-to-day politics can no longer be ignored. Indeed, the *Charter* has made an important contribution to Canadian political life by creating what Roland Penner calls a "culture of liberty."[26] Legislators cannot enact laws without consideration of their impact on individual rights, and government legal officers play an important role in encouraging their political masters to respect *Charter* rights.

The *Charter* has the potential to strengthen the Canadian democratic tradition and commitment to toleration and equal respect for all, and judges have an appropriate part to play in protecting those values. As interpreted by the courts to date, the *Charter* neither precludes nor entrenches particular socio-economic outcomes but rather enriches the democratic process.[27]

---

26 Penner, above note 21 at 114–15.

27 This paragraph and the preceding one are adapted from R.J. Sharpe, "Constitutionalization of Rights and the Politicization of the Judiciary" in I. Cotler, B. Elman, & D. Schneiderman, eds., *Chartering Human Rights: Canada-Israel* (Edmonton: Centre for Constitutional Studies, forthcoming).

FURTHER READINGS

BAKAN, J., *Just Words: Constitutional Rights and Social Wrongs* (Toronto: University of Toronto Press, 1997)

BEATTY, D.M., *Constitutional Law in Theory and Practice* (Toronto: University of Toronto Press, 1995)

BOGART, W.A., *Courts and Country: The Limits of Litigation and the Social and Political Life of Canada* (Toronto: Oxford University Press, 1994)

CONKLIN, W.E., *Images of a Constitution* (Toronto: University of Toronto Press, 1989)

ELY, J.H., *Democracy and Distrust: A Theory of Judicial Review* (Cambridge: Harvard University Press, 1980)

HOGG, P., & A. BUSHELL, "The Charter Dialogue between Courts and Legislatures" (1997) 35 Osgoode Hall L.J. 75

HUTCHINSON, A.C., *Waiting for CORAF: A Critique of Law and Rights* (Toronto: University of Toronto Press, 1995)

KNOPFF, R., & F.L. MORTON, *Charter Politics* (Scarborough: Nelson Canada, 1992)

MANDEL, M., *The Charter of Rights and the Legalization of Politics in Canada*, 2d ed. (Toronto: Thompson, 1994)

MONAHAN, P., *Politics and the Constitution: The Charter, Federalism and the Supreme Court of Canada* (Toronto: Carswell, 1987)

PENNER, R. "The Canadian Experience with the *Charter of Rights*: Are There Lessons for the United Kingdom?" [1996] Pub. L. 104

SLATTERY, B., "A Theory of the Charter" (1987) 25 Osgoode Hall L.J. 701

CHAPTER 3

INTERPRETATION OF THE *CHARTER OF RIGHTS AND FREEDOMS*

Entrenching rights in the constitution does not end the debate about the legitimacy of judicial review. Rather, the debate takes on a different form, revolving around the justification for various approaches to constitutional interpretation. Some argue for a strict reading of the constitutional text, often maintaining that the words of the document should be understood in light of their meaning at the time of drafting. Others argue for a more "progressive" approach that will allow the content to adapt to new societal needs and values. Those who take this position turn to moral philosophy, international human rights norms, or evolving community values for help in the interpretive process.

In this chapter, we outline the structure of the *Canadian Charter of Rights and Freedoms* and then canvass some of the debates about its interpretation.

A. NATURE OF *CHARTER* RIGHTS

The Canadian *Charter* identifies and enshrines six broad categories of rights:

- the "fundamental freedoms" of conscience, religion, thought, belief, opinion, expression, assembly, and association;[1]

---

1   Section 2

- democratic rights, including the right to vote, the guarantee of regular elections, and annual parliamentary sessions;[2]
- mobility rights to enter and leave the country and the right to reside in and gain a livelihood in any province;[3]
- legal rights, particularly those pertaining to the criminal process, such as the rights to counsel, protection against unreasonable search and seizure, *habeas corpus*, trial within a reasonable time, and the presumption of innocence until proven guilty, as well as a more general right to life, liberty, and security of the person, and the right not to be deprived thereof except in accordance with principles of fundamental justice;[4]
- the right to equality before and under the law and to the equal protection and equal benefit of the law;[5] and
- language rights.[6]

These rights are both guaranteed and made subject to limitations in section 1 of the *Charter*, which states that the *Charter* "guarantees the rights and freedoms set out in it subject to such reasonable limits prescribed by law as can be demonstrably justified in a free and democratic society." Thus, the Canadian *Charter* follows the model of international human rights documents rather than the American constitution. While the American document sets out the rights as if they are absolute, international documents, such as the *International Covenant on Civil and Political Rights,* expressly acknowledge that rights can be limited to protect other individual rights or broader community interests.

The *Charter* also includes a number of distinctive interpretive provisions, including a clause ensuring that there will be no derogation from Aboriginal rights by the *Charter* in section 25,[7] a commitment to preserve and enhance our multicultural heritage in section 27, and a further guarantee of gender equality in section 28. Also significant to interpretive issues is the specific remedial clause in section 24, discussed in Chapter 17, as well as a mechanism to override certain *Charter* rights, found in section 33, which is discussed in Chapter 5.

The rights included in a constitutional document reflect the concerns prevalent at the time of drafting. To the extent that the goal of the

---

2   Sections 3–5.

3   Section 6.

4   Sections 7–14.

5   Section 15.

6   Sections 16–23.

7   Aboriginal rights are recognized and affirmed in s. 35 of the *Constitution Act, 1982,* which does not form part of the *Charter.*

constitution is to curtail majority tyranny and government excesses, the rights protected will tend to lie in those areas where there has been evidence of problems — for example, government measures against unpopular expression or the practices of some religions. Similarly, to the extent that the constitution expresses an aspiration to greater equality in society, the listed grounds of discrimination may reflect historical or contemporary bases for unfair treatment against individuals and groups. The Canadian *Charter*, for example, was one of the world's first to include disability, while South Africa's new constitution, in force since December 1996, goes further to include sexual orientation in its equality guarantee.[8]

The emphasis in many countries has been on a liberal approach that protects the individual *from* certain state actions. There is, however, pressure in many countries today for the inclusion of positive rights — that is, rights to make governments act in order to provide greater equality or human dignity. While the Canadian *Charter* does include the positive right to minority-language schools in section 23, it does not contain the range of positive rights found, for example, in the new South African constitution, which includes the right to a healthy environment, the right to have access to adequate housing, health-care services, sufficient food and water, and social security, and the right to a basic education.[9] Efforts were made to add a "social charter" to the Canadian constitution during the constitutional-reform discussions occurring between 1990 and 1992, but serious opposition from a wide range of opinion undermined the project.[10]

In sum, the Canadian catalogue of rights and freedoms in the *Charter of Rights* looks essentially liberal in nature, in the sense that its language of rights and freedoms seems to define a zone of autonomy for the individual within which the state may not intrude. This feature of the *Charter* has been a cause for concern on the part of those who fear that its emphasis upon traditional liberal values will have an Americanizing influence on a Canadian legal and political culture, which emphasizes the communitarian values of "peace, order and good government" rather

---

8   South African Constitution, s. 9

9   *Ibid.*, ss. 24, 26, 27, 29. These rights often contain qualifications — for example, the right to access to adequate housing states in subs. (2) that "[t]he state must take reasonable legislative and other measures, within its available resources, to achieve the progressive realisation of this right."

10   Some of the arguments pro and con are found in W. Kymlicka & W.J. Norman, "The Social Charter Debate: Should Social Justice be Constitutionalized?" (Ottawa: Network on the Constitution, 1992); J. Bakan & D. Schneiderman, *Social Justice and the Constitution: Perspectives on the Social Union for Canada* (Ottawa: Carleton University Press, 1992).

than the American ideal of the "right to life, liberty and the pursuit of happiness." Instead of seeing government as a positive force because of its capacity to create greater equality or help the vulnerable, the *Charter* may foster the view that the state is the enemy of individual freedom.[11]

In looking at the experience under the *Charter*, one would have to conclude that the Canadian legal system has moved closer to the American model. However, this conclusion should be tempered by a realization that both the text and the interpretation of the *Charter* reflect an attitude more receptive to affirmative state measures designed to advance certain collective interests than that found in American constitutional law. For instance, "affirmative action" measures that have as their object the amelioration of conditions of disadvantaged individuals or groups are explicitly protected from claims of "reverse discrimination" and, thus, denials of equality.[12] Provinces are constitutionally obliged to provide facilities for minority-language education.[13] The promise of equality itself has been found to require affirmative measures by the state.[14] The Supreme Court has hinted that even rights that are cast in negative terms may impose positive obligations in some situations.[15] Most important, section 1 of the *Charter*, the "reasonable limits" clause discussed in chapter 4, has been interpreted to permit legislative measures designed to enhance the values underlying the fundamental rights and freedoms and to acknowledge that the liberty of the individual is sometimes justifiably limited in the interests of broader community interests and values. Especially in the early years, American jurisprudence was frequently cited in *Charter* litigation and treated as relevant and sometimes persuasive. But American approaches have also been flatly rejected in some areas and American jurisprudence is certainly not determinative, as the Supreme Court of Canada has frequently stated, given the differences in Canadian and American political and legal traditions.[16]

---

11   This passage echoes the criticisms of Andrew Petter, among others, discussed above in chapter 2, "The Legitimacy of Judicial Review."

12   Section 15(2). In addition, s. 6(4) protects discriminatory labour practices against out-of-province workers in provinces with unemployment rates above the national average.

13   Section 23.

14   *Eldridge* v. *British Columbia (A.G.)*, [1997] 3 S.C.R 624, 151 D.L.R. (4th) 577; *Vriend* v. *Alberta*, [1998] S.C.J. No. 29 [*Vriend*].

15   *Haig* v. *Canada (Chief Electoral Officer)*, [1993] 2 S.C.R. 995, 105 D.L.R. (4th) 577 at 607; *Native Women's Association of Canada* v. *Canada* (1994), 119 D.L.R. (4th) 224 at 245 (S.C.C.); *Vriend*, above note 14 at para. 64.

16   See J. Cameron, "The Motor Vehicle Reference and the Relevance of American Doctrine in *Charter* Adjudication" in R.J. Sharpe, ed., *Charter Litigation* (Toronto: Butterworths, 1987) c. 4. Indeed, the Canadian Court has embarked on jurisprudence that is quite distinctive from the American in areas such as hate propaganda and pornography, equality rights, and the drawing of electoral boundaries.

B. INTERPRETATION OF *CHARTER* RIGHTS

The Canadian courts have adopted a two-step process of interpretation and justification to give the general language of the *Charter* concrete meaning. First, the courts interpret the meaning of the right or freedom at issue to determine whether the matter complained of constitutes an infringement. Often, at this first stage, the courts have avoided narrow definitional limitations on rights that take into account the general social interest. It has been held, for example, that commercial advertising,[17] hate propaganda,[18] and pornography[19] are, subject to limitations justifiable under section 1, forms of expression protected by section 2(b). Only violence has been held to be excluded from the definition of expression.

With respect to some other rights, however, the courts have taken a more restrictive approach and defined certain limits to their scope. In interpreting the right to vote in section 3, for example, the courts have held that this provision gives a right to effective representation, not a guarantee of "one person, one vote."[20] Freedom of association has been limited by excluding group activities, such as the right to strike.[21] Section 15, the equality guarantee, can be invoked only by those discriminated against on the basis of the enumerated (for example, race, sex, or disability) or analogous grounds.[22] Certain rights are defined in terms requiring closer definition. For example, the section 8 right to be protected against unreasonable search and seizure requires the courts to take into account the limits on the right at the initial stage and define what searches and seizures are "unreasonable."[23]

A claimant can demonstrate that a right has been infringed either by looking at the government's purpose or at the effects of its actions. In some cases, the legislature's purpose will directly interfere with the exercise of the right — for example, a state-imposed compulsory religion for all would violate freedom of religion in section 2(a). In most cases, while the underlying objective of state action is not to interfere with a protected freedom, the legislation being challenged has that effect. For example, when a government prohibits individuals from fastening anything to telephone poles, the objective may be to prevent unsightly dis-

---

17   *Irwin Toy Ltd.* v. *Quebec (A.G.)*, [1989] 1 S.C.R. 927, 58 D.L.R. (4th) 577.
18   *R.* v. *Keegstra*, [1990] 3 S.C.R. 697, 61 C.C.C. (3d) 1 [*Keegstra*].
19   *R.* v. *Butler*, [1992] 1 S.C.R.. 452, 70 C.C.C. (3d) 129.
20   See chapter 11.
21   See chapter 10.
22   See chapter 15.
23   See chapter 14.

plays or even obstructions that may interfere with traffic safety. However, the effect of such a rule is to prevent the putting up of posters, which can be seen as an interference with freedom of expression.[24]

Once a right is infringed, the case is not over. The *Charter* recognizes that rights are not absolute; there are many situations when the interests of society at large or the rights of other individuals will require that the claimant's rights be limited. The consideration of whether these limits are justified under section 1 of the *Charter*, as reasonable limits prescribed by law in a free and democratic society, is left to the second step of a rights case — justification pursuant to section 1. The balance of this chapter discusses the initial interpretive stage, leaving the limitation of rights to the following chapter.

1) The Purposive Method

From the earliest *Charter* cases, the Supreme Court of Canada clearly recognized that *Charter* adjudication should be different from the traditional work of the courts. In *Law Society of Upper Canada* v. *Skapinker*,[25] the first *Charter* case to reach the Court, the judges indicated that they were prepared to assume responsibility for interpreting this "new yardstick of reconciliation between the individual and the community and their respective rights." Mindful that the "*Charter* is designed and adopted to guide and serve the Canadian community for a long time," Estey J. added that "narrow and technical interpretation" that could "stunt the growth of the law and hence the community it serves"[26] would be avoided.

In another early case, *Hunter* v. *Southam*,[27] the Court distinguished the method of statutory construction from that of constitutional interpretation. Insisting that the *Charter* must "be capable of growth and development over time to meet new social, political, and historical realities often unimagined by its framers," Dickson C.J.C. repeated Professor Paul Freund's plea that courts should not "read the provisions of the Constitution like a last will and testament lest it become one."[28] A similar note was struck by Beetz J. in *Manitoba (A.G.)* v. *Metropolitan Stores (MTS) Ltd.*[29] when dismissing the contention that the "presumption of constitutionality" should be weighed in the scales of *Charter* adjudication:

24 *Peterborough (City)* v. *Ramsden*, [1993] 2 S.C.R. 1084, 106 D.L.R. (4th) 233.
25 [1984] 1 S.C.R. 357, 9 D.L.R. (4th) 161.
26 *Ibid.* at 366 (S.C.R.).
27 [1984] 2 S.C.R. 145, 11 D.L.R. (4th) 641.
28 *Ibid.* at 649 (D.L.R.).
29 [1987] 1 S.C.R. 110, 38 D.L.R. (4th) 321.

"[T]he innovative and evolutive character of the Canadian *Charter of Rights and Freedoms* conflicts with the idea that a legislative provision can be presumed to be consistent with the *Charter*."[30] The rights and freedoms set out were not "frozen" in content and had to "remain susceptible to evolve in the future."[31]

These passages harken back to earlier decisions of the Privy Council and the Supreme Court of Canada interpreting the *Constitution Act, 1867*, in which the judges advocated an "organic" or "progressive" theory of interpretation with respect to the constitution. The judges rejected an approach advocated by some American scholars and judges which emphasizes the original intent of the framers of the constitution and interprets the document in light of the meaning of its terms at the time it was created. The "original intent" approach was soundly rejected by the Privy Council as being inconsistent with the idea of an enduring constitution that, if it is to last, must be capable of growth and expansion. In the *Edwards* case the Privy Council determined that, in the twentieth century, women were qualified "persons" for the purposes of eligibility for Senate appointments, even though in 1867, at the time the constitution was adopted, women were not eligible to hold public office. Viscount Sankey's words from that case have been frequently quoted:

> The *B.N.A. Act* planted in Canada a living tree capable of growth and expansion within its natural limits. The object of the Act was to grant a Constitution to Canada . . .
>
> Their Lordships do not conceive it to be the duty of this Board — it is certainly not their desire — to cut down the provisions of the Act by a narrow and technical construction, but rather to give it a large and liberal interpretation . . .[32]

The Supreme Court of Canada has specifically held that the supposed "original intent" of those who drafted the *Charter* will not be conclusive in its interpretation for two reasons.[33] First, statements of the intent of particular individuals are an unreliable guide to discerning the intent of many others who took an active role in the creation of the *Charter*. Furthermore, it is doubtful that there was a single or identifiable intent shared by all, given the number of federal and provincial pol-

---

30   *Ibid.* at 122 (S.C.R.)
31   *Ibid.* at 124 (S.C.R.).
32   *Edwards v. R.*, [1930] A.C. 124 at 136–37 [*Edwards*].
33   *Reference Re s. 94(2) of the Motor Vehicle Act (B.C.)*, [1985] 2 S.C.R. 486 at 508–9, 24 D.L.R. (4th) 536.

iticians and bureaucrats involved. Second, adoption of a strict interpretivist approach would freeze the meaning of the *Charter* at a particular time "with little or no possibility of growth, development and adjustment to changing societal needs."[34] Even if there were concrete evidence to help in determining the original understanding of the right, it would be wrong to fasten on to that meaning without question, for the original drafters themselves in all likelihood considered this to be an inappropriate method of interpretation. Constitutions are deliberately phrased in general, open-ended terms in order to let them adapt to changing circumstances and needs over the years. In the words of Ronald Dworkin, constitutions are meant to set out concepts, not conceptions, and thus, their content necessarily varies over time and place.[35]

Given the rejection of "original intent" to guide interpretation, how should a court proceed? In *Hunter v. Southam,* the Supreme Court of Canada first enunciated and applied the "purposive" method that has served as the standard approach in the elaboration of *Charter* rights and freedoms. This is a complex, value-laden exercise that draws upon a range of sources in the innovative spirit that the *Charter* demands. It calls upon the judge to reflect upon the purpose of and rationale for the *Charter* right at issue in the light of the overall structure of the *Charter*, our legal and political tradition, our history, and the changing needs and demands of modern society.

Perhaps the most often cited passage describing the nature of this exercise of purposive interpretation is from the judgment of Dickson J. in *R. v. Big M Drug Mart Ltd.*:

> In my view, this analysis is to be undertaken, and the purpose of the right or freedom in question is to be sought by reference to the character and the larger objects of the *Charter* itself, to the language chosen to articulate the specific right or freedom, to the historical origins of the concepts enshrined, and where applicable, to the meaning and purpose of the other specific rights and freedoms with which it is associated within the text of the *Charter*. The interpretation should be, as the judgment in *Southam* emphasizes, a generous rather than a legalistic one, aimed at fulfilling the purpose of the guarantee and securing for individuals the full benefit of the *Charter*'s protection. At the same time it is important not to overshoot the actual purpose of the right or freedom in question, but to recall that the *Charter* was not enacted in

---

34   *Ibid.* at 554 (D.L.R.), Lamer J.
35   R. Dworkin, *Taking Rights Seriously* (Cambridge: Harvard University Press, 1977) at 134.

a vacuum, and must therefore, as this Court's decision in *Law Society of Upper Canada* v. *Skapinker* illustrates, be placed in its proper linguistic, philosophic and historical contexts.[36]

The purposive method of interpretation is indicative of the most significant effect of the *Charter* upon the role of the judiciary. *Charter* adjudication is anything but the mechanical application of pre-established rules. The judges are called upon to delve deeply into the very foundations of our legal system and political culture to answer questions of the most fundamental nature, and many of these questions cannot be answered adequately by reference only to traditional legal sources.

2) Interpretive Sources

On the other hand, the task of *Charter* interpretation does have structure and discipline. The first source is obvious — the language of the *Charter* itself. For example, the recognition of Aboriginal rights, commitment to multiculturalism, and protection of affirmative action in section 15(2) all helped the Supreme Court determine that the meaning of equality in section 15(1) did not require that all must be treated in the same way, and that equality sometimes requires different treatment for different individuals and groups.[37]

Although the Court has avoided an overtly philosophical approach, many opinions are sprinkled with references to philosophical writings. In *Dolphin Delivery*, the first case to interpret the meaning of freedom of expression, reference was made to the writings of John Stuart Mill and John Milton in elaborating the meaning of freedom of expression.[38] In fact, Mill has been cited with some frequency in a range of cases,[39] as has Ronald Dworkin.[40] Justice Wilson was probably the most fre-

---

36   [1985] 1 S.C.R. 295 at 344, 18 D.L.R. (4th) 321 [*Big M*].

37   *Andrews* v. *Law Society (British Columbia)*, [1989] 1 S.C.R. 143, 56 D.L.R. (4th) 1.

38   *R.W.D.S.U., Local 580* v. *Dolphin Delivery Ltd.*, [1986] 2 S.C.R. 573 at 583, 33 D.L.R. (4th) 174 [*Dolphin Delivery*].

39   *Reference Re Public Service Employee Relations Act (Alberta)*, [1987] 1 S.C.R. 313 at 365, 38 D.L.R. (4th) 161, Dickson C.J.C.; *Jones* v. *R.*, [1986] 2 S.C.R. 284 at 318, 31 D.L.R. (4th) 569, Wilson J.

40   *Edwards Books & Art Ltd.* v. *R.*, [1986] 2 S.C.R. 713 at 809, 35 D.L.R. (4th) 1, Wilson J.; *Operation Dismantle Inc.* v. *R.*, [1985] 1 S.C.R. 441 at 481, 18 D.L.R. (4th) 481, Wilson J.; *R.* v. *Therens*, [1985] 1 S.C.R. 613 at 638, 18 D.L.R. (4th) 655, LeDain J.

quent user of philosophical materials in her years on the bench as she strove to give meaning to the rights and freedoms in the early days of *Charter* interpretation.[41]

While the Court rejected appeals to original intent, the judges have nevertheless looked to historical material and traditions to inform the meaning of the rights. In *Big M Drug Mart*, the first major case on freedom of religion, Dickson J. looked back in history to determine the rationale for protecting individuals' choice of religion, noting the many excesses of governments in the past to suppress religions with which they did not agree.[42] McLachlin J., in the first case on electoral boundaries under section 3, looked closer to home to determine the meaning of the right to vote within Canadian history. In rejecting an interpretation that guaranteed "one person, one vote," as in the United States, she drew on Canada's history (and geography) to explain why the right in Canada should aspire towards equality of voters in various electoral constituencies while at the same time emphasizing a right to effective representation. With quotes from our first prime minister, Sir John A. Macdonald, and other references to tradition, she concluded:

> [T]he history of our right to vote and the context in which it existed at the time the *Charter* was adopted support the conclusion that the purpose of the guarantee of the right to vote is not to effect perfect voter equality, in so far as that can be done, but the broader goal of guaranteeing effective representation . . . [D]emocracy in Canada is rooted in a different history than in the United States . . .[43]

McLachlin J. made it clear that she did not accept history or tradition as definitive. However, she did insist that the *Charter* should be seen as a

---

41 For example, in an opinion in a case dealing with language rights under s. 133 of the *Constitution Act, 1867*, she includes an extensive discussion of the views of various legal philosophers — Hohfeld, Austin, Hart, Stone, and Salmond — on the meaning of rights: *MacDonald v. Montreal (City)*, [1986] 1 S.C.R. 460 at 515–18, 27 D.L.R. (4th) 321. She also cites the writings of various philosophers when elaborating the meaning of "liberty" in s. 7: *R. v. Morgentaler*, [1988] 1 S.C.R. 30 at 178–79, 44 D.L.R. (4th) 385; *Jones v. R.*, above note 39 at 318–19; *Reference Re ss. 193 and 195.1(1)(c) of the Criminal Code (Canada)*, [1990] 1 S.C.R. 1123, 56 C.C.C. (3d) 65 at 135.

42 *Big M*, above note 36.

43 *Reference Re Provincial Electoral Boundaries (Saskatchewan)*, [1991] 2 S.C.R. 158 at 184, 81 D.L.R. (4th) 16.

Canadian document rooted in certain cultural and historical traditions that courts should take into consideration.[44]

The Supreme Court has also been asked to look outside Canada's borders to assist in the interpretation of the rights. In some cases, the meaning of a right in other countries is discussed. Often but not always, American sources are used. The Court takes this information into consideration, but in no case has it been determinative.[45] Sometimes, reference is made to norms of international law, such as Canada's commitments under conventions of the International Labour Organization or the *Convention on the Elimination of Racial Discrimination*.[46] While international law is not directly enforceable in Canadian courts, the Supreme Court does see international commitments as a valid consideration, concluding that the *Charter* should be interpreted, where possible, in a manner consistent with Canada's international obligations.[47]

C. CONCLUSION

Judges are subject to significant restraints when interpreting the *Charter*. They must pay heed to its language, to past decisions under the doctrine of precedent, and to the respective institutional roles of the courts and the legislatures, albeit redefined by the *Charter*. Yet it is apparent that judicial interpretation of the rights and freedoms guaranteed by the *Charter* has proved to be a complex and controversial task. Our legal regime does not provide judges with precise rules to guide them in this exercise. Indeed, our constitutional tradition directs the courts to resist the argument that the language of the constitution has a rigid and fixed meaning. The constitution is seen as an organic document that must grow with the times and remain capable of responding to the demands of a changing society. The debate about the *Charter's* meaning is legal in

---

44   For example, she stated at p. 187:

> This is not to suggest, however, that inequities in our voting system are to be accepted merely because they have historical precedent. History is important in so far as it suggests that the philosophy underlying the development of the right to vote in this country is the broad goal of effective representation. It has nothing to do with the specious argument that historical anomalies and abuses can be used to justify continued anomalies and abuses, or to suggest that the right to vote should not be interpreted broadly and remedially as befits *Charter* rights.

45   Sources cited above, note 16.

46   For example, in *Keegstra*, above note 18.

47   For example, see the reasons of Dickson C.J.C. in *Slaight Communications Inc. v. Davidson*, [1989] 1 S.C.R. 1038 at 1056–57, 59 D.L.R. (4th) 416.

structure, but the purposive approach adopted by the Supreme Court requires the judges to consider a rich array of historical, philosophical, and comparative sources.

FURTHER READINGS

BAKAN, J., *Just Words: Constitutional Rights and Social Wrongs* (Toronto: University of Toronto Press, 1997)

BAYEFSKY, A., *International Human Rights Law: Use in Canadian Charter of Rights and Freedoms Litigation* (Toronto: Butterworths, 1992)

BEATTY, D.M., *Talking Heads and the Supremes: The Canadian Production of Constitutional Review* (Toronto: Carswell, 1990)

HOGG, P.W., "The Charter of Rights and American Theories of Interpretation" (1987) 15 Osgoode Hall L.J. 87

HOGG, P.W., "Interpreting the Charter of Rights: Generosity and Justification" (1990) 28 Osgoode Hall L.J. 817

TRACKMAN, L.E., *Reasoning with the Charter* (Toronto: Butterworths, 1991)

CHAPTER 4

LIMITATION OF
CHARTER RIGHTS

A central task in the interpretation of any instrument guaranteeing fundamental rights and freedoms is to reconcile the rights of the individual with the interests of the community at large. The effect of the *Charter* is to shift an important share of responsibility for this task from the elected representatives of the people to the judiciary. In light of the Supreme Court's generous definition of most enumerated rights through the purposive method of interpretation described in chapter 3, it is not surprising to find that the court places heavy reliance on the second stage of *Charter* adjudication defining the limitation of rights. This is mandated by section 1, which, as noted above, provides that the rights and freedoms guaranteed are "subject only to such reasonable limits prescribed by law as can be justified in a free and democratic society." The Supreme Court has interpreted that provision as encompassing both a formal and a substantive element — the formal element is caught by the words "prescribed by law" and the substantive element is contained in an examination of the state's justification for limiting the right and its chosen means for doing so.

A. LIMITS PRESCRIBED BY LAW

The first requirement for a justifiable limit is that it be, in the words of section 1, "prescribed by law." Initially, the courts refused to uphold laws that conferred an open-ended or vaguely defined discretion to limit protected freedoms. Thus, for example, the courts struck down as too ill-defined a customs regulation that allowed officials to restrict entry into Canada of materials that they considered to be "immoral."[1] Similarly, a provincial scheme conferring the power of censorship on a film board without setting out the criteria by which such powers were to be exercised was struck down as a violation of freedom of expression which was not prescribed by law.[2]

In the words of LeDain J., "the requirement that the limit be prescribed by law is chiefly concerned with the distinction between a limit imposed by law and one that is arbitrary."[3] Therefore, government actions that infringe *Charter* rights should provide fair notice to citizens of the conduct that is permitted and prohibited so that they can regulate their activities accordingly. Another important consideration is that the law should set adequate limits on officials who exercise discretion in applying and enforcing the law.

Despite these concerns expressed in some of the early cases, the more recent trend has been to apply a relatively relaxed standard under the "prescribed by law" requirement. The Supreme Court has stated that merely because a law is subject to various shadings of interpretation does not render it unacceptably vague.[4] In some instances, laws that appear more than unusually vague and uncertain have been upheld.[5] The cases that have considered the vagueness point in most detail have arisen under the fundamental justice guarantee in section 7 and are discussed in chapter 13. As will be seen there, the Supreme Court has said that, since laws define standards of general application, there is an inherent element of uncertainty in all laws. While there must be some limit to open-ended and ill-defined standards, the vagueness argument is not one that has found favour with the Supreme Court in recent years.

B. PROPORTIONALITY

The text of the *Charter* says little about how limitations on rights are to be justified, but the Supreme Court of Canada, employing the purposive

---

1   *Luscher v. Deputy Minister of National Revenue (Customs & Excise)*, [1985] 1 F.C. 85, 17 D.L.R. (4th) 503.
2   *Re Ontario Film & Video Appreciation Society and Ontario Board of Censors* (1984), 5 DL.R. (4th) 766 (Ont. C.A.).
3   *R. v. Therens*, [1985] 1 S.C.R. 613, 18 D.L.R. (4th) 655 at 680.
4   *R. v. Lucas*, [1998] S.C.J. No. 28.
5   *Little Sisters Book and Art Emporium v. Canada (Minister of Justice)* (1996), 131 D.L.R. (4th) 486 (B.C.S.C.).

approach, established the basic framework for analysis in *R. v. Oakes*.[6] In that case, it was established that the initial burden of proving a violation of rights rests with the individual asserting a *Charter* violation. In light of the generous definition accorded many *Charter* rights, this burden is relatively easy to discharge in many cases. Once a *prima facie* violation is proved, the burden shifts to the party attempting to justify the infringement as a reasonable limit. It is at the justification stage that the court must consider the interest in limiting a right or freedom and weigh collective interests or the competing rights of other individuals against the right of the claimant. The reconciliation of the competing interests against individual rights is achieved by focusing on the legitimacy of the government's objective and the "proportionality" between the means chosen to achieve that objective and the burden on the rights claimant.

The proportionality test has three steps. First, it must be established that there is an objective "of sufficient importance to warrant overriding a constitutionally protected right or freedom."[7] In *Oakes*, the Supreme Court of Canada said that the objective must "relate to concerns which are pressing and substantial in a free and democratic society." The courts have been relatively deferential to legislative judgment of the importance of the objective. However, the government has failed on a number of occasions to satisfy this requirement. In one case, the Supreme Court held that Quebec legislation limiting the rights of English-speaking parents to have their children attend English-language schools unless the parents had been educated in English in Quebec constituted a direct attack on the very right enshrined in section 23 of the *Charter*, and hence the law was not motivated by a proper objective.[8] Similarly, in an Ontario case, the Court of Appeal held that legislation requiring the recital of the Lord's Prayer in non-denominational public schools constituted an attempt to impose a form of religious observance and that such an objective was not permitted by the guarantee of freedom of

---

6   [1986] 1 SC.R. 103, 26 D.L.R. (4th) 200 [*Oakes*]. For a good discussion of the evolution of s. 1, see P.W. Hogg, "Section 1 Revisited" (1991) 1 N.J.C.L. 1; E. Mendes, "The Crucible of the Charter: Judicial Principles v. Judicial Deference in the Context of Section 1" in G.A. Beaudoin & E. Mendes, eds., *The Canadian Charter of Rights and Freedoms*, 3d ed. (Toronto: Carswell, 1996).

7   *R. v. Big M Drug Mart Ltd.*, [1985] 1 S.C.R. 295 at 352, 18 D.L.R. (4th) 321, Dickson C.J.C.

8   *Quebec (A.G.) v. Quebec Association of Protestant School Boards*, [1984] 2 S.C.R. 66, 10 D.L.R. (4th) 321. The language of s. 23, discussed further in chapter 16, grants the right to the children of parents educated anywhere in Canada in English.

religion.[9] In another case, the Court dealt with a challenge to a vague law prohibiting the spreading of "false news."[10] Given the ancient origin of the law, it was unclear what its objective was at the time it was enacted. While it was now used to deal with hate propaganda, it had not been designed for that pupose, and the majority of the Court held that it was not acceptable for the government to advance a new objective not in the mind of Parliament when the law was enacted. In *Vriend* v. *Alberta*,[11] the Supreme Court found that Alberta had failed to articulate any objective or purpose that would be achieved by denying the protection of its human rights law to gays and lesbians. As Iacobucci J. stated, to sustain a limit on a protected freedom, a goverment must offer more than an explanation why it chose to deny the right — it must be pursuing some objective: "An 'objective', being a goal or an 'explanation' which makes plain that which is not immediately obvious."[12] Cases in which the government fails to satisfy this first branch of the section 1 test are, however, the exception rather than the rule, and in most cases the state is readily able to satisfy the court that the law being challenged is motivated by a permissible objective of sufficient weight.

The next phase in proportionality review is to consider the means chosen to achieve that objective. The first step involves asking whether there is a rational, non-arbitrary, non-capricious connection between the legislative objective and the law that is challenged. Second, the limitation on the right must pass the minimal-impairment test — that is, it should impair the right or freedom "as little as possible." Is the law carefully tailored to meet the objective? Finally, there is a balancing stage, at which the court asks whether there is proportionality between the *effects* of the measure in question and its objectives.

With respect to the rational-connection test, the courts again have been deferential, and it is rare to find that there is no rational connection between the legislative objective and the law that is subject to scrutiny. In the *Oakes* case itself, the Supreme Court held that there was no rational connection between the objective of curbing traffic in drugs and a law that reversed the usual onus of proof in criminal cases and required anyone found in possession of drugs to prove that he or she did not have the intent to traffic. In the Court's view, there was a lack of internal rationality in the legislation, because the reverse-onus provision

9   *Zylberberg* v. *Sudbury Board of Education (Director)* (1988), 52 D.L.R. (4th) 577 (Ont. C.A.).

10   *R.* v. *Zundel*, [1992] 2 S.C.R. 731, 95 D.L.R. (4th) 202.

11   [1998] S.C.J. No. 29.

12   *Ibid.* at para. 114.

assumed that an individual in possession of even a very small amount of a drug would be likely to traffic. In the words of Dickson C.J.C.:

> [P]ossession of a small or negligible quantity of narcotics does not support the inference of trafficking. In other words, it would be irrational to infer that a person had an intent to traffic on the basis of his or her possession of a very small quantity of narcotics. The presumption required under s. 8 of the *Narcotic Control Act* is overinclusive and could lead to results in certain cases which would defy both rationality and fairness.[13]

Most commentators suggest that the Court might more readily have justified striking down the law under the minimal-impairment test, discussed below. There is a rational connection between the objective of suppressing drug trafficking and making convictions easier for the state by a reverse-onus clause.[14] However, the Court in *Oakes* not only looked at the rationality of the means to meet the objective from the state's point of view, but also considered the arbitrariness of the law with respect to the rights claimant, a consideration now more likely to be addressed under the minimal-impairment component.[15] In subsequent cases, the rational-connection component of proportionality review has rarely been determinative.

The core element of proportionality review is the minimal-impairment test. While *Oakes* described this as the principle of "least intrusive means," later cases discussed below seemed to relax the test, asking whether there was some other reasonable way for the legislature to satisfy the objective that would not impair the right or freedom at issue or that would have less impact on the right or freedom than does the law under review.[16] In one of the most notable cases to be decided by the Supreme Court in this area, it was held that a Quebec law prohibiting

---

13   *Oakes*, above note 6 at 142 (S.C.R.)

14   See, for example, P.J. Monahan and A.J. Petter, "Developments in Constitutional Law (The 1986–87 Term)" (1988) 10 Supreme Court L.R. 61.

15   The way in which Dickson C.J.C. phrased this stage of inquiry in *Oakes* is as follows: "[The measures] must not be arbitrary, unfair or based on irrational considerations. In short, they must be rationally connected to the objective" (above note 6 at 227 (D.L.R.)).

16   Specifically, in *Edwards Books and Art Ltd.* v. *R.*, [1986] 2 S.C.R. 713, 35 D.L.R. (4th) 1 [*Edwards Books*], Dickson C.J.C. reformulated the test to ask whether the right was impaired "as little as reasonably possible," which suggested that the limitation need not be the least intrusive, but the least intrusive given the legislature's objective and other competing interests — that is, the test more openly balanced the interests of the state and the rights claimant.

the display of commercial signs in English could not survive scrutiny under the minimal-impairment test.[17] The Court was prepared to find that the preservation and enhancement of the French language was a sufficiently important objective in the province of Quebec to justify limiting the guarantee of freedom of expression, and that a law that required such signs to be in French and forbade signs in English was rationally connected to this objective. However, the Court found that the law went too far in prohibiting English altogether. The province could, in the Court's view, have satisfied the legitimate objective of preserving and enhancing French by requiring that commercial signs display a marked predominance of French. Such a law would achieve the goal of enhancing the goal of a "visage linguistique" appropriate to a predominantly French society but at the same time would respect, to the extent possible consistent with the attainment of that goal, the right of non-francophones to use their language. The Court was not persuaded that a total ban on English was necessary, and the law therefore failed, since it was not the least intrusive means of satisfying the legislative objective.

The final step in proportionality review, in the words of *Oakes*, requires that there "be a proportionality between the *effects* of the measure which are responsible for limiting the *Charter* right or freedom, and the objective which has been identified as of 'sufficient importance.'"[18] This final step applies when all the other aspects of proportionality have been satisfied. It engages the court in a balancing exercise, weighing the significance of the infringement of the right against the importance of attaining the objective of the legislation. In a later case, Lamer C.J.C. refined this test by saying that the third step requires "both that the underlying *objective* of a measure and the *salutary effects* that actually result from its implementation be proportional to the deleterious effects the measure has on fundamental rights and freedoms."[19]

In the cases decided by the Supreme Court, this balancing step has never been decisive. It appears unlikely that the Court would ever find that the objective was of sufficient importance to justify overriding a protected freedom, that the least intrusive means had been employed, and yet that on balance the effects on the right were disproportionate.

---

17 *Ford v. Quebec (A.G.)*, [1988] 2 S.C.R. 712, 54 D.L.R. (4th) 577. The case was decided under the Quebec *Charter of Human Rights and Freedoms*, but the Supreme Court made it clear that the same principles applied as under the Canadian *Charter*.

18 *Ibid.* at 227 (D.L.R.).

19 *Dagenais v. Canadian Broadcasting Corp.*, [1994] 3 S.C.R. 835 at 887, 120 D.L.R. (4th) 12.

In cases like *Keegstra* (upholding the federal hate-propaganda offence in the *Criminal Code*) and *McKinney* (upholding mandatory retirement), the Court fairly quickly concluded that they passed the balancing test, having found that they were justified under the minimal-impairment stage.[20]

C. THE *OAKES* TEST: STRICT RULES OR GUIDING PRINCIPLES?

The key issue is really how strictly the *Oakes* test is applied. The decided cases indicate that the stringency of review and particularly the application of the minimal-impairment tests are both controversial and variable. Indeed, some judges quarrel with the term the *Oakes* "test." For example, La Forest J. rejected the term, stating that *Oakes* did no more than establish some principles or guidelines to help in making a decision and insisted that these principles should be applied "flexibly, having regard to the specific factual and social context of each case."[21] However, the majority view is that the *Oakes* approach remains helpful, provided it is applied flexibly, with a sensitivity to the context of the particular law at issue.[22]

The central element in the application of section 1 is the principle of least intrusive means. It is this aspect of the *Oakes* test that is the focus of most litigation under the *Charter*. The least intrusive means principle is significant in assessing the impact the *Charter* has upon the role of the judiciary. Proportionality review, especially the minimal-impairment test, requires the judges to weigh and assess the choices made by the legislature and the other policy options that were available. This is not an exercise considered to fall within the realm of judicial competence in non-constitutional cases, yet it is very often the central question in *Charter* litigation. It is now clear that the Supreme Court will not apply the minimal-impairment test literally to strike down a law simply because it is possible to conceive of another measure that might be less intrusive on a protected freedom. Even Wilson J., a staunch defender of the minimal-impairment test, held that it is only where there are measures "clearly superior to the measures currently in use"

---

20   *R. v. Keegstra*, [1990] 3 S.C.R. 697, 61 C.C.C. (3d) 1 [*Keegstra*]; *McKinney* v. *University of Guelph*, [1990] 3 S.C.R. 229, 76 D.L.R. (4th) 545 [*McKinney*].
21   *RJR-MacDonald Inc.* v. *Canada (A.G.)*, [1995] 3 S.C.R. 199, 127 D.L.R. (4th) 1 at 46 (dissenting judgment) [*RJR*].
22   *Ibid.*, at 88–90, McLachlin J; *Libman* v. *Quebec (A.G.)*, [1997] 3 S.C.R. 569, 151 D.L.R. (4th) 385 at 407 [*Libman*].

that a law will fail on this ground.[23] A unanimous judgment of the Court adopted the following formulation of the test by McLachlin J.:

> The impairment must be "minimal," that is, the law must be carefully tailored so that the rights are impaired no more than necessary. The tailoring process seldom admits of perfection and the courts must accord some leeway to the legislator. If the law falls within a range of reasonable alternatives, the courts will not find it overbroad merely because they can conceive of an alternative which might better tailor objective to infringment . . . .[24]

While the Supreme Court has yet to acknowledge openly that there are varying levels of scrutiny, it would seem that the standard of review is influenced by at least three factors.[25] First, the Court has demonstrated a marked tendency to defer to legislative judgment and apply a relatively deferential standard of review in cases involving broad issues of social and economic policy, especially where the problem is complex and the implications of various solutions are not fully understood. Courts are experts in the matter of liberty, but not in the realm of social policy. The Court has recognized that the making of social policy "is a role properly assigned to the elected representatives of the people, who have at their disposal the necessary institutional resources to enable them to compile and assess social science evidence, to mediate between competing social interests and to reach out to protect vulnerable groups."[26]

One of the most striking examples of a relaxed standard of section 1 review is the case dealing with mandatory retirement.[27] The Court found that mandatory retirement at age sixty-five violated the right conferred by section 15 not to be discriminated against on grounds of age, but it held that the legislation permitting this form of discrimination should be upheld under section 1. In the view of the majority of the

---

23   *Lavigne v. Ontario Public Service Employees Union*, [1991] 2 S.C.R. 211 at 296, 81 D.L.R. (4th) 545.

24   *Libman*, above note 22 at 415 (D.L.R.), adopting McLachlin J.'s statement from *RJR*, above note 21.

25   The American Supreme Court has developed different standards of review depending on the particular right at issue or, in the case of the equal-protection clause, the basis for differential treatment. For example, differential treatment on the basis of race triggers "strict scrutiny," while differential treatment on the basis of a characteristic such as veteran's status leads to a much more deferential "rationality" review.

26   *Libman*, above note 22 at 416 (D.L.R.), adopting a passage from the dissenting judgment of La Forest J. in *RJR*, above note 21.

27   *McKinney*, above note 20.

Court, the issue was "whether the government had a reasonable basis, on the evidence tendered, for concluding that the legislation interferes as little as possible with a guaranteed right, given the government's pressing and substantial objectives."[28] This is plainly a much more relaxed standard of review than that applied in cases dealing with those rights or freedoms which do not pose complex social-policy questions.

Second, the Court has explicitly stated that a more relaxed standard of scrutiny is called for where the legislation challenged represents an attempt by the legislature to reconcile competing claims or protect vulnerable groups. In these cases, the majority judges in *Irwin Toy* indicated:

> If the legislature has made a reasonable assessment as to where the line is most properly drawn, especially if that assessment involves weighing conflicting scientific evidence and allocating scarce resources on this basis, it is not for the court to second guess. That would only be to substitute one estimate for another.[29]

In a case dealing with a Sunday closing law,[30] the Court noted that the legislature had been motivated by a secular purpose, namely, to provide workers with a common day of rest. The legislation did attempt to accommodate non-Sunday observers, but those exemptions were drafted with a view to protecting retail-sales workers, a particularly vulnerable group, from being forced to work. The exemptions were less than perfect from the perspective of non-Sunday observers. However, the majority held that, in such circumstances, the legislature had to be given a certain latitude to ensure that the *Charter* "does not simply become an instrument of better situated individuals to roll back legislation that has as its object the improvement of the condition of less advantaged persons."[31]

This line of analysis was later expanded when the Court indicated that a distinction should be drawn between cases where "the government is best characterized as the singular antagonist of the individual whose right has been infringed" and those where the government is "mediating between the claims of competing groups" and attempting to strike a balance that will protect the vulnerable while impinging as little as possible upon protected freedoms "without the benefit of absolute certainty concerning how that balance is best struck."[32] In the former case, a rigorous standard of review should be applied under section 1,

28 *Ibid.* at 666 (D.L.R.), LaForest J.
29 *Irwin Toy Ltd. v. Quebec (A.G.)*, [1989] 1 S.C.R. 927, 58 D.L.R. (4th) 577 at 623 [*Irwin Toy*].
30 *Edwards Books*, above note 16.
31 *Ibid.* at 49 (D.L.R.), Dickson C.J.C.
32 Irwin Toy, above note 29 at 993 & 994 (S.C.R.).

while in the latter, the legislature will not be held to such a strict test. In practical terms, the line between these two types of laws cannot be sharply drawn, for many laws affecting the criminal process, while placing the state in opposition to the individual, also implicate the interests of other groups. The Court has held, for example, that hate-crimes laws, provisions limiting access to the medical records of sexual-assault victims, or rules about the prior sexual conduct of a sexual assault victim all raise equality issues and the interests of competing groups.[33]

Third, a definitional element has been introduced into proportionality review. As noted above, the Court has often avoided definitional limitations and given *Charter* rights a liberal and generous meaning. For example, both commercial expression and hate propaganda have been found to fall within the definition of "expression" and accordingly are *prima facie* protected by section 2(b).[34] Any limits imposed upon those forms of expression must be justified under section 1 to survive *Charter* scrutiny. However, definitional considerations seem to affect the strictness of review under section 1, especially with respect to expression cases. The Court has spoken of a "core" meaning of freedom of expression, leading to a strict application of section 1 when a form of expression lies at or near that "core" — for example, political speech. But when the form of expression at issue is peripheral to the core, legislation imposing limitations is much more likely to survive. While neither commercial speech nor hate propaganda are excluded at the stage of defining *Charter* rights, it is equally the case that neither lie at or near the "core" meaning of freedom of expression and, as a result, a relatively relaxed level of *Charter* scrutiny is applied. Again, the motivation is to avoid an unduly burdensome standard of *Charter* review when the legislature is acting to protect vulnerable groups. In the children's advertising case, *Irwin Toy*,[35] the law at issue was designed to protect children from exploitative commercial messages, and the Court felt that the government had struck a reasonable balance in limiting advertising directed at children under thirteen years of age. In upholding the hate-propaganda law designed to protect ethnic minorities[36] and the pornography law aimed at protecting women from degrading portrayals, the Court noted that the expression at issue was far from the core.[37]

---

33 See, for example, *R. v. Seaboyer*, [1991] 2 S.C.R. 577, 83 D.L.R. (4th) 193 (rape shield case).

34 *Irwin Toy*, above note 29; *Keegstra*, above note 20.

35 *Irwin Toy*, above note 29.

36 *Keegstra*, above note 20.

37 *R. v. Butler*, [1992] 1 S.C.R. 452, 89 D.L.R. (4th) 449.

This does not mean, however, that speech further from the core is without *Charter* protection, for challenges to legislation in some commercial-speech cases have succeeded because the bans — advertising dentists' services and tobacco products — did not pass the minimal-impairment test.[38]

D. SECTION 1 EVIDENCE

The Supreme Court in *Oakes* indicated that governments seeking to justify limitations on rights will generally be required to present evidence in support of their argument. The result has been a significant expansion in the kind of materials coming before the courts. Historical, philosophical, and economic data are presented, sometimes through expert witnesses; so, too, are government reports, both domestic and international. Occasionally, the Court seems demanding with respect to evidence — for example, in the tobacco advertising case, the majority judges commented on the failure of the federal government to show why an alternative to a total ban on advertising would undermine the government's objective. Not only had the government failed to show that it was necessary to have a complete ban; it had refused to disclose a study of alternatives to a total ban, despite the request by the party challenging the law to have the information.[39] In other cases, the Court seems to have taken a relaxed approach to the evidence. In an earlier case, for example, the Court relied on government data justifying Sunday closing legislation that was imprecise and over fifteen years old.[40]

E. CONCLUSION

Much of the debate about the Court's treatment of section 1 of the *Charter* revolves around the issue of deference. When should the courts intervene to protect rights and when should they leave decisions about rights and limits to the legislatures? There is no easy answer. Too much deference can easily undermine the purpose of the *Charter* — to protect individual rights against the majority. Yet a court that demands an

---

38 *Rocket v. Royal College of Dental Surgeons of Ontario*, [1990] 2 S.C.R. 232, 71 D.L.R. (4th) 68; *RJR*, above note 21.
39 *RJR*, above note 21 at 101, 108 (D.L.R.).
40 *Edwards Books*, above note 16.

extensive factual record and least intrusive means for rights impairment in all cases could unduly constrain the legislature's efforts to govern in the broad public interest. In the end, while the *Oakes* test provides the basic framework for analysis, the courts have not adhered to a single test that serves in all cases to determine where to draw the line between protection for rights and respect for the legislative role and competing rights and claims. As the Supreme Court has made clear,[41] the context of a particular case is of fundamental importance in the application of section 1 of the *Charter*.

FURTHER READINGS

COLKER, R., "Section 1, Contexuality and the Anti-Disadvantage Principle" (1992) 42 U.T.L.J. 77

HOGG, P.W., "Section 1 Revisited" (1991) 1 N.J.C.L. 1

MENDES, E., "The Crucible of the Charter: Judicial Principles v. Judicial Deference in the Context of Section 1" in G.A. Beaudoin & E. Mendes, eds., *The Canadian Charter of Rights and Freedoms*, 3d ed. (Toronto: Carswell, 1996)

---

41   *Edmonton Journal* v. *Alberta (A.G.)*, [1989] 2 S.C.R. 1326, 64 D.L.R. (4th) 577.

CHAPTER 5

THE LEGISLATIVE OVERRIDE

There is a significant qualification in the Canadian constitution on the power of judicial review under the *Charter*, namely, the legislative override or notwithstanding clause found in section 33. This provision represents an important compromise reached at the time of the entrenchment of the *Charter* to meet concerns about the enhanced power of judicial review. It reflects the judgment that, while a strong element of judicial review is justifiable in a democracy, judicial power also needs to be constrained. Although the override has been rarely used, it is a fundamental structural feature of the *Charter* which shapes the respective responsibilities of the courts on the one hand and Parliament and the legislatures on the other.

Section 33 of the *Charter of Rights and Freedoms* permits Parliament or a provincial legislature to declare that a law shall operate "notwithstanding a provision included in section 2 or sections 7 to 15" of the *Charter*. In other words, a law containing a simple declaration from Parliament or a legislature that it is to have effect "notwithstanding" one of these sections will be protected from judicial review, and the law will remain in effect despite violating a *Charter* guaranteed right or freedom. This means that the fundamental freedoms (expression, religion, association, and assembly) are subject to being overridden by legislative decision, as are the legal rights and, subject to section 28, the right to equality. The reach of the legislative override does not extend to democratic rights (the right to vote and the requirement of regular sessions of Parliament and the legislatures), mobility rights (the right of citizens to enter, leave, and move about the country), or language rights.

These declarations can be in effect for a maximum period of five years, which is roughly tied to the life of a Parliament. As a result, the decision to renew an override will come before a newly elected Parliament or legislature and will have to be debated again by another group of elected legislators.

There is, as might be expected, enormous controversy concerning the wisdom of including the override clause in the constitution but it was a fundamental compromise without which Canada probably would have no *Charter of Rights*. The notwithstanding clause was modelled on similar clauses in human rights codes and a provision in the *Canadian Bill of Rights*.[1]

The Supreme Court of Canada has clearly stated that it will not engage in reviewing the legitimacy of a legislative decision to invoke the override clause.[2] The Court made this pronouncement in a case involving the Quebec government's decision to enact an omnibus override clause shortly after the enactment of the *Charter*. Through one stroke of the legislative pen, all Quebec statutes were exempted from the *Charter* by a blanket repeal and then re-enactment with the inclusion of a standard override clause. In addition, all new Quebec statutes were enacted with an override clause. The result was to protect all Quebec statutes from judicial review under the *Charter*. The decision to enact the override was taken by the separatist Parti Québécois government, which had opposed the 1982 amendments to the constitution including the *Charter*. Maintaining that the government of Quebec should have a veto over any such fundamental constitutional changes, the Quebec National Assembly refused to recognize the legitimacy of the *Charter*.

These override measures were challenged. The Quebec Court of Appeal held that such a sweeping and general declaration of override was invalid and that a much more specific approach was called for.[3] The Supreme Court of Canada disagreed, holding that, so long as the form of section 33 was observed, the courts had no business second-guessing or reviewing the exercise of the override power by a legislature. According to the Supreme Court, section 33 requires only a formal declaration expressly referring to the sections of the *Charter* being overridden. The Court did, however, impose one significant limitation — a declaration under the override power could not have retroactive effect.

---

1   See, for example, Ontario *Human Rights Code*, R.S.O. 1990, c. H.19, s. 47(2); *Canadian Bill of Rights*, S.C. 1960, c. 44, s. 2.
2   *Ford v. Quebec (A.G.)*, [1988] 2 S.C.R. 712, 54 D.L.R. (4th) 577 [*Ford*].
3   *Alliance des professeurs de Montréal v. Quebec (A.G.)* (1985), 21 D.L.R. (4th) 354 (Que. C.A.).

The override clause has been resorted to infrequently and some politicians, including former prime minister Brian Mulroney, have stated that their governments would never use it. The most dramatic invocation of the override clause, apart from the general declaration exempting Quebec from the reach of the *Charter*, was the decision to override the Supreme Court of Canada's decision that the Quebec "signs law" was contrary to freedom of expression.[4] As noted in chapter 4, the Court recognized Quebec's right to act to preserve and enhance the French language but held that it had failed to justify the virtual total prohibition of the use of English and other languages on such signs. The Quebec legislature immediately resorted to the override clause in enacting a new signs law (the general override enactment having expired after five years), thereby provoking an enormously negative reaction in the rest of Canada that significantly eroded support for the package of constitutional amendments known as the Meech Lake Accord.[5]

There are many who argue that the override clause represents a significant defect in the Canadian constitution, since fundamental rights should never have to yield to majoritarian decisions regarding the general welfare.[6] It is argued that the courts should have the exclusive and final say in matters of fundamental rights and that the majority must forever comply with their interpretations of the *Charter*.

Another school of thought is more accepting of the override clause.[7] The override is seen as a useful safety valve which can be invoked to escape significant errors or departures by the courts in the interpretation of constitutional guarantees. But for the override clause, nothing short of a subsequent case reversing the earlier decision or a constitutional amendment will correct the error.

Defenders of section 33 also argue that the override is deeply rooted in the Canadian political and constitutional tradition, which accepts that Parliament itself has an important role in the protection of rights.[8] Rather than seeing Parliament and the legislatures as being inevitably at odds with the courts in this sphere, the override clause recognizes the

---

4   *Ford*, above note 2.
5   While the Accord was much favoured in Quebec, it did not generate enough support in the rest of Canada to be enacted within the three-year time-frame necessary under the amendment process. As a result, it died in June 1990.
6   See especially J.D. Whyte, "On Not Standing for Notwithstanding" (1990) 28 Alta. L. Rev. 347.
7   See especially P.H. Russell, "Standing Up for Notwithstanding" (1991) 29 Alta. L. Rev. 293.
8   See B. Slattery, "A Theory of the *Charter*" (1987) 25 Osgoode Hall L.J. 701.

legitimate role of legislators in defining an appropriate balance between the rights of the individuals and the interests of society at large.

Finally, the override clause may be seen as creating a check on the power of both legislatures and the courts. On the one hand, the *Charter* confers a broad mandate upon the judiciary to act to protect fundamental rights and freedoms, thereby significantly curtailing legislative power. On the other hand, the override clause ensures that the courts' power is not unlimited. Taken as a whole, section 33 ensures that no one has the last word. Even if the clause is invoked to overcome judicial review, the five-year limitation period on any use of the override ensures that the issue will have to be revisited after another election in which the people can hold accountable their democratically elected representatives. The net effect of the section is to achieve a subtle and effective check on both legislative and judicial power.[9]

It is impossible to know whether the override clause has had an impact on the Supreme Court of Canada's interpretation of the *Charter*. Some commentators have speculated that the availability of the override has made the judges more willing to engage in a rigorous protection of rights.[10]

The only province other than Quebec to invoke the override was Saskatchewan in an effort to protect back-to-work legislation introduced during a labour dispute. The Supreme Court of Canada subsequently upheld the constitutionality of the legislation, thereby removing any need for the override. The suggestion by the Alberta government in 1998 that it intended to use the override to protect legislation limiting compensation for victims of forced sterilization provoked an outcry. Shortly thereafter, the same government refused to employ the override to reverse the decision of the Supreme Court extending the protection of the human rights legislation to gays and lesbians.[11] The override gives the majority a legal mechanism to have its way, but it may well be that the people will rarely, if ever, assume the moral burden of overriding protected rights and freedoms.

---

9   The theme of dialogue between the courts and the legislature is developed by Slattery, above, and by P.W. Hogg & A.A. Bushell, "The Charter Dialogue between Courts and Legislatures" (1997) 35 Osgoode Hall L.J. 75. It is also discussed by Iacobucci J., in *Vriend* v. *Alberta*, [1998] S.C.J. No. 29 [*Vriend*], at para. 138.

10   Russell, above note 7.

11   *Vriend*, above note 9.

FURTHER READINGS

RUSSELL, P.H., "Standing Up for Notwithstanding" (1991) 29 Alta. L. Rev. 293

SLATTERY, B., "A Theory of the *Charter*" (1987) 25 Osgoode Hall L.J. 701

WEINRIB, L.E. "Learning to Live with the Override" (1990) 35 McGill L.J. 541

Whyte, J.D., "On Not Standing for Notwithstanding" (1990) 28 Alta. L. Rev. 347

CHAPTER 6

APPLICATION

Section 32 of the *Canadian Charter of Rights and Freedoms* states that the *Charter* applies to "the Parliament and government of Canada in respect of all matters within the authority of Parliament . . ." and "to the legislature and government of each province in respect of all matters within the authority of the legislature of each province." In the early years of the *Charter*, there was considerable debate and uncertainty as to the appropriate interpretation of this section. It was not clear whether all legal relationships were subject to *Charter* scrutiny. In all provinces except Quebec, the residual source of law is the common law, which does not depend upon any explicit legislative enactment. Common law rules of contract, property, and tort govern an enormous range of social and economic activity. Does the *Charter* apply to the common law? Another aspect of the common law tradition is the concept that individuals are free to do as they please in the absence of some specific legal measure restraining their freedom. Does the *Charter* reach areas of human activity that are not subject to any specific legislation? Despite the importance of these issues, the text of the *Charter* was ambiguous. Some commentators thought that the purpose of section 32 was to limit the application of the *Charter* to *government* action. They argued that it would be wrong to subject the entire legal regime to *Charter* review, and that the essence of a constitutional charter of rights was to deal with the relationship between the individual and the state, not all relationships between individuals. Others argued that the supremacy clause in section 52 of the *Constitution Act, 1982,* made the *Charter* applicable to all action, public and private, and that section 32 was included simply as a precautionary measure to ensure that all levels of governments were bound.

A. *DOLPHIN DELIVERY* — LIMITING THE APPLICATION OF THE CHARTER

This debate was largely put to rest in *Dolphin Delivery*, a case involving unlawful secondary picketing by a union.[1] The employer sought an injunction to prevent the picketing. While most provincial labour codes regulate secondary picketing, this dispute was governed by the *Canada Labour Code*, which was silent on the issue. The employer argued that the union's activity was unlawful on the basis that it amounted to a tort, or civil wrong, recognized by the common law. The union argued that an injunction would violate the guarantee of freedom of expression under section 2(b) of the *Charter*, and the issue arose as to whether the *Charter* had any application to the activities of non-governmental private actors and to the judge-made common law in areas such as tort, contract, and property.

The Supreme Court of Canada concluded that the *Charter* applies only to government. The court determined that "government" includes the legislative, executive, and administrative branches. Therefore, all laws and regulations are subject to *Charter* scrutiny, as are the actions of the police or other governmental officials in their treatment of individuals. The Court also concluded that the *Charter* must apply to the common law, but only to the extent that the government relies upon it. For example, had the picketers been protesting some public matter and faced a suit by the government, the *Charter* would apply to any common law rules relied upon by the government.[2]

Some commentators have argued that the judicial branch and the judge-made common law should be included within the definition of "government." McIntyre J., writing for the majority, rejected the argument that a court order constitutes government action.[3] In McIntyre J.'s words:

> The courts are, of course, bound by the *Charter* as they are bound by all law. It is their duty to apply the law, but in so doing they act as neutral arbiters, not as contending parties in a dispute. To regard a court order as an element of governmental intervention necessary to invoke

---

1   R.W.D.S.U., *Local 580* v. *Dolphin Delivery Ltd.*, [1986] 2 S.C.R. 573, 33 D.L.R.(4th) 174 [*Dolphin Delivery*].

2   *Dolphin Delivery*, above note 1 at 194–95 (DL.R.).

3   This had been the holding in the leading American case on the point, *Shelley* v. *Kraemer*, 334 U.S. 1 (1948).

the *Charter* would, it seems to me, widen the scope of *Charter* application to virtually all private litigation.[4]

The Supreme Court's decision in *Dolphin Delivery* generated a great
deal of criticism. Many argued that the *Charter* should apply to the common law, since it is an important source of law in Canada.[5] Others were
critical of the public/private distinction drawn, which would subject the
government — but not other actors — to the *Charter*. In the view of
some critics, the Court's decision ignored the fact that private power,
often exercised by corporate entities, could just as easily undermine
individual liberty and equality as could government action.[6]

Yet there are countervailing arguments to an expansive application
of the *Charter*. Was the *Charter* really meant to govern all aspects of
individual relationships? For example, should parents' constraints on
children's expression or the refusal of a women's bridge group to
include male members be subject to Charter review?[7] To invite the
courts to scrutinize all private as well as public action would greatly
extend the reach of the *Charter*, the scope of *Charter* litigation, and the
power of the courts. Ironically, many of those who criticize *Dolphin
Delivery* for restricting the reach of the *Charter* also contend that the
Charter represents an unjustifiable expansion of judicial power.

Despite the academic invitation to rethink its approach, the Supreme
Court of Canada affirmed its holding in *Dolphin Delivery* in later cases. The
explanation for the Court's conclusion lies in its particular vision of the
role of the *Charter*. La Forest J. developed this conception in the mandatory-retirement case. He wrote: "[T]he *Charter* is essentially an instrument
for checking the powers of government over the individual . . . To open up
all private and public action to judicial review could strangle the operation
of society and . . . could seriously interfere with freedom of contract."[8] In

---

4   *Dolphin Delivery*, above note 1 at 196 (D.L.R.).

5   B. Slattery, "The *Charter's* Relevance to Private Litigation: Does *Dolphin* Deliver?"
     (1987) 32 McGill L.J. 905; D.M. Beatty, "Constitutional Conceits: The Coercive
     Authority of Courts" (1987) 37 U.T.L.J. 183. Slattery, for example, pointed out the
     irrationality of having the *Charter* apply to the *Civil Code* in Quebec, which is
     found in statute, but not to common law.

6   A.C. Hutchinson and A.J. Petter, "Private Wrongs/Public Wrongs: The Liberal Lie
     of the *Charter*" (1988) 38 U.T.L.J. 278.

7   See, for example, J. Whyte, "Is the Private Sector Affected by the *Charter*?" in
     L. Smith et al., eds., *Righting the Balance: Canada's New Equality Rights* (Saskatoon:
     Canadian Human Rights Reporter, 1986) at 145; R. Elliot and R. Grant, "The
     Charter's Application in Private Litigation" (1989) 23 U.B.C. L. Rev. 459.

8   *McKinney v. University of Guelph*, [1990] 3 S.C.R. 229, 76 D.L.R. (4th) 545 at 633–44
     [*McKinney*].

other words, the Supreme Court of Canada sees the exclusive focus of the *Charter* as a judicially enforceable check on government, necessary to protect fundamental rights from the unreasonable actions of politicians and public officials. Absent the Court's intervention, the excesses of government could be curbed only by political action. As noted in chapter 2, the philosophy underlying the constitutional guarantee of rights is that ordinary politics may not always be adequate to protect individuals and minorities from abuse by majorities. With respect to non-governmental action, this argument for the need for judicial oversight has no application. The legislature has the power to decide the appropriate scope of individual liberty or the balance between equality and liberty, as well as the power to intervene where necessary to check abuses of private authority that undermine individual rights.[9] To say that the *Charter* does not apply to private actors is not to ignore the potential for abuse of private power. Rather, it is to say that the locus of authority for legal controls is best left with the legislature and that it would be inappropriate for the courts to assume responsibility for all issues of social justice for all elements of society.[10]

B. WHAT IS GOVERNMENT?

In the cases following *Dolphin Delivery*, the task for the courts has been to determine what constitutes governmental action for the purposes of the *Charter*. The Supreme Court has held that the *Charter* applies to Cabinet decisions[11] but not to actions of legislative assemblies protected by parliamentary privilege.[12] The Court has found that professional bodies exercising regulatory power delegated by the government, such as law societies, are subject to the *Charter*.[13] Similarly, an adjudicator appointed under the federal labour code to determine whether an employee was unjustly dismissed was held to have issued a remedial order contrary to the *Charter* when he ordered the former employer to issue a specific letter of reference. The fact that the statute was the

9 In *Dolphin Delivery*, McIntyre J. noted that there are instruments such as human rights codes available to check private abuses.
10 Compare J. Bakan, *Just Words: Constitutional Rights and Social Wrongs* (Toronto: University of Toronto Press, 1997).
11 *Operation Dismantle Inc. v. R.*, [1985] 1 S.C.R. 441, 18 D.L.R. (4th) 481, a case involving a Cabinet decision to allow missile testing.
12 *New Brunswick Broadcasting Co. v. Nova Scotia (Speaker of the House of Assembly)*, [1993] 1 S.C.R. 319, 100 D.L.R. (4th) 212, which refused to subject to *Charter* scrutiny a decision to ban television proceedings in the legislative assembly.
13 *Black v. Law Society of Alberta*, [1989] 1 S.C.R. 591, 58 D.L.R.(4th) 317; *Rocket v. Royal College of Dental Surgeons of Ontario*, [1990] 2 S.C.R. 232, 71 D.L.R. (4th) 68.

source of the authority for the order made the exercise of the adjudicator's discretion subject to *Charter* principles.[14]

Cases have also considered, with varying results, the application of the *Charter* to a number of institutions in the broader public sector. In *McKinney* and *Harrison*, the Supreme Court of Canada held that the *Charter* does not apply to universities, even though they receive government funding, are created by statute, and may have government appointees on their governing bodies.[15] Despite these close links to government, the Court focused on the independence of universities from government control in their day-to-day operations and academic decision making, and it concluded that the *Charter* did not apply to the mandatory-retirement policies of these institutions. Similarly, in *Stoffman*, a hospital was held not to be subject to the *Charter*, despite government funding and some degree of oversight, since here as well there was a sufficient element of day-to-day independence.[16]

In contrast, community colleges in both British Columbia and Ontario have been held to be part of government for purposes of the *Charter*.[17] In the British Columbia case, the Court found that the college was an agent of the Crown. In both cases it was noted that there was greater control of college operations and programs by governmental officials than with universities. The result in the Ontario case was to find not only that the college was part of government but also that the collective agreement signed with a union was subject to the *Charter*. The Court concluded that government, through the college, was bound by the *Charter* not only with respect to its legislative function but also when making a contract or engaging in commercial activity. As a result, public-sector employment rules are subject to *Charter* scrutiny.

In sum, the test for determining whether entities such as hospitals, public broadcasters, or the post office are "government" for purposes of the *Charter* turns on the degree to which there is significant control by government ministers or their officials in their day-to-day operations.[18]

---

14   *Slaight Communications Inc.* v. *Davidson*, [1989] 1 S.C.R. 1038, 59 D.L.R. (4th) 416.

15   *McKinney*, above note 8; *Harrison* v. *University of British Columbia*, [1990] 3 S.C.R. 451, [1991] 77 D.L.R. (4th) 55.

16   *Stoffman* v. *Vancouver General Hospital*, [1990] 3 S.C.R. 483, 76 D.L.R. (4th) 700.

17   *Douglas/Kwantlen Faculty Assn.* v. *Douglas College*, [1990] 3 S.C.R. 570, 77 D.L.R. (4th) 94; *Lavigne* v. *Ontario Public Service Employees Union*, [1991] 2 S.C.R. 211, 81 D.L.R. (4th) 545.

18   Just as the Canadian test for what is government is developed on a case-by-case basis, so, too, do the American courts struggle with what constitutes "state action." See, for example, the discussion in K.E. Swinton, "Application of the Canadian *Charter* of Rights and Freedoms" in W.S. Tarnopolsky & G.A. Beaudoin, eds., *The Canadian Charter of Rights and Freedoms: Commentary* (Toronto: Carswell, 1982) at 41.

C. APPLYING THE *CHARTER* TO THE COMMON LAW

In *Dolphin Delivery*, the Supreme Court concluded that the *Charter* did not apply to the common law unless government relied on it. Nevertheless, the Court went on to say that, although the *Charter* did not apply to disputes between private parties, this was "a distinct issue from the question whether the judiciary ought to apply and develop the principles of the common law in a manner consistent with the fundamental values enshrined in the Constitution. The answer to this question must be in the affirmative."[19] Accordingly, the courts are to consider *Charter* principles when developing the common law. This is potentially a significant exception to the otherwise restrictive view of the *Charter's* application reflected by the *Dolphin Delivery* decision.

In a decision rendered shortly after *Dolphin Delivery*, the Supreme Court of Canada held that the *Charter* applied in a proceeding involving an *ex parte* injunction.[20] The injunction was issued to restrain picketing of a court-house during a lawful strike, on the basis that this constituted criminal contempt of court. The rules about contempt of court were found in the common law, but the Supreme Court held that the *Charter* nevertheless applied because the judge, in issuing the injunction, acted in a public capacity and invoked criminal law powers: "The criminal law is being applied to vindicate the rule of law and the fundamental freedoms protected by the *Charter*. At the same time, however, this branch of the criminal law, like any other, must comply with the fundamental standards established by the *Charter*."[21]

The *Charter* was similarly invoked in proceedings challenging a judge's order restraining the broadcast of a docudrama while a criminal trial on similar issues was ongoing or about to start.[22] The accused feared that the program might influence jurors and thereby affect the fairness of their criminal trials. On that basis, they obtained an order from a superior court judge prohibiting the broadcast until the completion of the criminal trials. The media then challenged the publication ban under section 2(b) of the *Charter*. Lamer C.J.C. stated that the discretion at common law to order a publication ban in criminal proceed-

---

19   *Dolphin Delivery*, above note 1 at 198 (D.L.R.)
20   *B.C.G.E.U. v. British Columbia (A.G.)*, [1988] 2 S.C.R. 214, 53 D.L.R. (4th) 1, also discussed in chapter 9, "Freedom of Expression."
21   *Ibid.* at 244 (S.C.R.).
22   *Dagenais v. Canadian Broadcasting Corp.*, [1994] 3 S.C.R. 835, 120 D.L.R.(4th) 12, also discussed in chapter 9.

ings must be exercised so as to conform to the *Charter*. In his view, the pre-*Charter* common law rule emphasized the right to a fair trial over the right to freedom of expression. The enhanced protection accorded by the *Charter* to freedom of expression called for reformulation of the common law rule.[23] Applying the new rule to the facts in the case, Lamer C.J.C. concluded that the initial ban was not justified, since there were alternative measures to safeguard the trial process.[24]

In both these cases, the application of the common law arose in the context of the administration of the criminal law by the courts. In *Hill v. Church of Scientology*,[25] the Court considered the interaction of the *Charter* and the common law in a purely private context. Hill, then a Crown prosecutor, sued the Church of Scientology and its counsel for libel because of various statements made about his conduct. The defendants challenged the validity of the common law of libel, claiming that it violated their right to freedom of expression. Speaking for the Court, Cory J. explained why it was necessary to interpret the common law in a manner consistent with *Charter* principles:

> Historically, the common law evolved as a result of the courts making those incremental changes which were necessary in order to make the law comply with current societal values. The *Charter* represents a restatement of the fundamental values which guide and shape our democratic society and our legal system. It follows that it is appropriate for the courts to make such incremental revisions to the common law as may be necessary to have it comply with the values enunciated in the *Charter*.[26]

Cory J. was careful to insist that the *Charter* does not apply directly to private activity, and that it cannot be applied in the same manner as

---

23   *Ibid.* at 38 (D.L.R.):
     A publication ban should be ordered when:
     (a)   Such a ban is *necessary* in order to prevent a real and substantial risk to the fairness of the trial, because reasonably available alternative measures will not prevent the risk; and
     (b)   The salutary effects of the publication ban outweigh the deleterious effects to the free expression of those affected by the ban.
24   *Ibid.* at 40. The *Charter* was also used to modify the common law rules allowing the Crown prosecutor to introduce evidence of an accused's insanity in *R. v. Swain*, [1991] 1 S.C.R. 933, 63 C.C.C. (3d) 481.
25   *Hill v. Church of Scientology of Toronto*, [1995] 2 S.C.R. 1130, 126 D.L.R. (4th) 129, also discussed in chapter 9. The Court rejected the argument that there was government action here because Hill was a government employee, concluding that the defamation had been made against him personally, not against the government.
26   *Ibid.* at 1169 (S.C.R.).

when government action is involved. Judicial law making is constrained. The courts will effect only incremental changes to the common law; more far-reaching change should be left to the legislature. The limitations clause in section 1 and the *Oakes* test do not apply to the modification of the common law in private litigation. Rather, said Cory J., a more flexible balancing of interests is required, with *Charter* values weighed against the principles underlying the common law. While the Court refused to make significant changes to the common law of libel, the Court did alter the common law rule relating to the reporting of court proceedings as being inconsistent with the *Charter* value of freedom of expression.

The Court's recognition of the application of *Charter* values to the common law in a private context is significant. By expanding the powers of the courts to modify common law rules, the Supreme Court has softened the impact of the strict public/private distinction drawn in *Dolphin Delivery*.

D. CLAIMING *CHARTER* RIGHTS

To this point, the focus has been on whether the *Charter* applies to particular actions or entities. There is another important application issue that should also be mentioned: namely, who can invoke *Charter* rights? Some of the rights are framed as "everyone has the right" (for example, the fundamental freedoms of expression and religion in section 2 and the right to life, liberty, and security of the person in section 7). Others are available to "any person," as in the legal rights in section 11, or to an "individual," as in the equality rights in section 15. Some are available to citizens or permanent residents (for example, mobility rights in section 6 and minority-language education rights in section 23).

Some *Charter* rights have been held to be unavailable to corporations. For example, the equality rights in section 15 and the right to life, liberty, and security of the person in section 7 have been deemed to be rights that can be exercised only by human beings. Corporations can, however, invoke certain rights which have been seen as appropriate for a corporate entity — for example, freedom of expression.

Even if a corporation cannot directly claim that its rights have been violated, it may have standing to raise a *Charter* issue in criminal or regulatory proceedings, where a law under which it is being prosecuted is alleged to be in violation of others' *Charter* rights. For example, if a corporation is prosecuted under a law prohibiting Sunday shopping, it can challenge the law as a denial of freedom of religion even though section

2(a), the guarantee of freedom of religion, does not apply directly to a corporation.[27] The reason for this lies in the concept of the rule of law: that no one should be subject to prosecution under an unconstitutional law.[28]

E. CONCLUSION

Dolphin Delivery determined that the basic principle of *Charter* application is that the purpose of the constitution is to check the power of government over the individual. There is no question but that this represents a significant constraint on the reach of the *Charter*, especially in an age of shrinking government. The sharp distinction between the public and private domains and the immunity of powerful private interests from *Charter* scrutiny is thought by many to be unduly restrictive. On the other hand, the courts have also been criticized for assuming too much power under the *Charter* and indeed the reach of the *Charter* would be unlimited were it not for *Dolphin Delivery*. In the end, the question is an institutional one: which body is best able to deal with the power of private interests, the courts or the legislatures? The Supreme Court has determined that it is simply not prepared to assume responsibility for all issues of social justice, and that it should focus its efforts under the *Charter* to resolving conflicts between the individual and the state. That having been said, it must not be forgotten that *Dolphin Delivery* does leave scope for extending the *Charter*'s reach. The residual common law is not directly subject to the *Charter*, but it is a form of judge-made law, and the courts are directed to pay heed to *Charter* values in its development. While this has produced few changes to date, it does represent a potentially significant escape from the strictures of *Dolphin Delivery*.

---

27 *R. v. Big M Drug Mart Ltd.*, [1985] 1 S.C.R. 295, 18 D.L.R. (4th) 321.
28 Further discussion of constitutional litigation is found in chapter 7.

FURTHER READINGS

BEATTY, D.M., "Constitutional Conceits: The Coercive Authority of Courts" (1987) 37 U.T.L.J. 183

ELLIOT, R., & R. GRANT, "The *Charter's* Application in Private Litigation" (1989) 23 U.B.C. L. Rev. 459

SLATTERY, B., "The *Charter's* Relevance to Private Litigation: Does *Dolphin* Deliver?" (1987) 32 McGill L.J. 905

SWINTON, K.E., "Application of the Canadian *Charter* of Rights and Freedoms" in W.S. Tarnopolsky & G.A. Beaudoin, eds., *The Canadian Charter of Rights and Freedoms: Commentary* (Toronto: Carswell, 1982) 41

WHYTE, J., "Is the Private Sector Affected by the *Charter*?" in L. Smith et al., eds., *Righting the Balance: Canada's New Equality Rights* (Saskatoon: Canadian Human Rights Reporter, 1986)

CHAPTER 7

CHARTER LITIGATION

Charter issues are decided in the ordinary course of litigation.[1] Any citizen whose rights are affected is entitled to raise a constitutional issue in a civil proceeding or by way of defence to a criminal prosecution. Canadian law follows the Anglo-American legal tradition and does not assign particular responsibility to a specialized court for the adjudication of constitutional disputes. The court that has jurisdiction over the dispute has, by virtue of that jurisdiction, authority to decide the constitutional issue.

This method of dealing with constitutional cases has important implications for the manner in which constitutional issues are decided. It means that *Charter* issues will almost always arise in a fact-specific context and be decided in the course of a concrete dispute between two parties. The primary task of the court is to decide the case before it, not to pronounce at large upon the constitution or its meaning. It is an established practice in Canadian law that, if a judge can decide a case without dealing with a constitutional issue, he or she should do so. Moreover, because proceedings in Canadian courts are strictly adversarial, a judge will not ordinarily comment upon a constitutional issue unless one is raised by the parties. Even if there is believed to be a constitutional issue that may be dealt with on the facts, it would be unusual

---

1   Both this chapter and chapter 17 draw freely on a contribution to a collection on Canadian constitutional law published in Italian, "Ordinamento giudiziarrio e giustizia costituzionale" in *L'ordinamento costituzionale del Canada* (Torino, G. Giappichelli Editore, 1997).

for a judge to deal with the issue if the parties do not raise it. It is for the parties to the dispute to define the issues before the court. Similarly, the parties control the presentation of evidence and argument.

A. INTERVENTION BY THE ATTORNEY GENERAL AND PUBLIC-INTEREST GROUPS

While constitutional cases generally follow the same procedural path as other cases, there are some important exceptions and special procedural rules to reflect the wide range of interests implicated and the importance of any decision for the future. The first concerns the representation of the public and other interests. A party who challenges the constitutional validity of a statute is required to give notice to the attorney general, provincial, federal, or both, as appropriate.[2] The attorney general has the right to intervene in the proceeding and to present whatever evidence or argument he or she deems necessary to defend the constitutionality of the law. This may seem to depart from the adversarial system by allowing for non-party participation, but, in fact, interventions by the attorney general reflect the underlying values of the adversarial system. A constitutional case implicates the public interest and it is a basic tenet of the adversarial system that rights should not be affected without affording the right-holder a hearing. The intervention of the attorney general ensures that the public interest will be represented before the courts when the constitutionality of a statute is attacked.

A second important development in constitutional litigation, particularly at the level of the Supreme Court of Canada, is the generous allowance for public-interest groups to appear as intervenors.[3] While the courts were initially cautious in this area,[4] the discretion to permit public-interest groups to intervene has been frequently exercised. Once again, this is a reflection of the fact that the decision of the court on a constitutional matter will have broad public ramifications. Those who have particular interests that are affected and who can assist the court should be heard.

Certain public-interest groups have appeared regularly before the Supreme Court of Canada in *Charter* litigation and they have had a sig-

---

2   See B.L. Strayer, *The Canadian Constitution and the Courts: The Function and Scope of Judicial Review*, 3d ed. (Toronto: Butterworths, 1988) at 73–86.

3   P.R. Muldoon, *Law of Intervention: Status and Practice* (Aurora, ON: Canadian Law Book, 1989).

4   K. Swan, "Intervention and Amicus Curiae Status in Charter Litigation" in R.J. Sharpe, ed., *Charter Litigation* (Toronto: Butterworths, 1987).

nificant influence. Notable are the interventions of the Canadian Civil Liberties Association, a body that exists to defend the interests of civil liberties, and the Women's Legal Education and Action Fund, or LEAF, a feminist group concerned with equality rights. There can be little question but that the reasoning of certain Supreme Court judgments has been influenced by, or even based upon, arguments presented by some of these groups. To be accepted as an intervenor, a group must apply to the court before the case is heard and demonstrate both that it has a serious interest in the issues to be litigated and that it has a distinctive perspective to bring to bear upon those issues. If given intervenor status, the group will have the opportunity to file written argument and often be permitted to make brief oral submissions.

B. REFERENCES

There is one significant exception to the general rule that constitutional disputes are decided in the course of ordinary litigation. The *Supreme Court Act* provides that the federal government may refer directly to the Court questions of law or fact concerning the interpretation of the constitution or the constitutionality or interpretation of any federal or provincial legislation.[5] There is similar legislation in each province permitting provincial governments to refer questions to the provincial Court of Appeal.[6] References have become a familiar and distinctive feature of Canadian constitutional law.[7] Most countries that follow the common law tradition do not permit references, and the device has been rejected as unconstitutional in both the United States[8] and Australia[9] and exists only in a very different and modified form in England.[10] Technically, a reference asks the court for an advisory opinion and, accordingly, the answer given by the court lacks the formal quality of a judgment for purposes of the doctrine of precedent. However, in practice, opinions rendered on references are almost invariably followed in subsequent litigation and treated in the same way as a judgment given in an ordinary case.

---

5 R.S.C. 1985, c. S-26, s. 53.
6 See, for example, *Courts of Justice Act*, R.S.O. 1990, c. C-43, s. 8.
7 See Strayer, above note 2 at 315–18.
8 L. Tribe, *American Constitutional Law*, 2d ed. (Mineola: Foundation Press, 1988) at 73–77.
9 *Re Judiciary and Navigation Acts* (1921), 29 C.L.R. 257.
10 See J. Jaconelli, "Hypothetical Disputes, Moot Points of Law, and Advisory Opinions" (1985) 101 L.Q.R. 587.

References have often been used when a government considers it to be in the public interest to have an immediate resolution by the appellate court of a constitutional issue. The procedure circumvents the normal process of trial, appeal, and further appeal to the Supreme Court of Canada and allows the government to obtain a relatively quick answer to a constitutional issue. It is also possible for one government to direct a reference as to the constitutionality of another government's law or proposed course of action. There are important examples of this being done by the federal government,[11] and the technique has also been used by provincial governments.

The most notable instance of a provincial reference with regard to a proposed federal course of action arose in connection with the patriation of the constitution in 1981.[12] The federal government had indicated that it would proceed to request the United Kingdom Parliament to amend the Canadian constitution although it had the consent of only two of the ten provinces. Three provincial governments referred the question to their courts of appeal and those cases were then appealed to the Supreme Court of Canada, which ruled that constitutional convention precluded the federal government from proceeding in the manner proposed. The result was that all governments were sent back to the bargaining table for a further round of talks and negotiation and significant changes were made to the constitutional amendments which were eventually enacted.[13]

One of the shortcomings of the reference procedure is that the court lacks the usual factual foundation because it is presented with an abstract question. Canadian judges are often troubled by this, since it is out of keeping with the fact-specific manner in which constitutional issues are ordinarily presented. On occasion, the Supreme Court has complained of being asked to answer a constitutional question without a specific factual context.[14] The Court has even said that it is not obliged to answer a reference if there is an insufficient basis for adjudication,[15] but the right to decline has been exercised infrequently and never in a significant case.

---

11   *Reference Re Alberta Legislation*, [1938] S.C.R. 100, [1938] 2 D.L.R. 81.
12   *Re Resolution to amend the Constitution*, [1981] 1 S.C.R. 753, 125 D.L.R. (3d) 1.
13   For an account of the process and negotiations, see R.J. Romanow, J. Whyte, & H.A. Leeson, *Canada . . . Notwithstanding: The Making of the Constitution, 1976–1982* (Toronto: Carswell Methuen, 1984).
14   *Manitoba (A.G.) v. Manitoba Egg and Poultry Association*, [1971] S.C.R. 689 at 704–5, 19 D.L.R. (3d) 169.
15   *Reference Re Legislative Authority of Parliament to Alter or Replace the Senate*, [1980] 1 S.C.R. 54, 102 D.L.R. (3d) 1.

References have been used to resolve pressing *Charter* issues. In Ontario, the provincial government employed the reference procedure when it decided to extend full funding to Roman Catholic separate schools. A variety of interests, including private and religious schools, which did not enjoy like support, attacked this measure as being contrary to the section 15 guarantee of equality. Prolonged litigation could have disrupted the administration of Ontario schools for years and the government decided that it would be in the public interest to have the matter resolved quickly. A reference was directed to the Ontario Court of Appeal,[16] and an appeal was then taken to the Supreme Court of Canada.[17] Both courts upheld the constitutionality of the scheme.

C. DECLARATORY PROCEEDINGS AND STANDING

A private citizen is not entitled to direct a reference but may, in certain specific situations, bring what is known as a declaratory action in which no relief or remedy is sought other than an order of a court that a statute is contrary to the constitution. Canadian courts, like other common law courts, are wary of declaratory proceedings and have established certain rules of standing that must be met. Rules of standing are thought to be necessary to avoid a flood of litigation, to conserve judicial resources and limit judicial power, and to ensure that constitutional disputes arise in the usual adversarial setting where only interested parties motivated to present strong arguments are represented. Ordinarily, a citizen must indicate a specific legal interest or right that is threatened by the statute challenged. However, the Canadian courts have also carved out generous exceptions to the rules of standing and have said that the courts have a discretion to permit a declaratory suit to proceed even where the plaintiff does not present the usual specific legal right or interest.[18] First, the citizen must demonstrate that the case raises a serious legal issue.

---

16 *Reference Re Bill 30, An Act to Amend the Education Act (Ontario)* (1986), 53 O.R. (2d) 513 (C.A.).

17 *Reference Re Bill 30, An Act to Amend the Education Act (Ontario)*, [1987] 1 S.C.R. 1148, 40 D.L.R. (4th) 18.

18 *Thorson v. Canada (A.G.)*, [1975] 1 S.C.R. 138, 43 D.L.R. (3d) 1; *Nova Scotia Board of Censors v. McNeil*, [1976] 2 S.C.R. 265, 55 D.L.R. (3d) 632; *Borowski v. Canada (Minister of Justice)*, [1981] 2 S.C.R. 575, 130 D.L.R. (3d) 588. For a general account of standing in Canadian law, see T.A. Cromwell, *Locus Standi* (Toronto: Carswell, 1986).

Second, it must be shown that the citizen has some genuine interest in bringing the proceeding. Third, there must be no other reasonable or effective way to bring the issue before the court. Certain statutes do not specify penalties or other sanctions, or, if they do, it is unlikely that those who are subjected to such penalties or sanctions would challenge the statute. In these situations, a private citizen who lacks the usual special interest will be permitted to bring a declaratory proceeding. The underlying rationale to this exception to the standing rules is that no statute should be immune from judicial review.

D. THE SYSTEM OF COURTS AND JURISDICTION IN *CHARTER* CASES

As noted above, the general rule is that *Charter* issues are resolved in the ordinary course of litigation. The Supreme Court of Canada has rejected the proposition that the *Charter* itself confers jurisdiction, and, accordingly, authority to decide a *Charter* issue turns on the pre-1982 court structure.

1) Provincial Courts

Each of the ten provinces has its own judicial system with trial courts and a Court of Appeal. At the trial level, provincial courts deal with minor criminal offences and also have jurisdiction over more serious offences with the consent of the accused. In addition, provincial courts deal with small civil claims and some family matters. The judges of these courts are appointed by the provincial governments. As many *Charter* issues arise in criminal cases, the provincial courts are often the court of first instance for a *Charter* challenge. However, because these courts are statutory and exercise only the jurisdiction that is specifically assigned to them, there are limits upon their authority to resolve *Charter* issues.

2) Superior Courts

The most important trial courts in Canada are the superior courts of each province. These courts exercise general and "inherent," or residual, jurisdiction over civil and criminal matters. The judges of these courts are appointed by the federal government. Superior courts also possess the authority of judicial review with respect to administrative agencies and have some appellate jurisdiction over the provincial courts. The provincial superior courts have authority to apply both federal and provincial laws. Thus, it follows that the provincial superior courts have the broadest possible authority to decide *Charter* issues in the first instance.

3) Federal Court

The Federal Court of Canada has specific jurisdiction over certain matters that fall within federal legislative competence as enumerated by the division of powers. Yet it does not have inherent jurisdiction and there are strict limits on its jurisdiction.[19] The Federal Court has authority over federal administrative law as well as certain special subjects such as admiralty, intellectual property, and suits against the federal government. Given its jurisdiction over federal administrative law and suits against the federal government, many *Charter* issues are decided by the Federal Court. However, the provincial superior courts also have full jurisdiction with respect to the constitutionality of federal laws, including declaratory suits brought against the federal Crown.[20] Hence, the provincial superior courts retain a much broader jurisdiction than the Federal Court and play a more important role in the adjudication of *Charter* issues.

4) The Supreme Court of Canada

Appeals from judgments from the provincial courts and the provincial superior courts are taken to the provincial Court of Appeal, and from there to the Supreme Court of Canada. Appeals from the Federal Court, Trial Division, are taken to the Federal Court of Appeal, and then to the Supreme Court of Canada.

The Supreme Court of Canada, sitting at the top of the judicial hierarchy, is Canada's most important court. The common law doctrine of precedent or *stare decisis* makes its decisions binding upon all other courts. Accordingly, the Supreme Court exercises a considerable law-making role both in constitutional and in non-constitutional matters. The Supreme Court is seen, not only by lawyers and judges but also by the public at large, as one of our most important national institutions.

The high public profile of the Supreme Court is, however, a relatively recent phenomenon. The Court is not mentioned in the original

---

19 P.W. Hogg, "Comment" (1977) 55 Can. Bar Rev. 550; P.W. Hogg, "Federalism and the Jurisdiction of Canadian Courts" (1981) 30 U.N.B.L.J. 9; J.M. Evans, "Comment" (1981) 59 Can. Bar Rev. 124; B. Laskin & R.J. Sharpe, "Constricting Federal Court Jurisdiction" (1980) 30 U.T.L.J. 283.

20 *Jabour* v. *Law Society of British Columbia*, [1982] 2 S.C.R. 307, 137 D.L.R. (3d) 1.

1867 constitution; indeed, despite an obscure and confusing reference to the Court in the amending formula enacted in 1982,[21] the Court lacks formal status in the written constitution to this day. The Court was created by an Act of Parliament in 1875 pursuant to the power conferred upon Parliament by section 101 of the *Constitution Act, 1867*, to establish a general court of appeal for Canada.[22] At the time of the Court's establishment, there were many who thought it unnecessary since there already existed a supreme appellate authority for constitutional as well as non-constitutional issues, namely, the Judicial Committee of the Privy Council in England.[23] This body, consisting essentially of members of the English House of Lords, heard appeals from the colonial courts and, after the creation of the Dominion of Canada in 1867, entertained cases directly from the provincial courts of appeal. In the early years of Canada's history, it was thought that the establishment of the Supreme Court of Canada would merely add another costly and unnecessary level of appeal.

For a long time, the Supreme Court of Canada was supreme in name only: the Judicial Committee of the Privy Council functioned as Canada's highest appellate court until 1949 when appeals to the Privy Council were abolished. This body of English judges had an important influence upon the evolution of the Canadian constitution, and its judgments remain significant today. The Privy Council established the principles of interpretation of Canada's federal structure and, throughout Canadian history, many have argued that its judgments unduly favoured provincial interests to the detriment of a strong and effective central government.[24]

---

21   Section 41(d) provides that amendments to the constitution in relation to "the composition of the Supreme Court of Canada" require the unanimous consent of the federal Parliament and the provincial legislatures, while s. 42(1)(d) provides that other amendments in relation to the Court fall under the usual formula (federal Parliament and at least seven provinces having at least 50 percent of the population of all the provinces). For varying views as to the effect of these provisions, see: P.W. Hogg, *Canada Act 1982 Annotated* (Toronto: Carswell, 1982) at 92–94; Strayer, above note 1 at 30–31; R.I. Cheffins, "The *Constitution Act, 1982* and the Amending Formula: Political and Legal Implications" (1982) 4 Supreme Court L. R. 43 at 53; W.R. Lederman, "Constitutional Procedure and Reform of the Supreme Court of Canada" (1985) 26 Cahiers de Droit 195.

22   For the history of the Supreme Court, see J.G. Snell & F. Vaughan, *The Supreme Court of Canada: History of the Institution* (Toronto: University of Toronto Press, 1985).

23   See G. Bale, *Chief Justice William Johnstone Ritchie: Responsible Government and Judicial Review* (Ottawa: Carleton University Press, 1990).

24   See, for example, B. Laskin, "Peace, Order and Good Government Re-Examined" (1947) 25 Can. Bar Rev. 1054. Compare, however, A.C. Cairns, "The Judicial Committee and Its Critics" (1971) 4 Can. J. Pol. Sci. 301.

An important step in the evolution of the Supreme Court of Canada to its present status occurred in 1975 when an amendment to the *Supreme Court Act* gave the Court control over the cases it hears. Most appeals as of right to the Court were abolished, and a leave-to-appeal procedure was introduced whereby the Court is able to screen cases and permit only those cases with national importance to proceed. This change has permitted the Court to focus its efforts on those cases that have the most legal and public significance. It has altered the role of the Supreme Court from that of error correction to one of law making.

The final significant step in the evolution of the Supreme Court of Canada occurred in 1982 with the enactment of the *Charter of Rights and Freedoms*. As noted in chapter 1, the *Charter* significantly increased the scope for judicial review and brought the Supreme Court of Canada into public prominence.

a) Composition of the Court and Appointment of Judges

The composition of the Supreme Court is fixed by the *Supreme Court Act*. The Court consists of nine judges. The *Supreme Court Act*, section 6, requires that three of the nine judges be appointed from the judges or bar of the province of Quebec. This provision is designed to ensure that there are at least three judges trained in Quebec's distinctive civil law tradition. By practice or convention, there are ordinarily three judges from Ontario, as it is Canada's most populous province, one judge from the eastern provinces, and two judges from the western provinces. A quorum of the Court is five judges but it is usual for the Court to have all nine judges sit on important cases.

The office of chief justice usually, but not invariably, alternates between an English- and French-speaking judge. The chief justice has important public and administrative responsibilities, including the assignment of judges to each case. However, in terms of the Court's decisions, the chief justice has no special authority and exercises the usual functions of a justice of the Court, sitting on cases and voting as any other judge.

The qualifications for appointment to the Court are specified in section 5 of *the Supreme Court Act*. One must be a judge of a superior court or a barrister of ten years' standing. The same qualification is specified by the *Judges Act* for appointment to the superior and provincial appellate courts.[25] Most Supreme Court judges have had prior judicial experience. Of the present nine justices, five previously sat both as trial and appellate judges and three previously sat as appellate judges only. It is not unusual,

---

25 *Judges Act*, R.S.C. 1985, c. J-1, s. 3.

however, for one or more of the judges to have been appointed directly from the bar and to have no prior judicial experience. In recent years, academics have frequently been appointed to the Court. There are currently three members of the Court who started their legal careers as law professors, but all had judicial experience prior to their appointment to the Court. The *Supreme Court Act* also provides (section 9) that judges of the Court hold office until reaching the age of seventy-five.

Judges of the Supreme Court of Canada and of the superior courts are appointed by the federal cabinet on the advice of the minister of justice. In the case of Supreme Court appointments, it has become the practice for the prime minister to make the appointments. While there is an informal consultation process in which the views of leading members of the bench and bar are sought, there is no public scrutiny of appointments to the Court. There is no involvement by Parliament nor do the provincial governments have any formal say in the appointments process. Most observers recognize that the quality of individuals appointed to the Court has been high, but the secretive nature of Supreme Court appointments has come under increasing criticism.[26] It is felt by many critics that the public should have some prior knowledge of the background and abilities of the candidates. Provincial governments have long complained that it is unfair for the federal government to have the exclusive decision with respect to appointments since the Supreme Court acts as the referee in disputes between the federal government and the provinces. Had constitutional amendments proposed in the Meech Lake and Charlottetown packages been enacted, the federal government would have been obliged to select Supreme Court justices from lists supplied by the provinces.

While it is unlikely that Canada would ever adopt the American practice of confirmation hearings whereby nominees to the Court are subjected to lengthy partisan questioning, it seems inevitable that demands for a less secretive and more open process will grow.[27] The federal government has also come under increasing pressure to appoint

---

26   See D.M. Beatty, *Talking Heads and the Supremes: The Canadian Production of Constitutional Review* (Toronto: Carswell, 1990).

27   For an interesting proposal, see M.L. Friedland, *A Place Apart: Judicial Independence and Accountability in Canada* (Ottawa: Canadian Judicial Council, 1995) at 256–57. Appointments to the provincial superior courts are now made after candidates have been privately reviewed by committees of senior judges, lawyers, and lay people. In some provinces, appointments to the provincial bench are made after a similar process that involves lay participation. For discussion, see Ontario Law Reform Commission, *Appointing Judges: Philosophy, Politics and Practice* (Toronto, 1991).

more women and members of cultural and ethnic minorities to the bench, an experience shared by provincial governments in their sphere of judicial appointments. Though this pressure stems partly from changing demographics and social attitudes, it is undoubtedly tied as well to the enhanced power of the courts in the *Charter* era. Since the *Charter* requires the courts to decide important public-policy issues, it is thought in many quarters that a diversity of backgrounds among judges is necessary to ensure that judicial decisions reflect a wide range of values.

b) The Hearing of Appeals

The Supreme Court of Canada hears between 120 and 140 appeals each year.[28] In addition, it receives 400 to 500 applications for leave to appeal. Approximately 50 percent of the cases heard by the Court are criminal, while the remaining 50 percent are civil. The Court exercises important jurisdiction in private law, but it has become predominantly a public law court that focuses on the *Charter of Rights and Freedoms*.

The Supreme Court receives the full record of the proceedings in the lower courts, including all of the evidence led at trial and all judgments rendered in the case. The parties present written argument, ordinarily limited to forty pages, and they are afforded one hour each for oral argument. The procedure is adversarial, in keeping with the common law tradition.

After the presentation of oral arguments, all deliberations of the Court are confidential until the judgment is released. Following the oral argument, the Court retires to a conference of all the judges sitting on the case. Each judge is asked to present his or her view of the case, commencing with the most junior judge. One of the judges who is in the majority undertakes to prepare the first opinion. In the absence of a volunteer, the chief justice assigns the task to one of the judges. The first opinion is circulated among the judges sitting on the case and each judge either agrees with the opinion as drafted or prepares concurring or dissenting reasons. It has become increasingly apparent that law clerks, recent law school graduates who serve for a period of one year with the justices, play an important role in doing background research and assisting in the preparation of the final opinions. It is the practice of the Court to publish all opinions, including dissents, and dissenting opinions not infrequently provide the foundation for future developments in the jurisprudence. When all judges sitting on the case have

---

28 Statistics on the work of the Court are published regularly in the Supreme Court *Bulletin*.

signed an opinion, the judgment of the Court is released to the parties and to the public in both English and French.

E. CONCLUSION

Charter cases are essentially dealt with in the same manner as any other litigation. It is apparent, however, that *Charter* issues pose special challenges for our courts. Special procedural rules relating to standing and intervention by attorneys general and interested groups reflect the public significance of *Charter* rulings.

The role of judges in dealing with complex social issues under the *Charter* has altered the mandate of our courts and resulted in increased public scrutiny of the judicial process. The method of appointing judges has come under particular criticism. Many observers have asked whether the traditional approach is adequate, especially for the selection of those who sit on our highest court. Though rarely, if ever, is exception taken to particular appointments, it may be expected that there will be continuing pressure to have a more open appointments process.

FURTHER READINGS

ROACH, K., *Constitutional Remedies in Canada* (Aurora, ON: Canada Law Book, 1994)

SHARPE, R.J., ed., *Charter Litigation* (Toronto: Butterworths, 1986)

STRAYER, B.L., *The Canadian Constitution and the Courts: The Function and Scope of Judicial Review*, 3d ed. (Toronto: Butterworths, 1988)

FREEDOM OF CONSCIENCE AND RELIGION

Section 2(a) of the *Charter* provides that "freedom of conscience and religion" is a fundamental right of all Canadians. Yet, while the *Charter* respects every individual's freedom of conscience and religion as a necessary element of personal dignity, autonomy, and self-development, this does not mean that it offers protection to all actions dictated by religious belief. Can the state interfere with the wearing of distinctive clothing, such as a turban? Can it prevent religious practices, such as female circumcision, that are regarded by the majority as harmful? Does the state have a positive duty to provide funding for religious schools? Does section 2(a) protect only the right to hold beliefs, or does it include the right to express those beliefs, free from state interference? As with the other *Charter* rights, the courts have had to determine the scope of the right to freedom of conscience and religion guaranteed by section 2(a), as well as the range of acceptable limitations under section 1.

A. SUNDAY CLOSING LAWS

Sunday closing laws may be characterized as having a religious purpose. Their origins lie, at least in part, in the desire to protect against the profanation of the Christian Sabbath and to maintain Sunday as a holy day. Over time, however, Sunday closing laws have also taken on a secular purpose, that of providing workers with a day of rest or a "pause day." From this perspective, Sunday was chosen not because of its religious significance but because it historically has been a day without work. On the other hand, even if there is a secular purpose behind Sunday closing laws, they do impose burdens on those who observe another day of rest for religious reasons.

R. v. Big M Drug Mart,[1] a case dealing with the constitutionality of the federal *Lord's Day Act* prohibition of Sunday shopping, was the Supreme Court's first decision on the *Charter* guarantee of freedom of religion. As a corporate entity, the drug store could not claim a right to freedom of religion for itself, but, since it had been prosecuted, it was allowed to challenge the constitutionality of the *Lord's Day Act* on the theory that no one should be prosecuted under an unconstitutional law.

The distribution of powers between federal and provincial governments in the Canadian federal system allows the federal Parliament to enact laws designed to protect religion and to prevent profanation of the Sabbath. The *Lord's Day Act* was enacted pursuant to this authority to legislate with respect to the criminal law under section 91(27) of the *Constitution Act, 1867*. However, under the division of powers, the federal Parliament does not have jurisdiction to enact Sunday closing laws with a secular purpose. Legislation of that kind falls within the general provincial jurisdiction under section 92(13) over "property and civil rights," which includes labour relations and regulation of business within the province. Accordingly, any attempt to justify the *Lord's Day Act* as having a secular "day of rest" purpose would make it vulnerable to a finding of invalidity on federalism grounds. As a result, when considering the challenge to the law as violating the *Charter* guarantee of freedom of religion, the conclusion that the underlying purpose of the law was to promote observance of the Christian Sabbath was inescapable.

That purpose was held to violate section 2(a) of the *Charter*. Writing for the majority, Dickson J. took the opportunity to interpret the guarantee broadly, as protecting not only the right to hold religious beliefs but also the right to express beliefs through observance, teaching, and practice. The state would violate an individual's freedom if it coerced religious observance. In his words,

> [F]reedom means that, subject to such limitations as are necessary to protect public safety, order, health, or morals or the fundamental rights and freedoms of others, no one is to be forced to act in a way contrary to his beliefs or his conscience.[2]

---

1   *R. v. Big M Drug Mart Ltd.*, [1985] 1 S.C.R. 295, 18 D.L.R. (4th) 321.
2   *Ibid.* at 337 (S.C.R.).

Dickson J. concluded that the *Lord's Day Act* was coercive in nature because its purpose was to compel universal observance of the Christian Sabbath:

> Non-Christians are prohibited for religious reasons from carrying out activities which are otherwise lawful, moral and normal. The arm of the State requires all to remember the Lord's day of the Christians and to keep it holy. The protection of one religion and the concomitant non-protection of others imports disparate impact destructive of the religious freedom of the collectivity.[3]

In reaching this conclusion, Dickson J. referred to section 27 of the *Charter*, which requires that the document be interpreted in a manner "consistent with the preservation and enhancement of the multicultural heritage of Canadians." The preferred position of the Christian religion was seen as undermining respect for the religions of other groups in Canadian society.

The government's attempt to defend the legislation as a reasonable limit under section 1 of the *Charter* was unsuccessful. Given the source of its authority to enact the law under the division-of-powers, it was impossible for the federal government to establish a valid legislative objective. The result was a dilemma fatal to the law. Its purpose for the division of powers analysis, the protection of the majority's religion, was repugnant to the *Charter's* protection of religious freedom for the minority. The law could not be defended as a worker-protection law, since that purpose would render it invalid on federalism grounds.

In light of the religious foundation of the law, *Big M* was not a particularly difficult case. More troublesome for the Supreme Court was the next Sunday closing case, *Edwards Books*.[4] This case involved Ontario legislation, secular in purpose, which was enacted to give retail workers a day of rest. The law made a concession to those who, for religious reasons, observed a different day of rest. It contained an exemption from the requirement that retail businesses close on Sundays if a store had closed the previous Saturday, had seven or fewer employees, and was smaller than 5,000 square feet.

On its face, the legislation did not require religious observance. However, in *Big M*, the Supreme Court had stated that rights could be infringed under the *Charter* not only by legislation whose purpose was to infringe the right but also by laws which had the effect of interfering

---

3   *Ibid.*
4   *Edwards Books and Art Ltd.* v. *R.*, [1986] 2 S.C.R. 713, 35 D.L.R. (4th) 1 [*Edwards Books*].

with the right. Not every burden on the practice of religion will constitute a *Charter* violation. The Court had said that a *Charter* breach will
be made out only where the burden is more than trivial and insubstan-
tial.[5] However, many apparently "neutral" laws — that is, laws enacted
for a perfectly proper reason unrelated to religion — may run afoul of
the *Charter* guarantee because of their impact on religious practice.

In *Edwards Books*, five judges concluded that the effect of the closing law interfered with freedom of religion. For Dickson C.J.C. and the
majority of the Court, the problem was the impact of Sunday closing on
those whose day of worship was Saturday (for example, those of the
Jewish or Seventh Day Adventist faiths). Retailers whose holy day was
Sunday were able to close their establishments and observe that day
without any financial disadvantage. Saturday observers were faced with
a dilemma: they could close Saturday, as required by their religion, but
they would suffer a financial loss as a result. Alternatively, faced with
the burden imposed by the law requiring them to close on Sunday, they
might feel pressured to open on their holy day. Dickson C.J.C. found
that the Sunday closing law was not neutral in its effect. It put Saturday
observers at a disadvantage compared to Sunday observers who enjoyed
statutory protection for their holy day. This financial burden was found
to violate freedom of religion.

In dissent, Beetz J. concluded that there was no interference with
freedom of religion. In his view, when an individual closed a store on
Saturdays to observe his or her faith, the cause of the closure was the
individual's religious beliefs, not any action by the state. The fact that
Sunday observers might get a financial advantage from the Sunday closing law did not affect the *Charter* claim. For Beetz J., it was telling that,
if the Sunday closing law was repealed, the Saturday observers (as well
as the Sunday observers) would still be at a business disadvantage in
relation to the non-observant retailer who could open any day, while
religious individuals would choose not to work. This, he thought,
proved that it was religious belief that caused the decision to close and
the consequent loss of income on Saturday, and that the Sunday closing
law did not interfere with freedom of religion.

While the majority concluded that the section 2(a) guarantee of
freedom of religion was violated, the law was upheld under section 1 of
the *Charter*, Wilson J. dissenting.[6] The judges were split as to why the
law was justified. In Dickson C.J.C.'s view (supported by two other

5   *Jones v. R.*, [1986] 2 S.C.R. 284, 31 D.L.R. (4th) 569 [*Jones*], discussed below.
6   The importance of the *Edwards Books* s. 1 analysis is considered in chapter 4
    "Limitation of *Charter* Rights."

judges), the exemption given to small retailers who observed Saturday was necessary to sustain the validity of the Act under section 1. He found that the state was justified in trying to protect a pause day for vulnerable workers in the retail industry. Further, he found that it was not necessary, under the *Oakes* minimal-impairment test, to require that all retailers close. Small retailers could be allowed to open, without undue interference with their employees' interests or the general nature of the pause day. La Forest J. held that no exemption was needed, since any effort to provide an exemption would create problems in enforcing the legislation and could undermine the protection of employees. He concluded that the courts should defer to the legislatures of the various provinces and allow them to determine whether they wanted to provide an exemption or not, and, if so, how to structure it.

Wilson J. dissented on the basis that the exemption for only some Saturday observers and not others was an unprincipled decision that did not satisfy the *Oakes* test. If religious freedom was important and deserving of *Charter* protection for some members of a religious group, there was no reason, in her view, that it should not be provided for all members of that group.

The debate in *Edwards Books* may seem dated today, given the current widespread adoption of Sunday shopping in Canada. However, the issues remain significant with regard to challenges to statutory holidays such as Christmas Day, Good Friday, and Easter Sunday. The requirement of retail closure on such days seems rooted in Christian tradition, although the argument will be made that these holidays now have a largely secular basis in the minds of many.

B. PARENTAL RIGHTS

Freedom of religion has been an issue in a number of cases involving the family and parental rights. For example, in *B. (R.)*,[7] parents of the Jehovah's Witnesses religion refused to allow their infant child to undergo a blood transfusion thought by doctors to be required to save the child's life. When the Children's Aid Society brought an application to take the child into care to ensure that she could be given necessary treatment, the parents argued that this application violated their freedom of religion. The Supreme Court of Canada upheld the order placing the child under the protection of the Society. Five of the judges agreed that the

---

7   *B. (R.)* v. *Children's Aid Society of Metropolitan Toronto*, [1995] 1 S.C.R. 315, 122 D.L.R. (4th) 1 [*B. (R.)*].

parents' right to freedom of religion was violated, concluding that the guarantee protected religious beliefs even if those beliefs could harm another. However, the limitation on the parents' rights was justified under section 1 in order to protect the child. In contrast, four judges argued that the guarantee of freedom of religion should not extend to conduct endangering the life or seriously endangering the health of the child.

This case followed an earlier pair of decisions dealing with restrictions on parents' rights to discuss religion with their children as a condition of access to their children following marriage breakdown. In *Young* v. *Young*,[8] the trial judge had given custody of the children to the mother and permitted access to the father. However, the order had forbidden the father, a Jehovah's Witness, from taking his children to religious services or on his proselytizing activities or from commenting unfavourably on the mother's religion. This restriction was overturned by the British Columbia Court of Appeal as violating section 2(a). The Supreme Court of Canada, by a narrow majority, agreed that the father should not be forbidden from discussing his religion with his children. By this time, he had promised not to take them to services or to involve them in proselytizing. The majority reasoning noted that custody and access decisions are made on the basis of the "best-interests of the child." Where a parent's religious beliefs are harmful to a child, the best-interests test will apply to protect the child from those beliefs. In the Court's view, there would be no *Charter* violation associated with such a determination, since the right to freedom of religion does not permit one to harm another. In light of the father's promises with respect to services and proselytizing, it was found that the child would not be harmed by discussions about his religious beliefs.

C. RELIGION AND EDUCATION

Another area of controversy under section 2(a) has been with respect to religion and education. There are a number of issues that arise: the extent to which there is room for religious instruction and practice in the public school system, the right of parents to withdraw their children from the public schools for religious reasons, and the extent of the state's obligation to fund independent religious schools.

---

8   *Young* v. *Young*, [1993] 4 S.C.R 3, 108 D.L.R. (4th) 193. In *P. (D.)* v. *S. (C.)*, [1993] 4 S.C.R. 141, 108 D.L.R. (4th) 287, the majority upheld a condition of access forbidding the father to indoctrinate the child in the Jehovah's Witness religion, although he was allowed to teach her about religion.

1) School Prayer and Religious Instruction

The Supreme Court of Canada has not dealt directly with the issue of the role of religion in the public school system. However, two important decisions of the Ontario Court of Appeal struck down provincial laws and regulations requiring school prayer and religious education in the public schools. In *Zylberberg*,[9] the Court dealt with a requirement that public schools open with religious exercises consisting of the reading of scripture or other suitable works and the repeating of the Lord's Prayer or other suitable prayers. The regulations provided that a pupil could be excused from participating if his or her parent requested this. The province defended the legislation on the basis that there was no denial of freedom of religion, given the right to claim an exemption. The majority of the Court of Appeal disagreed. It found that the requirement of prayers and scripture reading violated the rights of both Christians and non-Christians by compelling religious observance. The right to claim an exemption did not negate the coercive quality of the regime, for the reality was that members of minority religions or those opposed to the practices felt pressured to conform. Indeed, the exemption provisions were described as imposing a penalty on religious minorities, "stigmatizing them as non-conforming."[10]

A similar result was reached in a subsequent case involving religious education.[11] Ontario legislation and regulations required two one-half-hour periods of religious instruction in each week in the public schools, although, again, children could be exempted. While the regulations provided that issues of a controversial or sectarian nature were to be avoided, the curriculum in Elgin County was delivered by members of a local Bible club and clergy, with the result that the instruction had a strong evangelical Christian tone. Again, the Ontario Court of Appeal concluded that the curriculum was a form of religious indoctrination, which placed a burden on both religious minorities and non-observers. The Court held that, while teaching children about religious perspectives is permissible under section 2(a), indoctrination is not.

---

9   *Zylberberg v. Sudbury Board of Education (Director)* (1988), 52 D.L.R.(4th) 577
    (Ont. C.A.).
10 *Ibid.* at 592. See also at 591: "The peer pressure and the class-room norms to which
    children are acutely sensitive, in our opinion, are real and pervasive and operate to
    compel members of religious minorities to conform with majority religious practices."
11 *Canadian Civil Liberties Assn. v. Ontario (Minister of Education)* (1990), 65 D.L.R.
    (4th) 1 (Ont. C.A.).

It might be noted that the result of these cases does not necessarily draw a strict line between church and state. Unlike the language of the First Amendment to the American constitution, which guarantees the free exercise of religion and prohibits the establishment of religion, section 2(a) of the *Charter* does not prohibit government support for religion nor does it require state neutrality with respect to religion.

2) Sectarian Schools

Because of the secular nature of public schools, some parents refuse to send their children to the public system for religious reasons. Section 2(a) clearly affords parents the right to provide their children with alternative schooling if their religious beliefs require them to do so. However, the state may validly require that the child be provided with an education that meets minimum standards. Thus, in *Jones*,[12] the Supreme Court of Canada found no violation of section 2(a) because a father, educating his children and others at a church school, had to obtain an exemption from the school board on the basis that he was providing "efficient instruction." In Wilson J.'s view, Jones had failed to show "any substantial impact of this legislation on his belief that God and not the State is the true source of authority over the education of his children."[13] Again, as in *Edwards Books*, the Court indicated that burdens on the practice of religion are not always in violation of the *Charter*.

While the *Jones* case indicated that members of religious groups could avoid public-school attendance, the case did not deal with the question whether the state was required to fund independent religious schools. In a number of provinces, constitutional guarantees ensure funding for certain denominational schools.[14] Schools operated by other religious groups argue that they, too, should be included — either on the basis of the equality guarantee in section 15 of the *Charter* (which includes protection against discrimination on the ground of religion) or on the basis of section 2(a). With respect to section 2(a), the argument is that the secular program of the public school system may be considered inappropriate by adherents of certain religions. Though such parents have the right to send their children to religious schools, the cost of private education may be burdensome. Many may be unable to afford the tuition at independent religious schools. Such individuals, who still pay taxes to support the public system, argue that their religious beliefs

---

12   Above note 5.
13   Above note 5 at 315 (S.C.R.). However, Wilson J., in dissent, did find a s. 7 violation.
14   *Constitution Act, 1867*, s. 93.

are burdened and that the state should fund their religious schools, to ensure that those whose religion requires distinctive teaching may effectively enjoy their rights.

The specific guarantees for religious schools found in the earlier constitutional documents have to be taken into account in relation to these claims. The *Constitution Act, 1867*, section 93, guaranteed that the rights of certain religious denominations to schools possessed by law at the time of Confederation will be maintained. This provision gave constitutional protection to the Roman Catholic schools in Ontario and both the Catholic and Protestant schools in Quebec. Some of the other provinces were made subject to similar guarantees when they joined Confederation. Recently, constitutional amendments have altered these rights in Newfoundland and Quebec.

Supporters of non-Catholic religious schools in Ontario contend that they, too, should be given public financial support for their schools. This argument was first raised in the *Bill 30* reference, a case arising when Ontario extended funding for the Roman Catholic school system to Grade 13.[15] Until that time, funding had stopped at Grade 10. The Supreme Court of Canada interpreted section 93 to require full funding to Grade 13 but dismissed the argument that sections 2(a) and 15 required equal funding for other religious schools. The government had relied on section 29 of the *Charter* to defend its decision not to fund other religious schools:

> Nothing in this *Charter* abrogates or derogates from any rights or privileges guaranteed by or under the Constitution of Canada in respect of denominational, separate or dissentient schools.

The Court held that, even without this "non-derogation" clause, the rights enjoyed by Roman Catholic school supporters in Ontario were specially protected. The denominational school guarantees in section 93 of the *Constitution Act, 1867,* were described as a "fundamental part of the Confederation compromise" immune from review under the *Charter*. The Court held that the general right to freedom of religion conferred by the *Charter* could not be used to qualify the specific rights conferred on religious minorities by the 1867 constitution.

Despite this ruling, adherents of independent religious schools tried again in the *Adler* case to seek public funding. As they were precluded by the *Bill 30* decision from basing their claim on the rights of the Roman

---

15 *Reference Re Bill 30, An Act to Amend the Education Act (Ontario)*, [1987] 1 SC.R. 1148, 40 D.L.R. (4th) 18 [*Bill 30 Reference*].

Catholic schools in Ontario, they focused on the effect of a secular school education on their freedom of religion and equality rights. They argued that the compulsion to support a secular public school system, coupled with mandatory schooling, imposed a financial burden on those who believe in religion as part of education. This burden both interfered with their freedom of religion and meant that they were being treated unequally.

The Supreme Court of Canada again rejected these arguments.[16] Writing for the majority, Iacobucci J. held that section 93 of the *Constitution Act, 1867,* was conclusive. Like Wilson J. in the *Bill 30 Reference*, he emphasized that section 93 was part of a historical compromise leading to Confederation. Not only did it guarantee funding for Roman Catholic schools in Ontario, it also implicitly contemplated public, secular schools. The constitution entrenched a power in the provincial legislature to legislate with respect to non-denominational schools. The province had the power to fund other denominational schools, but its decision not to do so was protected from *Charter* review.

While other judges found that section 93 was not conclusive, none found a violation of the section 2(a) guarantee of freedom of religion.[17] Four members of the Court held that the legislative decision not to fund independent religious schools was subject to *Charter* review. However, there was, in their view, no violation of section 2(a). According to Sopinka J., although parents have the constitutional right to educate their children in the religion of their choice, there was no state obligation to fund religious schools. In his view, the state's failure to act in order to facilitate the practice of an individual's religion did not constitute state interference with freedom of religion. Any disadvantage flowing from a decision to send a child to a religious school rather than a public school flowed from the tenets of the religion, not state action.

The result is that in certain provinces, including Ontario, there is an apparently anomalous situation in which Roman Catholic schools are guaranteed public funding but other religious schools get none. Implicit in the decision of the Supreme Court in *Adler* is a belief that secular education is important to Canadian society. Indeed, McLachlin J., dissenting on other grounds, would have upheld the decision not to fund inde-

---

16   *Adler* v. *Ontario*, [1996] 3 S.C.R. 609, 140 D.L.R. (4th) 385.

17   In the case, all nine judges found no violation of s. 2(a); McLachlin J. found a violation of s. 15 that was justified under s. 1, although she dissented on the issue of funding for school health services: the failure to provide them to independent religious schools violated s. 15 in her view. L'Heureux-Dubé J. dissented on both the broad funding issue and the health services issue, arguing that both decisions were unjustified violations of s. 15.

pendent religious schools under section 1, even though she found it to be a violation of the equality guarantee. In her view, the preservation of an education system designed to encourage tolerance and harmony in a multicultural society was an important objective, reasonably achieved by funding only the public system.

While the issue of religious school funding seems to have been resolved under the *Charter*, this is not likely to be the end of the issue. Advocates of religious school funding are now turning to the arena of international law. They claim that the failure to fund their schools, especially in light of the funding for the Catholic schools, is a violation of the *International Covenant on Civil and Political Rights*.

D. CONCLUSION

Freedom of religion and conscience lies at the heart of a free and democratic society. While the principle of religious freedom is taken for granted, difficult issues arise when deeply held religious views and practices collide with other important state interests. The courts have been asked to pronounce on a number of controversial issues involving religious freedom. A dominant theme is the judicial tendency to protect vulnerable minorities in this area. Sunday closing laws imposing the religious values of the majority have been found to offend the *Charter* guarantee, as have policies involving school prayer and religious instruction. As with other *Charter* guarantees, however, difficult questions arise when the state is asked to take positive measures to ensure the better enjoyment of a protected freedom. For certain religious groups, religious education is fundamental. While there seems to be little question that the Charter protects the right of religious minorities to educate their children as they see fit, the courts have been unsympathetic to the claims that religious freedom requires state support for religious schools even in the absence of a specific constitutional right to denominational schooling.

FURTHER READINGS

HORWITZ, P., "The Sources and Limits of Freedom of Religion in a Liberal Democracy: Section 2(a) and Beyond" (1996) 54 U.T. Fac. L. Rev. 1

SWINTON, K.E., "Freedom of Religion" in G.A. Beaudoin and E. Mendes, eds., *The Canadian Charter of Rights and Freedoms*, 3rd ed. (Toronto: Carswell, 1996)

CHAPTER 9

FREEDOM OF EXPRESSION

Even before the *Charter of Rights and Freedoms*, freedom of expression was recognized by the Supreme Court of Canada as inherent in our system of government.[1] Democracy rests on the premise that public issues be freely and openly debated. Indeed, the freedom to criticize those who exercise power in our society is the very lifeblood of our democratic tradition. Political debate is often heated and intemperate. Criticism of public institutions and officials will not always be respectful and measured: those who challenge established authority often have to resort to strong language and exaggeration in order to gain attention. "If these exchanges are stifled, democratic government itself is threatened."[2]

Freedom of expression is also vital in other areas of human activity outside the realm of politics. Artists and writers often push the limits of conventional values. Scholars question "sacred cows" and accepted wisdom. Freedom of expression represents society's commitment to tolerate the annoyance of being confronted by unacceptable views. As stated by the Ontario Court of Appeal in an early *Charter* case:[3] "[T]he constitutional guarantee extends not only to that which is pleasing, but also to that which to many may be aesthetically distasteful or morally offensive: it is indeed often true that 'one man's vulgarity is another's lyric.'"

---

1   *Reference Re Alberta Legislation*, [1938] S.C.R. 100, [1938] 2 D.L.R. 81.
2   *R. v. Kopyto* (1987), 62 O.R. (2d) 449 at 462, 47 D.L.R. (4th) 213 (C.A.) [*Kopyto*], Cory J.A.
3   *Re Information Retailers Association and Metropolitan Toronto* (1985), 22 D.L.R. 161 at 180, Robins J.A.

There are two rationales for extending the guarantee this widely. The first is instrumental in nature and is reflected by the metaphor of the "marketplace in ideas." The great American judge Oliver Wendell Holmes, echoing the thoughts of John Milton and John Stuart Mill, said that "the best test of truth is the power of the thought to get itself accepted in the competition of the market."[4] Suppression of ideas in the name of truth is notoriously dangerous. The rationale of the marketplace of ideas posits that the free flow of ideas is the best way to get at the truth.

The second important rationale values expression less for the results it produces than for its intrinsic worth to the individual. Expression is seen as a vital element of individual autonomy, personal growth, and self-realization. The ability to say what one thinks and to follow whatever lines of inquiry that occur to one's imagination is an essential attribute of a free society.

A. RECONCILING FREEDOM OF EXPRESSION WITH OTHER VALUES

Does freedom of expression preclude any law limiting what individuals can say or publish? The answer is surely no. To take a familiar example, freedom of expression does not protect the right, falsely, to shout "Fire!" in a crowded theatre.[5] As with the other rights and freedoms guaranteed by the *Charter*, freedom of expression is not absolute. There are situations in which the freedom of one individual must be curtailed so that other important social values may be respected and protected.

How should these competing claims be reconciled? The American approach has been to accord near-absolute respect to expression deemed worthy of the constitutional guarantee; however, the American courts define freedom of expression narrowly so as not to include forms of speech that do not qualify for protection. The Supreme Court of Canada has adapted a different method to reconcile respect for this vital freedom with competing claims. Our Court has said that the structure of the *Charter*, and in particular section 1, requires that freedom of expression be given a broad definition with virtually no limitations, and that any curtailment of expression be justified under section 1 as a limit that is reasonable in a free and democratic society.

---

4   *Abrams v. United States*, 250 U.S. 616 at 630 (1919).
5   *Schenk v. United States*, 249 U.S. 47 at 52 (1919), Holmes J.

In 1988 the Supreme Court heard two cases from Quebec in which it charted the course to be followed. *Ford* v. *Quebec (A.G.)*[6] involved a challenge to the Quebec "signs law" which prohibited, with virtually no exception, the display of commercial signs not written in French. *Ford* was argued at the same time as *Irwin Toy Ltd.* v. *Quebec (A.G.)*,[7] which involved a challenge to a Quebec statute that limited the right to broadcast advertising aimed at children. In both cases, the attorney general of Quebec argued that the law did not limit freedom of expression. In *Ford*, Quebec contended that the "signs law" did not limit in any way the message that could be conveyed. The language of the speaker was merely the medium for expression. It was contended in both cases that commercial expression is not worthy of constitutional protection and that the Court should adhere to a core definition of freedom of expression, limiting the right to the most vital areas of political speech and artistic expression. The Supreme Court rejected these arguments, holding that freedom of expression should be given a wide and generous definition admitting few exceptions. Yet at the same time the Court recognized that expression may be curtailed if the standard of section 1 is met.

In *Ford* the Court stated that language was an essential component of expression:

> Language is so intimately related to the form and content of expression that there cannot be true freedom of expression by means of language if one is prohibited from using the language of one's choice. Language is not merely a means or medium of expression; it colours the content and meaning of expression.[8]

The Court was also unsympathetic to the argument that expression should be limited to political speech, thereby excluding advertising. The Court found that the purpose of protecting freedom of expression was not limited to political speech and the enhancement of democratic self-government. Other values were also involved. The Court accepted as a valid rationale for protecting expression the concept of a "marketplace of ideas." It also recognized the important element of individual autonomy and self-development inherent in expression. Informed by these purposes, the Court found that freedom of expression embraced expressive conduct extending to most areas of human activity, including commerce and the arts.

---

6   [1988] 2 S.C.R. 712, 54 D.L.R. (4th) 577 [*Ford*].
7   [1989] 1 S.C.R. 927, 58 D.L.R. (4th) 577 [*Irwin Toy*].
8   Above note 6 at 748 (S.C.R.).

The Court has recognized that freedom of expression should be defined generously in other ways as well. Although we usually regard the right as that of the speaker, meaningful expression assumes an audience. The purposes underlying the guarantee contemplate a recipient of the message, and the Court has said that the right extends to the listener as well as to the speaker.[9] Cases of freedom of expression typically involve a restraint on speech. The Court has acknowledged, however, that the freedom also protects the individual from being required to express one particular view.[10]

In *Irwin Toy*, the Supreme Court described in a formal manner the framework for interpretative analysis to be followed in a freedom of expression case. The first stage is definitional. Here, the Court said, a broad approach is called for. Expression includes any activity that conveys or attempts to convey a meaning. The use of the word "activity" is significant as the Court recognized that, in some situations, actions without words may have expressive content. For example, parking a car ordinarily has no expressive feature, but, as the Supreme Court explained, if an unmarried person, as a protest, were to park in a space reserved for spouses, that action would have expressive content. The only restriction the Court placed on conduct of an expressive nature was for acts of violence. Violence is often used by terrorists as a means to convey a message, but, said the Supreme Court, it is obvious that the perpetrator of an act of violence for an expressive purpose cannot gain constitutional protection from the ordinary law of the land.

The second stage of the analysis is to determine if there has been a violation. Here, the Supreme Court distinguished content-based restraints from those that merely have the effect of limiting expression. The former category includes laws or practices that have as their purpose the restriction of the actual type of speech as well as restraints on a form of expression tied to content. Content-based restraints are the most familiar: examples include the law of defamation, the prohibition of pornography, and restrictions on advertising. An example of a restraint on a form of expression tied to content is a law that prohibits the handing out of pamphlets. While such a law is indifferent to the content of the pamphlet, it inevitably bans whatever content the pamphlet has and thus necessarily constitutes a restraint on expression. An effects-based restraint is one that is aimed at some other aspect of the

---

9   *Rocket v. Royal College of Dental Surgeons of Ontario*, [1990] 2 S.C.R. 232, 71 D.L.R. (4th) 68.

10 *RJR-MacDonald Inc. v. Canada (A.G.)*, [1995] 3 S.C.R. 199, 127 D.L.R. (4th) 1 [*RJR*].

activity but that may nevertheless have an impact on expression. A prohibition against littering has a valid purpose and is not aimed at expression. Yet it may have the effect of limiting expression depending upon
the circumstances. If enforced against someone handing out pamphlets,
it would have that effect, but if applied to someone carelessly discarding
a candy wrapper, it would not. In the case of an effects-based restraint,
the Supreme Court held, the party claiming the protection of the *Charter*
must be able to show that the activity in question promotes one of the
three principles underlying freedom of expression: political debate, the
marketplace of ideas, or autonomy and self-fulfillment.

Given the generous scope of this definition of expression, most
claims for *Charter* protection will survive these first two stages. The
Supreme Court has found, for example, that in addition to commercial
expression, pornography,[11] hate speech,[12] and even deliberate false-
hoods[13] qualify as expression. The purpose of these activities is to convey a message, however unpleasant, and the purpose of the *Criminal
Code* provisions criminalizing pornography and hate speech is to
restrict the very content of the messages being conveyed.

There remains, however, the third stage of analysis under section 1
of the *Charter*. Here, as seen in chapter 4, the burden is on the state to
justify the limit it seeks to impose as being reasonable in a free and democratic society. In virtually all of the freedom of expression cases to reach
the Supreme Court of Canada, the crucial analysis has been under section
1. The most significant decisions are discussed in the pages that follow.

B. COMMERCIAL EXPRESSION

The Supreme Court has decided a number of cases involving restraints
on commercial speech, with mixed results. In *Ford*,[14] the case involving
the Quebec "signs law," the issues extended well beyond what constitutes the permissible regulation of advertising. The Court struck down
the "signs law" on the ground that Quebec had failed to justify it as a
reasonable limit. While the Supreme Court was prepared to accept as a
legitimate purpose the protection and enhancement of the French language in Quebec, it held that the virtual total ban on public signs in any

---

11   *R. v. Butler*, [1992] 1 S.C.R. 452, 70 C.C.C. (3d) 129 [*Butler*].
12   *R. v. Keegstra*, [1990] 3 S.C.R. 697, 61 C.C.C. (3d) 1 [*Keegstra*].
13   *R. v. Zundel*, [1992] 2 S.C.R. 731, 95 D.L.R. (4th) 202 [*Zundel*]; *R. v. Lucas*, [1998]
     S.C.J. No. 28 [*Lucas*].
14   *Ford*, above note 6.

other language went too far. Quebec had failed to introduce evidence to show that such an extreme measure was necessary and the Court held that the law failed to meet the minimal-impairment test. In making the minimal-impairment assessment, the Court considered alternative measures that might satisfy the goal of protecting and enhancing the French language. It suggested that a law that required the use of French in commercial signs but that did not ban other languages might be acceptable, even if such a measure called for a marked predominance of French. A law along these lines would meet the aim of protecting and enhancing the French language while at the same time respecting the rights of non-French speakers.

In the companion case, *Irwin Toy*,[15] the Supreme Court was faced with a more typical case of commercial speech. At issue was the right of a toy manufacturer to advertise its products for commercial purposes. Quebec legislation prohibited commercial advertising directed at persons under thirteen years of age. The statute established certain criteria to determine whether the advertising was directed at children. A majority of the Court found that the Quebec law could be justified as a reasonable limit on the right of freedom of expression. As noted in chapter 4, the decision in *Irwin Toy* represents a significant statement by the Court on the application of section 1 where a law has been enacted to protect a vulnerable group. In the Court's view, the legislature had acted reasonably in protecting children who it deemed less than fully capable of making informed judgments on the basis of advertising. As in *Ford,* the law imposed a total ban, but in *Irwin Toy* there was some evidence that such a measure was required. The evidence, it must be said, fell well short of proving with certainty that the law enacted by Quebec was the only or even the least drastic way to achieve the goal of protecting children from advertising. However, the Supreme Court accepted that the evidence was sufficient to support Quebec's claim. The Court recognized that, in this area, the facts were not susceptible of clear proof and that the legislature had to be given some latitude:

> If the legislature has made a reasonable assessment as to where the line is most properly drawn, especially if that assessment involves weighing conflicting scientific evidence and allocating scarce resources on this basis, it is not for the court to second guess. That would only be to substitute one estimate for another.[16]

---

15   Above note 7.
16   Above note 7 at 990 (S.C.R.).

There is much to be said for the view that, while commercial expression does qualify for constitutional protection, Parliament and the legislatures are entitled to some latitude when enacting protective measures in the public interest. Commercial expression has only tenuous connection to the underlying values of democratic self-government and individual autonomy and self-development. There is an obvious connection with the rationale of the marketplace of ideas, although here the search for the truth is surely less elusive than in other areas of human activity such as politics or the arts. Regulation to ensure "truth in advertising" is familiar, yet it would surely be unthinkable to impose comparable measures in the areas of political or artistic expression.

The pattern revealed by *Ford*, striking down a total ban, and by *Irwin Toy*, reflecting a significant judicial tolerance for more specific laws restricting commercial expression, has been repeated by later decisions of the Court. The Court has upheld as a reasonable limit under section 1 of the *Charter* a *Criminal Code* provision making it illegal to solicit in a public place for the purpose of prostitution.[17] Dickson C.J.C. stated that, when considering the reasonable-limits test, the Court should have in mind the nature of the expression at issue. Solicitation had an overt "economic purpose" and it could "hardly be said that communications regarding an economic transaction of sex for money lie at, or even near, the core of the guarantee of freedom of expression."[18] However, where the law imposes a total ban on commercial speech rather than targeting the mischief with a more limited and specific measure, the Court has taken a tougher line. In *Rocket* v. *Royal College of Dental Surgeons*,[19] a dentist challenged regulations imposing a ban on professional advertising. The Supreme Court accepted that a professional body was entitled to regulate advertising by its members to protect the public and that "restrictions on expression of this kind might be easier to justify than other infringements."[20] Yet the Court struck down the regulations on the grounds that they went well beyond what was necessary to protect the public interest and that they prevented dentists from giving straightforward and useful information such as hours of operation and languages spoken. Similarly, in *RJR MacDonald*,[21] by a majority of five to four, the Supreme Court found that a law imposing a

---

17   *Reference Re ss. 193 and 195.1(1)(c) of the Criminal Code (Canada)*, [1990] 1 S.C.R. 1123, 56 C.C.C. (3d) 65.
18   *Ibid.* at 1136 (S.C.R.).
19   Above note 9.
20   Above note 9 at 247 (S.C.R.), McLachlin J.
21   Above note 10.

complete ban on advertising of tobacco products could not survive section 1 scrutiny as a minimal infringement of freedom of expression. While the majority accepted that Parliament could limit the right to advertise tobacco with a view to promoting the health of Canadians, the total ban was not shown to be necessary nor had the government shown that more limited alternatives would be ineffective.

C. POLITICAL EXPRESSION

As already noted, freedom of expression about political issues lies at the heart of our democratic tradition. But does this mean that Parliament is incapable of intervening in all situations? Expression in the real world of politics is closely tied to economic resources. Those who have money have the means to convey their message to the public; those who lack resources are at a disadvantage and to them the promise of freedom of expression may be ineffectual. Is Parliament entitled to alleviate economic inequalities by regulating election expenses? Such laws are designed to improve debate by ensuring that some voices do not drown out others. Does the laudable goal justify imposing restraints on the political expression of those who have more substantial resources? To these difficult questions, the Canadian courts have thus far given limited and, to some extent, conflicting answers.[22]

In an early *Charter* case, a federal law prohibiting anyone other that a registered party or candidate from spending money during an election campaign to promote a cause or a candidate was struck down.[23] The federal government contended that limiting the right of individuals to participate in campaigns was necessary to ensure the integrity of other provisions controlling expenditures by candidates. An Alberta judge held that the government had failed to prove its case. Given the importance of freedom of political expression, he was not satisfied that this significant constraint on the participation of individuals and groups who were not candidates was justifiable.

In 1996 the Alberta Court of Appeal came to a similar conclusion with respect to a federal law prohibiting any advertising between the date an election is called and the 29th day before voting day, as well as the day before and the day of the election.[24] The law also prohibited

22 American courts have been hostile to election-spending restraints: *Buckley* v. *Valeo*, 424 U.S. 1 (1976).
23 *National Citizens' Coalition* v. *Canada (A.G.)* (1984), 11 D.L.R. (4th) 481 (Alta. Q.B.).
24 *Somerville* v. *Canada (A.G.)* (1996), 136 D.L.R. (4th) 205 (Alta. C.A.).

third parties from spending more that $1,000 for advertising, promoting, or opposing a particular candidate. These measures followed the recommendations of a royal commission on elections. The "blackout" provision was intended to control escalating campaign costs and to limit the advantage of an incumbent. The third-party spending provision was intended to prevent circumvention of spending limits imposed on candidates and to enhance public confidence in the electoral process by avoiding the risk of patronage in return for such spending. The Alberta courts were unpersuaded by the evidence adduced by the attorney general that these measures were justified as limits on freedom of expression under section 1. In the Court of Appeal, Conrad J.A. found that the government's case failed to establish a sufficiently important objective to justify overriding a *Charter* right. In her view, the harm feared from unconstrained advertising and spending was essentially speculative. She also expressed the view that such restrictions, especially those effectively precluding participation by non-candidates, were fundamentally at odds with basic *Charter* values:

> An important justification for the *Charter* guarantees of free expression and association, and an informed vote, is the need in a democracy for citizens to participate in and affect an election. It follows that there can be no pressing and substantial need to suppress that input merely because it might have an impact.[25]

In a case dealing with Quebec's referendum law, the Supreme Court of Canada reached a conclusion similar to that of the Alberta Court of Appeal even while revealing a different perspective.[26] The Court struck down a law imposing spending restrictions but expressly stated that third-party spending limits of the kind at issue in the Alberta case could be justifiable. The Quebec referendum law limited expenditures and required that all expenses be paid from the funds of committees specifically authorized to represent one side or the other. The Court was entirely sympathetic to the view that limiting election expenses could be justified in order to ensure fairness in a campaign and to prevent the most affluent members of society from exercising a disproportionate influence, but it found that the Quebec law went too far. Individuals or groups not willing or able to affiliate with one of the authorized committees were precluded from even producing leaflets or posters to express their opinion. While limiting the rights of third parties to spend money during a campaign might be necessary to ensure the integrity of

---

25   *Ibid.* at 232, Conrad J.A.
26   *Libman v. Quebec (A.G.)*, [1997] 3 S.C.R. 569, 151 D.L.R. (4th) 385.

spending limits justifiably imposed on candidates or authorized committees, the Quebec law failed the minimal-impairment test by prohibiting all third-party expenditures and thereby effectively precluding any third-party expression of view.

The only other case on election funding to reach the Supreme Court, *MacKay* v. *Manitoba*,[27] dealt with public subsidies for the campaign expenses of candidates. The plaintiff challenged Manitoba legislation that gave candidates the right to be reimbursed from public funds for a portion of their campaign expenses, provided they secured a specified percentage of the vote. The Court found that there were serious deficiencies in the evidence and that it was being asked to rule in the abstract rather than in response to a specific factual situation. While dismissing the case on this narrow ground, Cory J. indicated that the Court would be receptive to the argument that election-funding laws designed to improve the quality of debate would be acceptable: ". . . the Act seems to foster and encourage the dissemination and expression of a wide range of views and positions. In this way it enhances public knowledge of diverse views and facilitates public discussion of those views."[28]

The most recent decision in this area indicates that the Supreme Court will impose a high standard of justification for restrictions on expression in connection with elections.[29] At issue was a federal law banning the publication of opinion polls in the three days prior to a federal election. The majority found that the law could not be justified under section 1. The contention that it was desirable to provide voters with a period of rest and reflection, free from opinion polls, was rejected as a pressing and substantial objective. Writing for the majority, Bastarache J. stated that "Canadian voters must be presumed to have a certain degree of maturity and intelligence" and that it was an insult to assume that "an individual would be so enthralled by a particular poll result as to allow his or her electoral judgment to be ruled by it."[30] While the Court accepted that measures to ensure an opportunity to assess the accuracy of opinion polls was a valid objective, it found that the law failed to meet the minimal-impairment test. There were other measures that would meet that objective in a manner less intrusive of freedom of expression, such as requiring the publication of the methodology used. Moreover, wrote Bastarache J., by imposing a complete ban on the publication of opinion polls within the three-day period, the law constituted

---

27   [1989] 2 S.C.R. 357, 61 D.L.R. (4th) 385.
28   *Ibid.* at 392 (D.L.R.).
29   *Thomson Newspapers Co.* v. *Canada (A.G.)* (1998), 159 D.L.R. (4th) 385.
30   *Ibid.* at 437.

such a serious infringement of freedom of expression that even if it satisfied the minimal-impairment test, its deleterious effects would have outweighed the benefit it sought to achieve.

D. HATE SPEECH

The *Criminal Code* prohibits the communication of statements, other than in private conversation, that wilfully promote hatred against an identifiable group.[31] The purpose behind this prohibition is readily understood. In view of Canada's multicultural and multiracial social fabric, Parliament considered it appropriate to take steps to ensure that the values of tolerance, equality, and non-discrimination are respected. But anti-hate speech laws are opposed by many advocates of free speech. While it is impossible to see any redeeming value in the utterances of the hatemonger, it is argued that such laws pose an unjustifiable risk to the competing value of freedom of expression. Race, religion, and cultural difference are important issues of public concern and often give rise to heated public debate. The issues are exceedingly sensitive and some may take offence at what others regard as fair comment. Is it possible to identify with sufficient clarity and precision that which is truly unworthy and reprehensible without posing a significant risk to honest and vigorous debate?

In *R. v. Keegstra*,[32] a majority of the Supreme Court of Canada answered yes. All members of the Court agreed that, despite its message, hate speech does convey a meaning and therefore constitutes expression within the ambit of the *Charter*. Following the course it had laid out in *Irwin Toy*, the Court refused to exclude hate speech from the protection of the *Charter* on definitional grounds. It held that, if this form of expression was to be limited, the law had to satisfy the reasonable limits test of section 1. All members of the Court also accepted the argument that the objective of the anti-hate speech law was sufficiently compelling to justify limiting a *Charter* right. Such a law is intended to avoid tangible harm in the form of feelings of humiliation and degradation felt by those targeted. Furthermore, it is designed to enhance a social climate of mutual respect and tolerance. Anti-hate laws, said the Court, were not only consistent with certain international obligations assumed by Canada but also enhanced other important and competing *Charter* values of equality and multiculturalism.

---

31   Section 319. See also the related provisions prohibiting the wilful promotion of genocide (s. 318).
32   Above note 12.

The judges of the Supreme Court divided, however, on the question of minimal impairment. A purposive analysis led the majority to conclude that the minimal-impairment test was to be applied less rigorously than in other contexts. While hate speech qualified as expression, in the majority's view, it had to be recognized that hate speech was inimical to the values underlying freedom of expression. It was clearly false, thereby not attracting support from the rationale of the marketplace of ideas. And, while democracy depends upon free and open debate, hate speech denies equal dignity and respect, a precondition for genuine debate. Hate speech also attacks the autonomy rights of those who are its targets. From this perspective, the majority concluded that the anti-hate law could be justified as a minimal impairment of freedom of expression. The law was, in their view, drawn with sufficient precision to avoid posing a threat to honest or worthy expression. It does not prohibit private communications, and the prosecution has to prove as an essential ingredient of the offence that the speech represents the wilful promotion of hatred. The accused is afforded a number of defences, including truth; the good-faith expression of opinion on a religious subject; the reasonable belief in the truth of statements relevant to the public interest, the discussion of which is for the public benefit; and the conviction that the statement was intended in good faith to remove feelings of hatred. The majority found that the Parliament had carefully tailored the law to its legitimate objective and that it should be upheld on the ground that it minimally impaired freedom of expression.

The dissenting judges saw the effect of the anti-hate law quite differently. While not disputing Parliament's laudable goals, the minority did not agree that the law had a rational connection to those goals. The effect of an anti-hate-law prosecution is to afford the hatemonger an otherwise unattainable platform and level of publicity. Attempts at suppression might only serve to create martyrs. Historical evidence of vigorous anti-hate law prosecution in pre-Nazi Germany was offered to suggest that such laws were at best ineffective and at worst counter-productive. The dissenting judges also disagreed that the law was sufficiently precise, pointing to instances where prosecutions had been brought or threatened against forms of expression plainly tolerable in a free society. Though such prosecutions might not succeed, the very threat of prosecution could well stifle expression on controversial matters.[33]

In a subsequent cases, the Supreme Court upheld the *Canadian Human Rights Act* provisions curtailing hate speech[34] and a decision of a

---

33   The American courts have tended to strike down restrictions on racist speech: see
     Collin v. Smith, 578 F.2d 1197 (1978); *R.A.V. v. City of St. Paul*, 112 S.Ct. 2538 (1992).
34   *Canada (Human Rights Commission) v. Taylor*, [1990] 3 S.C.R. 892, 75 D.L.R.
     (4th) 577.

provincial human rights tribunal ordering a school board to remove from the classroom a teacher who had expressed racist views.[35] However, in another case[36] the Supreme Court struck down the "false news" provision of the *Criminal Code* which had been used in an attempt to silence a well-known purveyor of anti-Semitic and Holocaust-denial literature. The law in question prohibited the publication of statements, known by the speaker to be false, that causes or is likely to cause injury or mischief to a public interest. All members of the Court agreed that, although the law was aimed at deliberate lies, freedom of expression was involved. Even lies convey a meaning, and if that meaning was to be suppressed, the Court held that the law had to satisfy the section 1 reasonable-limits test. However, as in the hate-speech case, the Court was sharply divided on the application of the minimal-impairment test. This time the majority ruled that the law could not be justified. While the "false news" law was being used to combat a modern problem, its objective was shrouded in the mists of time. Its origins could be traced to a thirteenth-century law designed to protect the reputations of the great men of the realm. In the view of the majority, it was impossible to say what objective Parliament had in mind in retaining this ancient provision in the modern *Criminal Code*. The law lacked a clear objective or purpose and the majority held that the objective of a law cannot shift to meet the demands of the reasonable-limits test. Even if the law could be said to relate to the pressing and substantial concern of promoting racial harmony, the majority found that it could not satisfy the minimal-impairment test. Unlike the anti-hate speech law, the "false news" provision was far too broad. Falsity was difficult to determine, and, combined with the virtually unlimited reach of the phrase "injury to a public interest," the provision created an offence that posed a serious threat to freedom of expression. Writing for the majority, McLachlin J. made reference to the significant "chilling effect" this provision could have on protected speech:

> To permit the imprisonment of people, or even the threat of imprisonment, on the ground that they have made a statement which 12 of their co-citizens deem to be false and mischievous to some undefined public interest, is to stifle a whole range of speech, some of which has long been regarded as legitimate and even beneficial to our society. I do not assert that Parliament cannot criminalize the dissemination of racial slurs and hate propaganda. I do assert, however, that such provisions

---

35   *Ross* v. *New Brunswick School District No. 15*, [1996] 1 S.C.R. 825, 133 D.L.R. (4th) 1.
36   *Zundel*, above note 13.

must be drafted with sufficient particularity to offer assurance that they cannot be abused so as to stifle a broad range of legitimate and valuable speech.[37]

McLachlin J. was unpersuaded by the argument that the authorities could be trusted to use the law only when appropriate:

> The whole purpose of enshrining rights in the Charter is to afford the individual protection against even the well-intentioned majority. To justify an invasion of a constitutional right on the ground that public authorities can be trusted not to violate it unduly is to undermine the very premise upon which the Charter is predicated.[38]

E. PORNOGRAPHY

Pornography poses a problem similar to that of hate speech. Pornography is a form of expression in that it does convey a meaning. However, pornography is degrading, dehumanizing, and inimical to other *Charter* values, especially the equality of women. Defining what constitutes pornography with sufficient precision to avoid threatening legitimate artistic or scientific treatment of eroticism and sexuality is notoriously difficult. Is it possible to criminalize that which is of no redeeming value without posing an unjustifiable risk to the freedom to explore the important human issues of sexuality and eroticism?

The Supreme Court of Canada was confronted with these issues in *R. v. Butler.*[39] The *Criminal Code* makes it an offence to make, publish, or circulate "obscene" materials. An obscene publication has as its "dominant characteristic" "the undue exploitation of sex, or of sex and any one or more of . . . crime, horror, cruelty, and violence."[40] This definition is vague and prosecutions for the offence are susceptible to misuse. The offence was enacted in an era when the use of criminal prosecutions to enforce standards of sexual propriety and decency was readily accepted. Prosecutions against sexually explicit works of literary or artistic merit are certainly not unheard of. On the other hand, the reach of the provision has been to some degree restricted in recent years by judicial decisions which viewed the law as aimed at a different harm, namely, the legitimization or encouragement of sexual violence and victimization of

---

37 *Ibid.* at 743 (S.C.R.).
38 *Ibid.* at 773 (S.C.R.).
39 Above note 11.
40 Section 163.

women. These decisions interpreted the law as a means to protect the values of equality, specifically with respect to women, and emphasized the harm of sexual violence, degradation, and dehumanization.

In *Butler*, faced with a challenge to the law on the ground that it infringed freedom of expression, the Supreme Court built upon this interpretive framework for the obscenity offence. The judgment of Sopinka J. described three categories: first, explicit sex with violence, which would almost always be punishable; second, explicit sex without violence but that is degrading and dehumanizing, which would be punishable if the risk of harm is substantial; and, third, explicit sex without violence and that is not dehumanizing or degrading, which would not be punishable unless children are employed in its production.[41] In effect, the Court found that it was possible to interpret an offence originally intended to protect a certain view of sexual morality as having evolved to the point where it now protects against sexual violence and the denial of equality for women. The Court reinterpreted the obscenity offence so that it became an anti-pornography provision.

The Court was unanimous in finding that the offence, interpreted in this way, could withstand *Charter* scrutiny. As with hate speech, the Court had little hesitation in holding that, however reprehensible, pornography is a form of expression since it is intended to convey a meaning. This meant that the law had to be subjected to section 1 analysis. The Court held that the enforcement of decency and sexual propriety is not an objective sufficient to override a *Charter* right because such an objective would be inimical to individual freedom of choice. However, the Court was satisfied, that with the refined definition it accorded to the offence, the law was aimed at values essential to a free and democratic society, namely, the dignity and autonomy of women and the avoidance of degradation and dehumanization. In the Supreme Court's view, this did not conflict with the "false news" case[42] where the Court had refused to accept that the purpose of the law could shift to meet a modern problem.

On the issue of proportionality, pornography, like hate speech, was found to lie outside the core values underlying freedom of expression, and hence a more relaxed form of scrutiny was applied. Indeed, in *Butler*, the Court adopted an unusually relaxed standard when assessing the strength of the evidence linking pornography to the harm it was

---

41   Two members of the Court, Gonthier and L'Heureux Dubé JJ., disagreed and said that the depiction of explicit sex could be punished if displayed in certain public settings.

42   *Zundel*, above note 13.

alleged to cause. The Court acknowledged that, in this area, the connection was difficult if not impossible to establish, but rather than hold that this gap in evidence was fatal to the section 1 analysis, Sopinka J. stated: "[I]t is reasonable to presume that exposure to images bears a causal relationship to changes in attitude and beliefs."[43] Even with its modern and refined interpretation, the pornography offence is anything but precise. However, the Court frankly admitted that past attempts at a more precise definition had floundered. In this context, the Court was prepared to find that the minimal-impairment test could be satisfied by a law which fell well short of perfection.

F. JUDICIAL PROCEEDINGS

The Supreme Court has recognized that, in view of the important role played by the courts in our society, "the courts must be open to public scrutiny and to public criticism of their operation by the public . . . The press must be free to comment upon court proceedings to ensure that courts are, in fact, seen by all to operate openly in the penetrating light of public scrutiny."[44] This principle led the Supreme Court to strike down legislation prohibiting publication of the details of matrimonial proceedings,[45] and it led the Ontario Court of Appeal to give a narrow definition to the offence of contempt of court for intemperate remarks critical of the judicial system.[46]

Yet another area in which freedom of expression collides with other *Charter* rights is the "free press versus fair trial" debate. The right of everyone charged with an offence to a fair trial on the basis of the evidence produced in court is reinforced by the *Charter*, section 11(d). The press is plainly entitled to provide the public with information about cases pending before the courts, but in some circumstances pre-trial publicity may be thought to affect the right to a fair trial. Before the *Charter*, there is little doubt but that Canadian courts accorded priority to the right to a fair trial. Where pre-trial disclosure of evidence, the identity of the accused, or details of the offence might possibly prejudice potential jurors against the accused or otherwise impair the right of the accused to a fair trial, the courts did not hesitate to impose gag orders

---

43 *Butler*, above note 11 at 502 (S.C.R.).
44 *Edmonton Journal v. Alberta (A.G.)*, [1989] 2 S.C.R. 1326 at 1337 & 1339, 64 D.L.R. (4th) 577.
45 *Ibid.*
46 *Kopyto*, above note 2.

delaying publication of such details until after the trial. Such orders plainly limited freedom of expression and freedom of the press, but since neither right was expressly guaranteed by the constitution, the courts were entitled to give priority to the statutory right to a fair trial.

In *Dagenais* v. *Canadian Broadcasting Corp.*,[47] the Supreme Court was asked to review this area in light of the *Charter* and the entrenchment of the rights of freedom of expression and freedom of the press. The Court found that the pre-*Charter* rule inappropriately emphasized the right to a fair trial at the expense of freedom of expression. Under the *Charter*, both freedom of expression and the right to a fair trial enjoy constitutional protection, and "*Charter* principles require a balance to be achieved that fully respects the importance of both sets of rights."[48] This led the Court to conclude that a more stringent test should be applied to publication bans so that the balance between these conflicting rights might be achieved. A ban should be ordered only where it was shown to be necessary to prevent a real and substantial risk to fairness of the trial, and where reasonably available alternative measures, such as adjourning the trial, allowing challenges for cause during jury selection, and strong instructions to the jury or change of venue, would not prevent the risk. To this, the Court added the requirement that it be shown that "the salutary effects of the publication ban outweigh the deleterious impact the ban has on free expression."[49]

The decision represents a significant change in the law with respect to gag orders. The case also provides further insight into the manner in which the Supreme Court responds to measures that limit freedom of expression in the name of protecting another *Charter* right or freedom. As in the cases dealing with hate speech and pornography, the Court has rejected the proposition that one right or freedom should be given priority over another. Rather, the Court has said that the appropriate approach is to reconcile the competing rights through the proportionality review of section 1, allowing measures intended to protect one right to limit another but only to the extent necessary and subject to the minimal-impairment test.

---

47   [1994] 3 S.C.R. 835, 120 D.L.R. (4th) 12.
48   *Ibid.* at 877 (S.C.R.), Lamer C.J.C.
49   *Ibid.* at 878 (S.C.R.).

G. PROTECTION OF REPUTATION

An individual's reputation enjoys the protection of law. Statements that defame and injure reputation may give rise to a civil right of action for libel or slander, permitting the targeted individual to claim damages for the injury to reputation. The law of libel is notoriously complex and difficult but essentially provides that, where the defendant publishes a statement injurious to the plaintiff's reputation, damages are recoverable. While certain defences are available, including the truth of the statement complained of, it is for the defendant to prove a defence, failing which damages are presumed. In recent years, Canadian juries have been willing to award substantial damages, both compensatory and punitive.

Here again, a laudable and important objective is said to require limiting the rights of freedom of expression and freedom of the press. Canadian law makes no distinction between private and public figures. The press must observe the same strict requirements when describing the activities of political and public figures as apply to ordinary citizens. The presumption of falsity means that any time the press makes a statement which might injure reputation, it must be able to prove the truth of what it has said according to the exacting standards of a court of law. Honest belief in the truth of the statement provides no defence, nor does absence of malice or negligence in the writing of the story. The press must, therefore, be more than cautious in what it says; it must be right. Journalists have to avoid publishing stories, even on matters of immediate public interest and concern, unless they are confident that the truth of statements capable of injuring reputation can be proved.

The courts of the United States[50] and Australia[51] have seen fit to modify the law of defamation and to accord significantly more weight to freedom of expression. In the United States, this change was premised on the constitutional guarantee of freedom of the press. American law distinguishes between public and private figures. In the case of a public figure, the presumption of falsity is removed and the plaintiff is required to prove that the defendant acted with malice, that is, that the defendant knew the story was false or was wilfully blind to its falsity.

In *Hill* v. *Church of Scientology of Toronto*,[52] the Supreme Court of Canada was asked to reconsider the common law of defamation, partic-

---

50 *New York Times Co.* v. *Sullivan*, 376 U.S. 254 (1964).
51 *Theophanous v. Herald and Weekly Times Ltd.* (1994), 124 A.L.R. 1 (H.C.).
52 [1995] 2 S.C.R. 1130, 126 D.L.R. (4th) 129.

ularly the presumptions of falsity and damage, in light of the *Charter* protection of freedom of expression. The plaintiff, a crown attorney, sued after a lawyer for the Church of Scientology publicly announced that his client intended to take proceedings alleging the crown attorney had breached an order of the court. These allegations proved to be without foundation, and the jury awarded over one million dollars in damages. As explained in chapter 6, the *Charter* does not apply directly to the common law in such circumstances. While the Supreme Court did not resist the proposition that the common law must evolve and change in light of *Charter* values, the Court was unwilling to make any significant change in the law.[53] Writing for the Court, Cory J. said that defamatory statements are only tenuously connected to the core values protected by freedom of expression, while the right to individual reputation, although not specifically protected by the *Charter*, represents and reflects the innate dignity of the individual, a value that underlies all *Charter* rights. Accordingly, the Court rejected the argument that the law of defamation was in need of reformulation and found the balance struck by the existing law in favour of the protection of reputation to be appropriate. The Court adopted a similar approach in *R. v. Lucas*,[54] upholding the *Criminal Code* provisions dealing with defamatory libel. Though finding that the law infringed freedom of expression, the Court reiterated the importance attached to the protection of reputation and held that the law was justifiable under section 1.

H. ACCESS TO PUBLIC PROPERTY

Individuals who wish to express themselves often seek to do so in a well-travelled public place. For those who lack the resources to place their message in newspapers or broadcast media, access to public property may be essential if the message is to find an audience. An audience may be found at public places such as roads, squares, parks, and airports. Yet each of these places has a public purpose. How should the individual's right to freedom of expression be reconciled with the rights of others to use these places for their intended purpose? Does the state have the right to control access to such places for the purposes of disseminating a message?

---

53   The Court did extend the defence of "qualified privilege" to reports of pleadings and other court documents yet to be filed.

54   Above note 13.

In *Committee for the Commonwealth of Canada* v. *Canada*[55] the Supreme Court of Canada considered this issue in relation to the claim of a group that sought to distribute pamphlets at a major Canadian airport. The Court rejected the contention that government could preclude the pamphleteers access to the airport. As Lamer C.J.C. noted, government property is held for the benefit of the community at large and ownership does not, by itself, justify refusal of access for expressive purposes. By the same token, however, the right of the individual asserting freedom of expression must be assessed with reference to the public purpose of the place in question. Six of the seven judges sitting on the case found it necessary to write reasons, and hence it is not possible to identify a single rationale for the decision. However, in the end, all the judges agreed that the exercise of the right to freedom of expression did, in the circumstances, include the right of access to the airport for expressive purposes.

A subsequent case[56] dealt with posters and came to a similar conclusion. A musician advertised performances of his band by placing posters on hydro poles. Charged under a municipal bylaw prohibiting the placing of posters on public property, he challenged the bylaw as an infringement of freedom of expression. Iacobucci J. was conscious of the importance of posters as a form of expression for those with limited resources: "[P]osters have communicated political, cultural and social information for centuries."[57] All members of the Court agreed that the bylaw's complete ban on posters constituted an undue restriction of freedom of expression.

I. CONCLUSION

The Supreme Court has identified freedom of expression as an important *Charter* guarantee that lies at the heart of a free and democratic society, but it has also refused to accord anything approaching absolute protection to this important freedom. The Court has given expression an exceptionally wide definition, leaving to the section 1 analysis the difficult issues of reconciling this important freedom with other values. The results have been mixed. Despite the importance it has attached to freedom of expression, the Court has demonstrated considerable tolerance for laws that limit freedom of expression in the name of protecting

---

55   [1991] 1 S.C.R. 139, 77 D.L.R. (4th) 385
56   *Peterborough (City)* v. *Ramsden* (1993), 2 S.C.R. 1084, 106 D.L.R. (4th) 233
57   *Ibid.* at 245.

minority interests. Laws prohibiting hate speech and pornography have been upheld under relatively relaxed section 1 scrutiny on the ground that significant countervailing equality values are at stake. Similarly, protection of reputation prevailed over freedom of expression when the Court was asked to reassess the laws of defamation. On the other hand, the courts have, for the most part, subjected laws constraining political speech during elections to close scrutiny. The law relating to reporting judicial proceedings has been significantly modified under the *Charter* in favour of the media. With respect to commercial speech, an area some observers predicted would not be affected by the *Charter*, the Court has insisted upon a relatively high level of proof that legal restraints are required to achieve state objectives.

It is thought by those who place special value on freedom of expression that this pattern of decisions is inconsistent.[58] While the Court has never denied the importance of freedom of expression, it has certainly been prepared to see this freedom limited in the name of protecting other important interests. Other observers applaud the judicial refusal to place freedom of expression on a special pedestal and welcome the Court's willingness to grant Parliament and the legislatures a degree of latitude in the protection of equality values.[59] These critics contend that, if anything, the Court has been too solicitous of expression in the area of commercial speech. In the end, as this range of opinion suggests, the Court has proceeded very much on a case-by-case basis, avoiding definitive pronouncements on other than the basic structure for analysis of a freedom of expression claim.

---

58 See, for example, Alan Borovoy, *When Freedoms Collide: The Case For Our Civil Liberties* (Toronto: Lester & Orpen Dennys, 1988) c. 2.

59 See, for example, Kathleen Mahoney, "The Canadian Constitutional Approach to Freedom of Expression in Hate Propaganda and Pornography" (1992) 55 Law & Contemp. Probs. 77.

FURTHER READINGS

BOROVOY, A.A., *When Freedoms Collide: The Case for Our Civil Liberties* (Toronto: Lester & Orpen Dennys, 1988) c. 2

DYZENHAUS, D., "Regulating Free Speech" (1991) 23 Ottawa L. Rev. 289

HUTCHINSON, A.C., "Money Talk: Against Constitutionalising (Commercial) Speech" (1990) 17 Can. Bus. L.J. 2

LEPOFSKY, M.D., "The Supreme Court's Approach to Freedom of Expression: *Irwin Toy* v. *Quebec (Attorney General)* and the Illusion of Section 2(b) Liberalism" (1993) 3 N.J.C.L. 37

MAHONEY, K., "The Canadian Constitutional Approach to Freedom of Expression in Hate Propaganda and Pornography" (1992) 55 Law & Contemp. Probs. 77

MOON, R., "The Supreme Court of Canada on the Structure of Freedom of Expression Adjudication" (1995) 45 U.T.L.J. 419

SCHNEIDERMAN, D., ed., *Freedom of Expression and the Charter* (Toronto: Thomson, 1991)

SHARPE, R.J., "Commercial Expression and the Charter" (1987) 37 U.T.L.J. 229

WEINRIB, L., "Hate Promotion in a Free and Democratic Society: *R.* v. *Keegstra*" (1991) 36 McGill L.J. 1416

CHAPTER 10

FREEDOM OF ASSOCIATION

Freedom of association, guaranteed by section 2(d) of the *Charter,* protects the right of individuals to come together to form a wide array of organizations and relationships, including those with political, religious, and social purposes. The difficult threshold issue for the courts has been whether the guarantee not only recognizes the right of individuals to come together in an organization but also confers constitutional protection on the activities essential to ensure the association's meaningful existence.

Nowhere has the issue of the scope of the guarantee of freedom of association been more hotly debated than with respect to the institutions and practices of collective bargaining. Most of the case law on section 2(d) deals with labour relations, especially in the public sector. If section 2(d) protects only the right to come together and form an association, its importance is relatively modest. On the other hand, if it were held also to protect the essential activities of the group, it would have enormous impact, particularly in the realm of labour relations. Another important issue for the collective bargaining regime is whether freedom of association includes the right to refuse to be associated with a group or its views and policies. Does section 2(d) include the right to join the trade union of one's choice, or to refuse to join a union or pay it dues?

A. THE RIGHT TO STRIKE

The Supreme Court of Canada answered these questions in a trilogy of cases limiting the right to strike. In the leading case, *Reference Re Public Service Employee Relations Act*,[1] a majority of the Court held that the guarantee of freedom of association did not encompass the right to bargain collectively or the right to strike. The legislation at issue removed the right to strike from public sector workers and, in the absence of agreement, prescribed mandatory arbitration to determine the contents of the collective agreement. LeDain J. held that the rights to bargain collectively and to strike are not fundamental rights or freedoms. Rather, they are the creatures of legislation that balances a number of competing interests. Clearly, LeDain J. felt that the area of labour relations was one requiring specialized expertise. He was influenced by the fact that this area of law had largely been removed from the courts and assigned to the supervision of labour relations tribunals. LeDain J. limited the protection of section 2(d), stating that ". . . the freedom to work for the establishment of an association, to belong to an association, to maintain it, and to participate in its lawful activity without penalty or reprisal is not to be taken for granted."[2]

The dissenting judges, Dickson C.J.C. and Wilson J., concluded that the guarantee of freedom of association did include the rights for workers to bargain collectively and to strike. In their view, section 2(d) protected not only the right to join together but also the right of members of the association to pursue together aims that could be lawfully pursued individually. Although there is no individual equivalent to the right to strike, the dissenting judges thought that this activity should be included in section 2(d), given its importance to the protection of the interests of working people. While they would have found the legislation to violate section 2(d), the dissenting judges conceded that certain restraints on the right to strike would be acceptable under section 1. Dickson C.J.C. noted that ensuring essential services during a labour dispute could be a pressing and substantial objective under section 1. However, the legislation at issue was not, in his view, justifiable because its prohibition on striking was too sweeping and included more than essential workers. Furthermore, Dickson C.J.C. wrote, the arbitration

---

1   *Reference Re Public Service Employee Relations Act (Alberta)*, [1987] 1 SC.R. 313, 38 D.L.R. (4th) 161. McIntyre J., writing alone and in much greater detail, concluded that s. 2(d) did not include a right to strike, although he did not specify whether it included a right to bargain collectively.
2   *Ibid.* at 391 (S.C.R.).

provisions did not adequately safeguard employees' interests, since they provided for government control of access to arbitration and placed restrictions on the items that could be bargained.

In the two companion cases, a majority of the Court held that limitations on the right to strike and bargain did not violate the right guaranteed by section 2(d). In one case, Saskatchewan legislation banning a strike in the dairy industry was upheld,[3] while the other upheld the federal government's price-and-wage control program, which banned strikes and altered the financial compensation scheme.[4]

Following these decisions, there was still some doubt whether section 2(d) might include a right to bargain collectively, even if it did not include a right to strike. However, in the *PIPS* case, the majority of the Court clearly rejected the argument that the right to bargain collectively was included in section 2(d).[5] The Professional Institute of the Public Service (PIPS) had represented a group of federal government employees transferred to employment with the Northwest Territories government. The public-service legislation of the Northwest Territories provided that a union could not obtain bargaining rights unless it was incorporated under legislation giving it the power to bargain collectively, and PIPS was not incorporated under this legislation. The majority of the Supreme Court held that there was no violation of section 2(d), because the transferred employees remained free to join any union. The incorporation provision was likened to the voluntary recognition provisions in other collective bargaining legislation, which allow employers to recognize a union's right to bargain on behalf of its employees. Here, incorporation was the means by which the Legislative Council of the Territories conferred bargaining rights on a public sector union. As to the argument that this left PIPS with no chance to represent its former members, the Court held that no union could demand collective bargaining rights vis-à-vis an employer, stating that "since the activity of bargaining is not itself constitutionally protected, neither is a legislative choice of the bargainer."[6] Writing for the majority, Sopinka J. turned to the reasons of

3   *R.W.D.S.U., Locals 544, 496, 635, 955* v. *Saskatchewan*, [1987] 1 S.C.R. 460, 38 D.L.R. (4th) 277. In this case, Dickson C.J.C. reached the same conclusion as the majority, while Wilson J. was alone in dissent.
4   *P.S.A.C.* v. *Canada (A.G.)*, [1987] 1 S.C.R. 424, 38 D.L.R. (4th) 249. Again Dickson C.J.C. and Wilson J. dissented.
5   *Professional Institute of the Public Service of Canada* v. *Northwest Territories (Commissioner)*, [1990] 2 S.C.R. 367, 72 D.L.R. (4th) 1 [*PIPS*].
6   *Ibid.* at 406 (S.C.R.).

McIntrye J. in the earlier Alberta reference and summarized his view of the meaning of section 2(d):

> ... first, that s. 2(d) protects the freedom to establish, belong to and maintain an association; second, that s. 2(d) does not protect an activity solely on the ground that the activity is a foundational or essential purpose of an association; third, that s. 2(d) protects the exercise in association of the constitutional rights and freedoms of individuals; and fourth, that s. 2(d) protects the exercise in association of the lawful rights of individuals.[7]

Sopinka J. concluded that collective bargaining is not protected by section 2(d): "Restrictions on the *activity* of collective bargaining do not normally affect the ability of individuals to form or join unions."[8]

Cory J., with two others, dissented. In his view, the Legislative Council had to comply with the *Charter* when implementing the decision to permit collective bargaining by its employees. Mandating the incorporation of bargaining agents was seen to be an interference with the employees' right to select, form, or change an association.

B. THE RIGHT NOT TO ASSOCIATE

To this point, the focus has been on the freedom to associate. But sometimes an individual may not want to associate with another. This claim arose in *Lavigne*, where a community college teacher who was not a union member objected to a collective agreement provision forcing him to pay dues to the union. The compelled payment of dues, known as the "Rand formula" (or the agency shop), differs from compelled membership in the union (or a closed shop provision). Even though Lavigne was not compelled to join the union, he disagreed with a number of purposes for which his union dues were being spent, including opposing cruise missile testing and supporting certain causes, such as abortion.

The collective agreement was subject to *Charter* scrutiny because the employer, the college's Council of Regents, was closely controlled by government and hence could be considered a Crown agent.[9] Four of seven judges held that the mandatory dues provision did not violate section 2(d). Wilson J. and two others concluded that section 2(d) did not

---

7 *Ibid.* at 402 (S.C.R.).
8 *Ibid.* at 404 (S.C.R.).
9 This point is discussed in greater detail in chapter 6.

include a right not to associate (sometimes called a "negative right"). In her view, however, this did not leave an individual unprotected from the harms that might come from forced association. The section 2(b) guarantee of freedom of expression would be available to an individual who was compelled to be associated with views he or she did not hold.[10] McLachlin J. concluded that some instances of compelled association might violate section 2(d), but not the requirement to pay union dues. In her view, section 2(d) protected only against "coerced ideological conformity." She did not think that Lavigne's payment of dues in fact associated him with the union's causes.[11]

La Forest J. disagreed and found that section 2(d) included a right not to associate, which had been breached in this case. In his view, it is contrary to the *Charter* either to prevent individuals from joining together or to compel them to do so in some circumstances. While certain forced associations are a reality of modern society, La Forest J. found there was a *Charter* violation, since Lavigne was required to contribute to causes beyond the immediate concerns of the bargaining unit. Compelling him to contribute funds to the union for bargaining purposes, including collective agreement administration, served to protect the common good and was consistent with section 2(d), but forced contribution to non-union purposes was not.[12] However, La Forest J. concluded that the compelled payment of dues was justified under section 1. He rejected the idea that individual objectors could be given an opportunity to opt out of paying for matters that were not purely "collective bargaining." Permitting such opting out would seriously undermine the union's financial security and invite paternalistic scrutiny of union activities by government.

C. CONCLUSION

The result of the collective bargaining cases in the Supreme Court has been to remove important aspects of the area of labour relations from *Charter* scrutiny. While criticized by some, the Court's posture may be characterized as middle-of-the-road. The Court has not granted unions new protection against legislative action curtailing bargaining and strikes, but neither has it given new tools to those opposed to the majori-

---

10 *Lavigne v. Ontario Public Service Employees Union*, [1991] 2 S.C.R. 211, 81 D.L.R. (4th) 545 at 582–85.

11 *Ibid.* at 645 (D.L.R.).

12 *Ibid.* at 635 (D.L.R.).

tarian nature of collective bargaining and intent on overturning agency and closed shop provisions. In concluding that section 2(d) does not apply to collective bargaining, the Supreme Court has emphasized that the purpose of the guarantee is to protect individual fulfilment. There are many critics who decry the Court's failure to protect union activity, because they had hoped that the *Charter* would expand the scope of collective bargaining.[13] However, the treatment accorded section 2(d) can be seen as consistent with the Court's tendency in other areas to refuse to recognize economic activity as worthy of *Charter* protection.[14]

FURTHER READINGS

BAKAN, J., *Just Words: Constitutional Rights and Social Wrongs* (Toronto: University of Toronto Press, 1997) c. 5

BEATTY, D.M., "Labouring Outside the Charter" (1991) 29 Osgoode Hall L.J. 839

BEATTY, D.M., *Putting the Charter to Work: Designing a Constitutional Labour Code* (Montreal: McGill–Queen's University Press, 1987)

SWINTON, K.E., "The *Charter of Rights* and Public Sector Labour Relations" in G. Swimmer & M. Thompson, eds., *Public Sector Collective Bargaining in Canada: Beginning of the End or End of the Beginning?* (Kingston, ON: I.R.C. Press, 1995)

WEILER, P., "The Charter at Work: Reflections on the Constitutionalizing of Labour and Employment Law" (1990) 40 U.T.L.J. 117

---

13   See, for example, D.M. Beatty, "Labouring Outside the Charter" (1991) 29 Osgoode Hall L.J. 839.

14   See chapters 3, 4, and 13 for further discussion of this point.

CHAPTER 11

DEMOCRATIC RIGHTS

A central argument favouring the entrenchment of rights in a constitution is that checks on the political process are needed in order to protect certain fundamental values. There is often disagreement about the specific rights that should be entrenched or the degree to which legislatures should be restricted by the constitution and subject to judicial review. Yet one area in which there is widespread consensus on the need for some judicial oversight is that of political activity. Participation in fair elections and vigorous public debate are the cornerstones of democracy.

The *Charter of Rights and Freedoms* contains three guarantees designed to ensure the healthy functioning of Canadian parliamentary democracy. Section 3 provides that every citizen has the right to vote in elections for the House of Commons or a provincial legislature and to be qualified for membership in those houses. Section 4 sets a maximum duration of five years for the life of the House of Commons or a provincial legislature, although that period can be extended in time of war or similar national crisis by a two-thirds vote of the members. Finally, section 5 guarantees a sitting of Parliament and the legislatures at least once in every year. The importance — and the primacy — of these sections is shown by the fact that they cannot be overridden by the exercise of the notwithstanding clause in section 33.

Section 4 of the *Charter* is designed to ensure that Canadians have a regular opportunity to elect federal and provincial representatives, while section 5 is designed to ensure that those elected representatives have a regular opportunity to examine and vote upon the actions of the executive branch of government. Sections 4 and 5 are long-standing parts of the Canadian constitution which derive from our British tradition of parliamentary democracy. Indeed, section 50 of the *Constitution Act, 1867*, also states that the life of the House of Commons is five years, unless an election is called earlier.

Not surprisingly, since sections 4 and 5 reflect constitutional conventions that have been widely accepted for a long time, they have not generated any litigation. However, section 3, the right to vote, is a much richer and more controversial provision that has given rise to a number of disputes. These include the legitimacy of residency and other qualifications on the right to vote and the drawing of electoral boundaries. Section 3 has also often been raised in conjunction with the guarantees of freedom of expression and association, discussed earlier.

A. VOTER QUALIFICATIONS

Read literally, the right to vote requires that every citizen have the opportunity to cast a ballot in every election — although the guarantee applies only to federal and provincial elections, not those at the municipal level.[1] However, election laws contain a number of qualifications, most commonly restricting the right to vote to those under a certain age and denying the vote to prison inmates. In addition, many laws require citizens to have been resident within a territory for a specified period, often several months, before they are eligible to vote.

The Supreme Court of Canada has not yet ruled on the constitutionality of most of these limitations on the right to vote in regular elections. During the 1992 referendum on constitutional amendments known as the Charlottetown Accord, the Court was asked to determine the validity of a residency requirement. Simultaneous referenda were held in all provinces and territories. In Quebec, the referendum was held under provincial legislation, which required six months' residence in the province. In all other parts of Canada, the referendum took place under federal legislation. Graham Haig, having recently moved to Quebec from Ontario, was disqualified under the Quebec legislation because he did not meet the provincial residency requirement. He could not qualify under federal legislation, which required residence in a polling division

---

1   The Ontario courts have held that s. 3 did not give a right to vote in municipal elections or to run for municipal office in *Jones v. Ontario (A.G.)* (1988), 53 D.L.R. (4th) 273 (Ont. H.C.); *Rheaume v. Ontario (A.G.)* (1992), 7 O.R. (3d) 22 (C.A.).

in the federal referendum area. Haig challenged the failure to include him under the federal election legislation, but his claim was dismissed on the ground that section 3 applied only to federal and provincial elections and did not guarantee the right to vote in a referendum.[2]

Several lower courts have ruled on issues relating to voter qualifications. Generally, residency requirements have been found to be reasonable limits on voting rights justifiable under section 1 of the *Charter*, in light of the widespread use of territorial representation in the Canadian system of government. As most representatives are elected in a geographically determined riding or constituency, a residency requirement ensures that only individuals with substantial ties to a locality have a right to select its representative. A period of residency also contributes to the voter's knowledge of the issues affecting that community. As well, residency requirements protect the integrity of the election process by preventing individuals from coming into the riding temporarily to disrupt voting patterns.[3]

Some voter qualifications are linked to the concept of competency. For example, the requirement that a voter be eighteen years of age, as specified by the *Canada Elections Act*, rests on the assumption that a certain age is a standard for measuring maturity and responsibility. Formerly, judges were disqualified from voting in order to preserve the appearance of judicial neutrality and independence from the political process. A successful *Charter* challenge to this disqualification[4] was followed by a 1993 change to the federal *Elections Act* to allow judges to vote.[5]

The most litigated voter qualification provision has been the denial of the franchise to prisoners in penal institutions. The traditional reason for denying inmates the vote was to register society's disapproval of those who had broken its laws and thereby were thought to have disqualified themselves from participating in one of the important elements of citizenship. In effect, the denial of the right to vote was a further penalty for the crime. It has also been argued, in some cases, that inmates must be denied the right to vote in order to preserve prison security. Finally, it has been suggested that, since prison inmates are

---

2   *Haig v. Canada (Chief Electoral Officer)*, [1993] 2 S.C.R. 995, 105 D.L.R. (4th) 577 at 602. Iacobucci J., Lamer C.J.C. concurring, dissented on the ground that the denial of the opportunity to vote violated the guarantee of freedom of expression in s. 2(b) of the *Charter*.

3   *Reference Re Yukon Election Residency Requirement* (1986), 27 D.L.R. (4th) 146 (Y.T.C.A.).

4   *Muldoon v. Canada*, [1988] 3 F.C.R. 628 (T.D.).

5   *Canada Elections Act*, S.C. 1993, c. 19.

detached from the community, they cannot participate meaningfully in the public debate necessary to inform themselves as educated voters.

In two 1992 decisions, appellate courts accepted the argument that the prisoner's section 3 right to vote was infringed and this was not a reasonable limit under section 1.[6] In *Belczowski*,[7] Hugessen J.A. observed that there were some crimes, such as treason, in which the denial of the right to vote was logically linked to the nature of the crime. However, the then existing provision barred an inmate from voting regardless of the nature of the crime committed. Moreover, he held, there was no necessary connection between imprisonment and lack of familiarity with political issues — indeed, many in society would be unfamiliar with important issues, yet they are still allowed to vote. Both decisions were upheld, with very brief reasons, by the Supreme Court of Canada in 1993.[8] The Court held that the blanket prohibition on inmate voting in section 51(e) did not meet the proportionality test under section 1, particularly the minimal-impairment component of the test. Subsequently, the *Canada Elections Act* was amended in 1993 to limit the prohibition on voting to those sentenced to a term of more than two years. The differentiation between those with less than two-year sentences and those with longer sentences denies the vote only to those who have been convicted of the most serious offences. On the other hand, those who advocate prisoners' right to vote will likely argue that, since no effort was made to tailor the prohibition to the type of offence, the prohibition remains too broad to survive, even in its amended form.

B. ELECTORAL BOUNDARIES

The most contentious issue litigated under section 3 has been the role of the courts in overseeing the design of the electoral system. Is the right to vote only a right to cast a ballot, or should it be interpreted to ensure that the electoral system does not give undue weight to the vote of some and insufficient weight to the vote of others?

---

6   *Sauvé v. Canada (A.G.)* (1992), 89 D.L.R. (4th) 644 (Ont. C.A.); *Belczowski v. Canada* (1992), 90 D.L.R. (4th) 330 (F.C.A.).

7   Above note 6.

8   *Sauvé v. Canada (A.G.)*, [1993] 2 S.C.R. 438. In *Re Reynolds and British Columbia (A.G.)* (1984), 11 D.L.R. (4th) 380, a prohibition on voting by those on probation was found to be unconstitutional by the British Columbia Court of Appeal.

The Canadian electoral system is based on territorial representation at both the federal and the provincial level. Individuals vote for a member to represent their constituency in the provincial legislature or the House of Commons. The government is selected on the basis of having the support of a majority of elected members in the House. The Canadian system is also a "first past the post" system, with the individual who receives the greatest number of votes winning the seat, even if he or she did not garner a majority of the votes.

Other countries have quite different electoral systems. Some use proportional representation of parties based on the percentage of votes received, with members of the legislature selected from party lists. Members are not necessarily attached to a particular constituency. Other systems also use proportional representation but still provide for the election of members in a particular constituency.

The rationale for proportional representation is to ensure, to the extent possible, that every vote is reflected by the members elected. On the other hand, the rationale for electing members from a geographic constituency is to facilitate the input of interests within that territory, while also ensuring that an elected member is available to play a problem-solving role for the citizens whom he or she represents.

In the Canadian system and others based on territorial representation, difficult issues arise when drawing electoral boundaries for constituencies. Should the goal be an equal number of voters in each constituency? Should there be departures from that goal in order to serve other interests — for example, to recognize the distinctive interests of communities, or to facilitate travel and contact between voters and their representative? Traditionally, rural voters were thought to have different concerns than urban voters, and electoral boundaries were drawn accordingly. With the increasing ethnic diversity in Canadian society, it might be argued that electoral lines should be drawn so as to maximize the opportunity for an ethnic or religious group to vote for a member of their community, rather than dispersing their votes among other ethnic and religious communities where they would have less voting power should they choose to vote as a block. One might argue that it is justifiable that rural or northern constituencies have smaller numbers of voters than urban ones because of the difficulties of campaigning and maintaining contact in less-populated areas.

Inevitably, the drawing of electoral-boundary lines raises the spectre of "gerrymandering," a term that connotes the exercise of distasteful self-interest on the part of those in control of the process. Not surprisingly, political incumbents have an interest in drawing boundaries in ways that can help them and undermine support for their opponents.

Where the process of constituency line drawing is left to politicians, rather than independent electoral-boundary commissions, there may be good reason for the courts to scrutinize the fairness of the outcome. But no matter the process, one cannot avoid difficult and debatable decisions about the size and design of constituencies. The courts have a delicate role in deciding when the electoral system improperly undermines the right to vote, guaranteed under section 3 of the *Charter*.

The most significant decision to date is that of the Supreme Court of Canada in the *Reference Re Provincial Electoral Boundaries (Saskatchewan)*.[9] Saskatchewan had established an independent electoral-boundaries commission but had also set a strict quota of urban and rural seats and required that the boundaries of urban ridings coincide with the existing boundaries of municipalities. Aside from two sparsely populated northern ridings, the ridings under consideration were within plus or minus 25 percent of the "provincial quotient," the figure determined by dividing the provincial voting population by the number of ridings.

While the Supreme Court of Canada split six to three in upholding the boundaries, all the judges agreed on the general principles underlying the right to vote espoused by the majority judgment of McLachlin J. In reasons supported by four others, she described the meaning of the right to vote as "not equality of voting power *per se*, but the right to 'effective representation.'"[10] The conditions of "effective representation" included not only relative parity of voting power (so that the weight of an individual's vote would not be unduly diluted) but also factors important to "fair" representation of Canada's diversity. In her words:

> Factors like geography, community history, community interests and minority representation may need to be taken into account to ensure that our legislative assemblies effectively represent the diversity of our social mosaic.[11]

McLachlin J. expressly rejected the American model of "one person, one vote," arguing that it is neither consistent with Canadian history nor a practical alternative in the search for effective representation in a country like Canada:

> Respect for individual dignity and social equality mandate that citizens' votes not be unduly debased or diluted. But the need to recognize

9   [1991] 2 S.C.R. 158, 81 D.L.R. (4th) 16.
10 *Ibid.* at 183 (S.C.R.).
11 *Ibid.* at 184 (S.C.R.).

cultural and group identity and to enhance the participation of individuals in the electoral process and society requires that other concerns also be accommodated.[12]

Applying these principles, McLachlin J. concluded that both the process
and the outcome of the Saskatchewan scheme were fair and consistent
with section 3 of the *Charter*. In particular, she noted that the division
of seats between rural and urban areas approximated the actual population division in the two areas. Moreover, she accepted the argument that
rural ridings are more difficult to serve, both because of transportation
and communication problems and because rural voters are said to make
more demands on their representatives. Finally, discrepancies between
ridings were justified on traditional bases such as geography, community interests, and projected population changes.

While accepting these general principles, Cory J., with two other
judges, dissented. He found that the underlying process in drawing
boundaries in Saskatchewan was contrary to section 3 because the strict
rural/urban division interfered with the rights of urban voters and that
this was not justifiable under section 1.[13]

The Saskatchewan case is interesting from several perspectives. As
in the area of freedom of expression, we see a distinctive Canadian
approach that takes into account concerns about the effectiveness of
representation as well as sensitivity to the interests of groups. The result
marks the reluctance of the Supreme Court to give the judiciary a central role in electoral map drawing. By accepting the legislation's allowance for as much as a 25 percent deviation from the provincial quotient
for constituency size, the Court gave a great deal of scope for electoral-
boundary commissions or legislatures in drawing boundaries.

At the federal level, variation in the size of electoral districts is indirectly mandated by the constitution itself. Section 51A of the *Constitution Act, 1867*, guarantees that no province will have fewer members in
the House of Commons than in the Senate. This ensures that Prince
Edward Island, a province with a population of about 140,000, will

---

12   *Ibid.* at 188 (S.C.R.).
13   Cases in Alberta and Prince Edward Island have applied the Saskatchewan
      principles, with the Alberta decisions upholding an electoral map that favoured
      rural over urban ridings (*Reference Re Electoral Boundaries Commission Act
      (Alberta)* (1991), 120 A.R. 70 (C.A.); and the Prince Edward Island finding of a
      Charter violation (*MacKinnon v. Prince Edward Island* (1993), 101 D.L.R. (4th) 362
      (P.E.I.T.D.).

always have four members in the House of Commons. Many of the urban ridings in provinces with rising populations such as Ontario and British Columbia are substantially larger than those in P.E.I.[14] Since the House of Commons is unlikely to grow substantially for both political and practical reasons, the result of the "Senate floor" rule is almost certainly to create a significant imbalance in constituency size.

It has been asked by some whether there is a requirement of "affirmative gerrymandering" to ensure that electoral boundaries are drawn to ensure maximum voting power to racial and ethnic groups.[15] Some argue that "effective representation" for groups traditionally underrepresented in Canadian legislatures requires positive action to promote the election of representatives from these communities. This could be facilitated within the existing system of geographic representation, if all that is required is to draw lines in a manner alert to ethnic or cultural difference. However, that approach will not work if a group is not concentrated territorially. For example, to ensure greater representation of women, one would have to argue that section 3 required a different kind of electoral system — either two-person constituencies with male and female members, or a shift to a proportional representation system.

Does the Supreme Court's decision in the Saskatchewan reference indicate that such challenges would be successful? The Court was clearly sympathetic to a system sensitive to the diversity of interests in Canadian politics which allows for deviation from the principle of "one person, one vote" or "treat all the same." Yet the Court did not go so far as to adopt a "mirror" concept of representation that requires individuals to be represented on the basis of sex or ethnicity. Nor did the Court signal any willingness to alter the "procedural representation" that is at the basis of the Canadian system. That system allows individuals, grouped geographically, to decide, from time to time, whether they see their interests aligning with others on the basis of sex, ethnicity, class, religion, or a combination of these and other characteristics.

---

14   This is discussed further in K. E. Swinton, "Federalism, Representation and Rights" in J. Courtney, P. MacKinnon, & D. Smith, eds., *Drawing Boundaries: Legislatures, Courts, and Electoral Values* (Saskatoon: Fifth House, 1992) at 17.

15   K.W. Roach, "Chartering the Electoral Map into the Future" in *Drawing Boundaries, ibid.* at 211–14.

C. CONCLUSION

The right to vote is one of the most fundamental rights possessed by citizens in a democracy. The right conferred by section 3 of the *Charter* has not been the subject of a significant volume of litigation. In the cases that have come before the courts, judges have shown little sympathy for laws that deny the right to vote to particular groups. On the other hand, the courts have respected the historical and representational underpinnings of electoral-boundary design and hesitated to interfere with legislative judgment.

FURTHER READINGS

COURTNEY J., P. MACKINNON, & D. SMITH, eds., *Drawing Boundaries: Legislatures, Courts, and Electoral Values* (Saskatoon: Fifth House, 1992)

CHAPTER 12

MOBILITY RIGHTS

An important element of individual freedom is the right to enter and leave one's country and to move about it freely. In countries with federal systems, such as Canada, it is fundamental to a sense of national citizenship that individuals be able to move to and work in other provinces without prejudice because of their province of origin. The mobility rights protected by section 6 of the *Charter* are designed to promote and foster these objectives.

Section 6 contains two kinds of mobility rights, one international and the other interprovincial. Section 6(1) guarantees the right of citizens to enter, remain in, and leave Canada, while section 6(2)(a) and (b) guarantees the right of citizens and permanent residents "to move and take up residence in any province; and to pursue the gaining of a livelihood in any province." The interprovincial guarantee is qualified in two ways. The right is subject to laws of general application in force in a province, provided those laws do not discriminate among individuals primarily on the basis of province of present or previous residence (section 6(3)(a)). Section 6(3)(b) permits reasonable residency requirements for the receipt of publicly provided social services. As well, section 6(4) protects from *Charter* challenge laws and programs aimed at relieving the plight of those who are socially or economically disadvantaged in provinces with rates of unemployment above the national rate. Finally, as with all *Charter* rights, a government may be able to justify laws that violate section 6 under section 1. However, mobility rights are among those rights in the *Charter* that are regarded as so significant that they are not subject to the legislative override in section 33.

A. THE RIGHT TO ENTER AND LEAVE CANADA

Section 6(1), the right of citizens to enter and leave Canada, has its origins in the *International Covenant on Civil and Political Rights*. Article 12(2) of that document provides that "[e]veryone shall be free to leave any country, including his own," while Article 12(4) states that "[n]o one shall be arbitrarily deprived of the right to enter his own country." However, the language of section 6(1) of the *Charter* is broader in that it includes a right to "remain in" Canada.

The most obvious uses for this section would be to challenge the denial of a passport, compelled expulsion from the country, or denial of re-entry. Yet, these scenarios are unlikely in a country with Canada's democratic traditions, and, not surprisingly, there has been no litigation in relation to any of them.[1]

Section 6(1) has been invoked most often when Canadian citizens try to resist extradition to another country for trial. Canada has numerous extradition treaties with other countries, which allow a foreign country to seek the surrender of a Canadian citizen who is alleged to have committed an offence according to that country's law. If the individual is found guilty, he or she would ordinarily be required to serve any sentence in the foreign country, although Canada has arrangements with some countries which allow the convicted person to serve the sentence in a Canadian prison.

In *United States* v. *Cotroni*,[2] the Supreme Court of Canada concluded that surrender of a citizen pursuant to the *Extradition Act* was a violation of section 6(1) of the *Charter*. Even though the surrender did not amount to an expulsion or banishment, since the individual could return after an acquittal at trial or after serving a sentence, the Court held that the rights in section 6(1) were infringed because the individual was denied the right to remain in Canada.

Although section 6(1) was violated, La Forest J., writing for the majority, concluded that the infringement caused by extradition lay far from the core values of section 6(1). In his view, the central thrust of section 6(1) was protection against exile and banishment, "the purpose of which is the exclusion of membership in the national community."[3]

---

1   The closest example is the deportation of a permanent resident under the *Immigration Act* after conviction for a serious offence. Section 6(1) is not applicable because it applies only to citizens, and s. 7 is not violated (*Chiarelli* v. *Canada (Minister of Employment and Immigration)*, [1992] 1 S.C.R. 711, 90 D.L.R. (4th) 289).
2   [1989] 1 S.C.R. 1469.
3   *Ibid.* at 1482.

This led the majority to take a more flexible approach to the application of section 1 of the *Charter* in the case of extradition. The Court had no difficulty in finding that there was a pressing and substantial objective underlying the extradition law. It aimed at the suppression of crime through international cooperative efforts. On the issue of proportionality of means and ends, the Supreme Court divided (five to two). Cotroni argued that, because he could have been tried in Canada for the same offence he was charged with in the United States, his extradition could not be justified as a reasonable limit. While the two dissenting judges accepted this proposition, the majority disagreed. Cotroni was alleged to have conspired to possess and distribute heroin. His actions occurred in Canada, the heroin was to be distributed in the United States, and most of the witnesses were in that country. Therefore, the Court held, it was reasonable to allow him to be surrendered to the United States for trial and the section 1 test was satisfied.[4]

B. INTERPROVINCIAL MOBILITY

Section 6 also protects interprovincial mobility. The section was part of a more ambitious set of proposals by the federal government to strengthen the Canadian economic union. Concerned about barriers to the mobility of labour, capital, goods, and services, the federal government proposed to bolster the common market clause in section 121 of the *Constitution Act, 1867*. That section provides that the articles produced or grown in a province shall be "admitted free" into other provinces. It has been narrowly interpreted by the courts as prohibiting customs duties, but it has been ineffective in protecting against rules discriminating against out-of-province labour, property ownership, or access to government contracts.[5] For example, Quebec for many years discriminated against workers from out-of-province in the construction industry, while Prince Edward Island restricted land ownership by non-residents.

Despite federal pressure for more ambitious constitutional language in various efforts at constitutional reform, section 6(2) deals only with mobility for citizens and permanent residents. It has been interpreted by the Supreme Court of Canada as guaranteeing a right of interprovincial mobility that ensures a right to move to another province to take up

---

4   A similar result was reached in *United States of America v. Ross*, [1996] 1 S.C.R. 469.
5   See, for example, the discussion of Laskin C.J.C. in *Reference Re Agricultural Products Marketing Act (Canada)*, [1978] 2 S.C.R. 1198 at 1266–268, 84 D.L.R. (3d) 257.

work there, and the right of a non-resident to work in another province without relocating. It is not, however, a free-standing guarantee of the right to work, and for the right to be invoked, there must be some element of interprovincial mobility at issue.[6] While the British Columbia Court of Appeal in *Wilson* interpreted section 7 as including a right of mobility *within* a province,[7] this must be contrasted with the Supreme Court of Canada's view that section 6(2) is designed to eliminate boundaries between the provinces.[8]

Nor has the section been interpreted as protecting new residents and non-residents from compliance with the general rules applicable to existing provincial residents — for example, occupational qualifications and licence requirements which affect everyone.[9] Section 6(3)(a) makes it clear that residents and non-residents are subject to laws of "general application" — that is, it safeguards laws that do not discriminate primarily on the basis of province of residence.

The leading case interpreting section 6(2) is *Black* v. *Law Society of Alberta*.[10] In an effort to control interprovincial law firms — specifically, a partnership between an Alberta and an Ontario firm — the Law Society of Alberta passed two rules. The first prohibited partnerships between lawyers resident in Alberta and non-residents, while the second prohibited partnerships by members in more than one firm. The three-member majority of the Supreme Court of Canada held that the rules infringed section 6(2)(b), because their effect was seriously to impair the ability of non-resident lawyers to carry on a viable business arrangement. These rules were not saved by section 6(3)(a), because they were not laws of general application. Their purpose and effect was to discriminate on the basis of residence.

The majority went on to examine the rules in light of section 1 of the *Charter* and concluded that they were not reasonable limits. Even though the Law Society had legitimate concerns about the proper governance of the legal profession, including avoiding conflicts of interest in the prac-

---

6   *Law Society of Upper Canada* v. *Skapinker*, [1984] 1 S.C.R. 357, 9 D.L.R. (4th) 161 [*Skapinker*].

7   *Wilson* v. *British Columbia (Medical Services Commission)* (1988), 53 D.L.R. (4th) 171 (B.C.C.A.).

8   In *Skapinker*, above note 6, Estey J. stated at 181 (D.L.R.): "The two rights (in paras. (a) and (b)) both relate to movement into another province, either for the taking up of residence, or to work without establishing residence."

9   See, for example, *Taylor* v. *Institute of Chartered Accountants of Saskatchewan* (1989), 59 D.L.R. (4th) 656 (Sask. C.A.).

10   *Black* v. *Law Society of Alberta*, [1989] 1 S.C.R. 591, 58 D.L.R. (4th) 317 [*Black*].

tice of law, there were other alternatives that would achieve their ends without impinging upon the rights secured by section 6 (2)(b).

McIntyre J., in dissent, argued that the rules about partnership between residents and non-residents or multiple partnerships might violate the right to freedom of association in section 2(d), but there was no violation of the mobility guarantee. In his words, "[n]obody is forbidden entry into Alberta and nobody is prohibited from practising law or forming a partnership in Alberta."[11] In considering section 1, he concluded that the rule forbidding partnerships between residents and non-residents was not a reasonable limit, although he would have upheld the rule against multiple partnerships.

Black dealt with provisions that were directed at non-residents. However, many provincial laws restrict the practice of an occupation and cause barriers to mobility, even though their purpose is not to restrict competition from non-residents or new residents. For example, one province may require higher levels of training for nurses than another. Quebec has rules about proficiency in the French language for those practising professions that create obstacles for non-francophones. Most provincial laws of this kind seem safe from a mobility-rights challenge Even if they have a disproportionate impact on non-residents, they will likely be characterized as laws of general application within section 6(3)(a) that do not discriminate on the basis of province of residence.

C. CONCLUSION

If section 6 was meant to have a major impact on the functioning of the Canadian economic union, its supporters have likely been disappointed, for its reach has been limited so far to cases of direct discrimination on the basis of provincial residence in the pursuit of an individual's livelihood or choice of residence. It does not catch many other barriers to the mobility of goods, services, people, and capital, leaving these to be addressed by other institutions and legal rules.[12]

---

11   *Ibid.* at 636.

12   See, for example, *Reference Re Prince Edward Island Lands Protection Act* (1987), 40 D.L.R. (4th) 1 (P.E.I.C.A.), where it was found that controls on non-residents' ownership of land did not violate s. 6. For further discussion of such barriers and their legal treatment, see K.E. Swinton, "Courting Our Way to Economic Integration: Judicial Review and the Canadian Economic Union" (1995) 25 Can. Bus. L.J. 280.

FURTHER READINGS

BLACHE, P., "Mobility Rights" in G.A. Beaudoin & E. Mendes, eds., *The Canadian Charter of Rights and Freedoms*, 3d ed. (Toronto: Carswell, 1996)

SWINTON, K.E., "Courting Our Way to Economic Integration: Judicial Review and the Canadian Economic Union" (1995) 25 Can. Bus. L.J. 280

CHAPTER 13

LIFE, LIBERTY, AND SECURITY OF THE PERSON

Section 7 of the *Charter* provides:

> Everyone has the right to life, liberty and security of the person and the right not to be deprived thereof except in accordance with the principles of fundamental justice.

The section is cast in broad language and the scope of the guarantee is potentially significant and far-reaching. However, the Supreme Court has made it clear that the process of elaborating the meaning of section 7 will necessarily be a gradual and case-by-case exercise.[1] This is understandable, for the interpretation of section 7 raises difficult questions. As we shall see, many of these questions involve fundamental moral and social issues and call for the courts to consider the scope and limits of judicial review under the *Charter*.

Section 7 has had significant impact in the criminal law context where it has been held to extend important procedural guarantees to persons accused of crime. That aspect of section 7 is discussed in chapter 14. This chapter considers the impact of section 7 outside the sphere of procedural guarantees in the criminal process.

Should section 7 be narrowly interpreted to protect little more than procedural fairness in the criminal process or does the requirement to

---

1   *R. v. Morgentaler*, [1988] 1 S.C.R. 30 at 51, 44 D.L.R. (4th) 385 [*Morgentaler*], Dickson C.J.C.

respect the "principles of fundamental justice" demand review of the substantive content of legislation to ensure that all laws are just and fair? Does section 7 protect the "liberty" to do as one pleases, or should "liberty" be given a narrower interpretation, embracing only physical freedom? All laws constrain "liberty" in its widest sense. It is a basic tenet of our legal system that one is at liberty to do as one pleases unless constrained by some positive law. Yet ours is also a society governed by law and a society that recognizes that laws, and hence constraints on liberty, are required to preserve order and protect the weak and vulnerable. Does "security of the person" entail the right to own property? If so, section 7 could help the "haves" in our society by significantly constraining governmental regulatory and redistributive measures. Does "security of the person" guarantee some minimal level of economic entitlement? If so, section 7 could help the "have-nots" by compelling the creation and extension of government welfare schemes. Opponents of abortion have argued that abortion denies the unborn of the right to "life," while pro-choice advocates contend that laws preventing abortion infringe a woman's rights to "liberty" and "security of the person."

In this chapter, we canvass the way the courts have responded to these and other questions. As we shall see, definitive answers have yet to be given in many contentious areas. After more than sixteen years of litigation, the task of defining the outer limits of "life, liberty and security of the person" as well as the "principles of fundamental justice" has only just started.

A. STRUCTURE FOR ANALYSIS

The courts have settled on the basic structure for analysis of a section 7 claim. First, it is necessary for the person claiming a violation of rights to show that the right he or she seeks to protect falls within the meaning of "life, liberty or security of the person" and that that right has been infringed. This, however, is insufficient by itself to make out a section 7 claim. For example, a person convicted of a criminal offence and sentenced to jail suffers a loss of liberty. But loss of liberty, standing alone, is not contrary to the *Charter* guarantee. The rights claimant must proceed to the second stage and show that the denial of a right protected by section 7 is contrary to the principles of fundamental justice. As will be seen, this phrase has been generously interpreted to include norms of substantive as well as procedural justice.

If the claimant establishes both that the right is included in the words "life, liberty and security of the person" and that the violation of the right is contrary to the "principles of fundamental justice," the party seeking to uphold the law being challenged will have an opportunity to show that the violation is a reasonable limit under section 1. However, section 7 contains its own internal qualifier. To make out a claim, it must be shown not only that the right to "life, liberty and security of the person" has been infringed, but also that the denial of rights is contrary to the principles of fundamental justice. It has been suggested that only in exceptional cases will a law found to infringe section 7 be upheld under section 1.[2]

B. PRINCIPLES OF FUNDAMENTAL JUSTICE

1) Substance and Procedure

Fair procedure is a matter that falls within the traditional expertise of the judiciary. Judges are experts at the fact-finding processes of the adversarial system and have a keen sense of the procedural values needed to ensure fairness to all who come before the courts. In the common law tradition, judges have also played an important role in monitoring the administrative apparatus of the state to ensure that individuals are dealt with fairly. The common law has evolved "rules of natural justice," which include the right to notice and a hearing if one's rights are affected. There is strong evidence to suggest that, at the time of the *Charter's* adoption, it was widely believed that the phrase "principles of fundamental justice" was restricted to procedural values of this kind.[3] However, in its first important judgment on section 7, the Supreme Court rejected that narrow interpretation. In *Motor Vehicle Act*,[4] the Court held that section 7 should be given a more generous meaning, namely, that it allowed the courts to review, from the perspective of substantive as well as procedural justice, laws infringing "life, liberty or security of the person." This means that the courts have the right to strike down laws that do not conform to the judicial view of what is fundamentally just. In *Motor Vehicle Act*, the Court struck down a law imposing a mandatory jail sentence upon conviction for driving while under suspension even when the accused was not aware of the suspension. In the Court's view, this was at odds with the fundamental principle

---

2 *Reference Re s. 94(2) of the Motor Vehicle Act (B.C.)*, [1985] 2 S.C.R. 486, 24 D.L.R. (4th) 536 [*Motor Vehicle Act*].

3 The relevance of the drafter's original intention in *Charter* interpretation is discussed in chapter 3, "Interpretation of the *Charter of Rights and Freedoms*."

4 Above note 2.

that the severe sanction of imprisonment should be imposed only in cases of moral blameworthiness.[5]

Lamer J., who wrote the majority opinion, recognized that the case raised "fundamental questions of constitutional theory, including the nature and very legitimacy of constitutional adjudication under the *Charter* as well as the appropriateness of various techniques of constitutional interpretation."[6] While finding that section 7 conferred a mandate on the courts to assess the substantive justice of laws, Lamer J. took pains to impose two important qualifications. First, he noted that the very structure of section 7 made it clear that the "principles of fundamental justice" were not a free-standing guarantee but rather could be invoked only where a law violated the right to "life, liberty or security of the person." Second, Lamer J. tied the principles of fundamental justice to what he described as "the basic tenets of our legal system" and to the "domain of the judiciary as guardian of the justice system," distinguishing the latter from what he described as "the realm of general public policy."[7] He made reference, as well, to "the spectre of a judicial 'super-legislature,'"[8] to the need to give meaningful content to section 7 while avoiding adjudication of policy matters, and to the necessity for "objective and manageable standards."[9] While this is admittedly imprecise, it does reflect a judicial awareness of the need to limit the power of judicial review to matters for which the courts have some claim to institutional competence and expertise.

Lamer J. made it clear in *Motor Vehicle Act*, as well as in subsequent cases, that in his view the reach of section 7 is essentially limited to the sphere of criminal and penal law, where the state imposes restrictions on an individual's physical liberty.[10] It will become apparent in the pages that follow, however, that not all judges share that view and that the reach of section 7 is potentially much wider.

2) Vagueness

It is a fundamental value of our legal system that citizens are entitled to fair notice of the conduct that is permitted or prohibited so that they can

---

5   This point is discussed in greater detail in chapter 14, "*Charter* Rights in the Criminal Process.

6   *Motor Vehicle Act*, above note 2 at 495 (S.C.R.).

7   *Ibid.* at 503.

8   *Ibid.* at 498.

9   *Ibid.* at 499.

10   B. *(R.) v. Children's Aid Society of Metropolitan Toronto*, [1995] 1 S.C.R. 315, 122 D.L.R. (4th) 1 [B. (R)], discussed below. See also *Reference Re ss. 193 and 195.1(1)(c) of the Criminal Code (Canada)*, [1990] 1 S.C.R. 1123, 56 C.C.C. (3d) 65 [*Prostitution Reference*].

regulate their activities accordingly. A related concept is that the law should set appropriate limits on officials who exercise discretion in applying and enforcing the law. In chapter 4, we considered these points from the aspect of section 1, the *Charter's* limitation clause, which requires a certain minimal level of precision in laws that impinge upon protected rights. Where government seeks to uphold a law that infringes a protected right on the ground that the law is justifiable as a reasonable limit, it must show that the limit is "prescribed by law."

The Supreme Court has accepted the argument that the "principles of fundamental justice" include the requirement that laws not be so vague as to fail to respect these values of fair notice and control of discretionary power.[11] On the other hand, the Court has made it clear that there is an inherent element of uncertainty in any legal standard of general application and that it is unrealistic to expect precision and predictability in all cases. While the Court has insisted that the standard supplied must be intelligible and capable of providing a basis for legal debate and rational decision making, it has consistently resisted the argument that a legal norm or standard must provide crystal clear and immediate answers.

In *Irwin Toy*,[12] the 1989 decision challenging a restraint on advertising as an infringement of freedom of expression that we considered in detail in chapter 9, the majority wrote:

> Absolute precision in the law exists rarely, if at all. The question is whether the legislature has provided an intelligible standard according to which the judiciary must do its work. The task of interpreting how that standard applies in particular instances might always be characterized as having a discretionary element, because the standard can never specify all the instances in which it applies. On the other hand, where there is no intelligible standard and where the legislature has given a plenary discretion to do whatever seems best in a wide set of circumstances, there is no "limit prescribed by law."

The notion of "an intelligible standard" was echoed in the judgment of Lamer J. in the *Prostitution Reference* where he speaks of "an ascertainable standard of conduct, a standard that has been given sensible meaning by courts."[13] The theme was taken up again by Gonthier J. in

---

11   The following discussion is taken from R.J. Sharpe, "The Application and Impact of Discretion in Commercial Litigation" (1998) 17 Adv. Soc. J. (No. 1) 4.

12   *Irwin Toy Ltd.* v. *Quebec (A.G.)*, [1989] 1 S.C.R. 927, 58 D.L.R. (4th) 577 at 617 [*Irwin Toy*].

13   *Above note 10 at 91 (C.C.C.)*

R. v. Nova Scotia Pharmaceutical Society.[14] There, the Court had to contend with the offence of conspiracy to lessen unduly competition under the *Competition Act,* a measure that was challenged as failing to respect the principles of fundamental justice:

> Legal rules only provide a framework, a guide as to how one may behave, but certainty is only reached in instant cases, where law is actualized by a competent authority . . .
>
> By setting out the boundaries of permissible and non-permissible conduct, these norms give rise to legal debate. They bear substance, and they allow for discussion as to their actualization. They therefore limit enforcement discretion by introducing boundaries, and they also sufficiently delineate an area of risk to allow for substantive notice to citizens.
>
> Indeed, no higher requirement as to certainty can be imposed on law in our modern state. Semantic arguments, based on a perception of language as an unequivocal medium, are unrealistic. Language is not the exact tool some may think it is. It cannot be argued that an enactment can and must provide enough guidance to predict the legal consequences of any given course of conduct in advance. All it can do is enunciate some boundaries, which create an area of risk. But it is inherent in our legal system that some conduct will fall along the boundaries of the area of risk; no definite prediction can then be made. Guidance, not direction, of conduct is a more realistic objective . . .
>
> A vague provision does not provide an adequate basis for legal debate, that is for reaching a conclusion as to its meaning by reasoned analysis applying legal criteria . . . [I]t fails to give sufficient indications that could fuel legal debate.[15]

These statements indicate a judicial recognition that the problem of uncertainty of result in any given case is pervasive and inherent in any standard phrased broadly enough to provide us with guidance in more than one situation.[16] The objective of law is not and cannot be complete predictability of results — that must be left to judgment in each case. At the same time, however, the idea of law does require a minimum "intelligible standard," "an ascertainable standard of conduct," a norm that "give[s] rise to legal debate" or "provide[s] an adequate basis for legal debate" and "give[s] sufficient indication that could fuel legal debate."

14   [1992] 2 S.C.R. 606, 93 D.L.R. (3d) 36.
15   *Ibid.* at 638–40 (S.C.R.).
16   For another case reiterating the point, see *R. v. Lucas,* [1998] S.C.J. No. 28, dealing with the offence of defamatory libel.

C. CONTROL OF THE BODY: ABORTION AND ASSISTED SUICIDE

The Supreme Court of Canada has had two opportunities to examine the extent to which section 7 protects the individual in making signifi-cant decisions about the body. The first was R. v. *Morgentaler*,[17] in which the Supreme Court of Canada held that the abortion provisions of the *Criminal Code* violated section 7; the second, *Rodriguez* v. R.,[18] narrowly upheld the prohibition on assisted suicide in the *Criminal Code*.

1) Abortion

R. v. *Morgentaler*[19] dramatically demonstrated the *Charter's* impact on highly contested matters of public policy. The *Criminal Code* provison at issue prohibited abortions but also provided an exemption if a woman seeking an abortion obtained a certificate from a therapeutic-abortion committee consisting of three physicians. Such a certificate could be issued if the committee concluded that the woman's life or health would be endangered by the continuation of the pregnancy. These committees could operate only in accredited hospitals, and the doctor performing the abortion could not be included on the commit-tee. Evidence was led to show that access to abortion varied significantly across the country. Many hospitals did not provide abortions at all, while others imposed rules more stringent than those set out in the *Code*, for example, denying abortions to married women.

The Supreme Court struck down the *Criminal Code* prohibition of abortion, but the Court was sharply divided in its reasoning. Beetz J., writing for himself and Estey J., found it possible to strike down the law on relatively narrow grounds. He focused on the fact that the law had a direct impact on a woman's health. In his view, the law infringed the woman's right to security of the person by requiring committee approval of medical treatment necessary to protect her life or health. He also found that the therapeutic-abortion committee procedure was not in accor-dance with the principles of fundamental justice, since it was applied in an arbitrary and uneven fashion, often based on factors not reasonably linked to the protection of the life or health of the woman or her foetus.

---

17 Above note 1.
18 *Rodriguez* v. R., [1993] 3 S.C.R. 519, 107 D.L.R. (4th) 342 [*Rodriguez*].
19 Above note 1.

Wilson J. adopted a much more expansive interpretation. In her view, there was a violation of both the right to liberty and the right to security of the person. The right to liberty, Wilson J. wrote, "guarantees to every individual a degree of personal autonomy over important decisions intimately affecting their private lives."[20] A woman's decision whether to continue a pregnancy is hers and hers alone, and state interference with her personal autonomy in making that decision violates her right to liberty. In addition, Wilson J. found, the state violated the woman's right to security of the person by forcing her to continue a pregnancy. The woman's autonomy right was infringed for she was being treated as "a means to an end which she does not desire," in that she was "the passive recipient of a decision made by others as to whether her body is to be used to nurture a new life."[21]

The third set of majority reasons was written by Dickson C.J., with Lamer J. concurring. Some of his language echoed that of Wilson J.:

> Forcing a woman, by threat of criminal sanction, to carry a foetus to term unless she meets certain criteria unrelated to her own priorities and aspirations, is a profound interference with a woman's body and thus a violation of security of the person.[22]

However, other passages suggest an approach closer to that of Beetz J., because of the emphasis on the threat to a woman's physical and psychological health created by procedures that prevented, or at least delayed, access to important medical treatment under the threat of criminal sanction.

McIntyre J. in dissent, with La Forest J. concurring, rejected the view that section 7 included a right to an abortion in any circumstances. In his view, neither the language of the *Charter* nor "the history, traditions and underlying philosophies of our society would support the proposition that a right to abortion could be implied in the *Charter*."[23]

While all the majority judges rejected arguments made under section 1 to save the legislation, they also made it clear that some restrictions on a woman's access to abortion could be justified under section 1 in order to protect the foetus. Beetz J., however, rejected the proposition that Parliament could prevent access to an abortion necessary to protect maternal life or health. Wilson J. suggested that Parliament's case for intervention to protect the foetus would became stronger as the

20   *Ibid.* at 171 (S.C.R.).
21   *Ibid.* at 173 (S.C.R.).
22   *Ibid.* at 56–57 (S.C.R.).
23   *Ibid.* at 143, 144 (S.C.R.).

pregnancy progressed. This suggested an approach similar to that of the United States Supreme Court, which, in *Roe* v. *Wade*,[24] had concluded that increasing restrictions on access to abortion were justified in the later stages of pregnancy.

Morgentaler generated much debate about whether Parliament could enact new legislation limiting abortions that would survive judicial scrutiny. The federal government attempted to do so shortly following the decision with the introduction of Bill C-43, which would have required a doctor to certify that a woman's health was endangered by the continuation of the pregnancy. The bill passed in the House of Commons but was defeated as a result of a tie vote in the Senate. The result is that there is currently no prohibition of abortion in Canada's criminal law. Some provinces have attempted to control access to abortion, particularly by restrictions on free-standing abortion clinics, but some of those initiatives have been found unconstitutional under the distribution of powers in the federal system. For example, in another *Morgentaler* decision, the Supreme Court of Canada struck down Nova Scotia's regulation as an attempt to legislate in the area of criminal law, which is within exclusive federal jurisdiction.[25]

There have also been attempts to litigate the abortion issue from the perspective of foetal rights. Joseph Borowksi, a pro-life activist, brought an action seeking a declaration that the abortion provisions in the *Criminal Code* violated the foetus's right to life under section 7. He was unsuccesful in the lower courts of Manitoba. By the time the case reached the Supreme Court of Canada, the Court had struck down the abortion provisions of the *Criminal Code* in *Morgentaler,* and the Court declined to consider his case on the merits on the basis that the issue was moot — that is, there was no legal issue, given the invalidity of the legislation.[26]

In *Daigle* v. *Tremblay*,[27] a man sought an injunction to prevent his former partner from obtaining an abortion. The case involved the interpretation of Quebec's *Charter of Human Rights and Freedoms*, specifically, the scope of the foetus's and prospective father's rights. The Supreme Court of Canada determined that a foetus is not a person with rights under the Quebec *Charter*, but it did not address the issue of whether "everyone" in section 7 of the Canadian *Charter* includes a foetus, since no law was being challenged and the Canadian *Charter* did not apply to a proceeding involving private parties.

---

24   410 U.S. 113 (1973).
25   *R. v. Morgentaler*, [1993] 3 S.C.R. 463, 107 D.L.R. (4th) 537 [*Morgentaler 1993*].
26   *Borowski v. Canada (A.G.)*, [1989] 1 S.C.R. 342, 57 D.L.R. (4th) 231.
27   [1989] 2 S.C.R. 530, 62 D.L.R. (4th) 634.

2) Assisted Suicide

Rodriguez v. *R.*[28] raised the issue of the scope of section 7 in relation to another important personal decision, namely, the right to determine the timing of one's death through assisted suicide. Sue Rodriguez was terminally ill, suffering from Lou Gehrig's disease, which had attacked her neurological system. She wanted to be able to end her own life when she felt that the quality of her life made it no longer worth living. Given the nature of her disease, at that point, she might be unable physically to accomplish the necessary acts, and hence she might need some assistance. Attempting suicide is not a crime, but section 241(b) of the *Criminal Code* makes it an offence for anyone to assist another person to commit suicide. Rodriguez argued that the section violated section 7 of the *Charter* by denying her the right to terminate her life when she wished.

The Supreme Court of Canada divided five to four on the issue of the constitutionality of the provision. Sopinka J., writing for the majority, held that the legislation did violate the right to security of the person. His reasons drew upon those of Wilson J. in *Morgentaler*. He concluded:

> . . . that personal autonomy, at least with respect to the right to make choices concerning one's own body, control over one's physical and psychological integrity, and basic human dignity are encompassed within security of the person, at least to the extent of freedom from criminal prohibitions which interfere with these.[29]

On the facts of the case, Sopinka J. held that denying Ms. Rodriguez assistance to commit suicide would deprive her of personal autonomy and cause physical pain and psychological distress. However, when Sopinka J. went to the next level of analysis, he found that the restriction on assisted suicide did not violate principles of fundamental justice. The purpose of the legislation, he found, was to protect those in a vulnerable situation from exploitation. The prohibition of assisted suicide was grounded in the state interest in the sanctity of human life, a fundamental value of Canadian society. Sopinka J. conceded that there are exceptions to the principle of the sanctity of life in our law. For example, the law allows for the termination of life through the refusal or consented withdrawal of medical treatment. On the other hand, Sopinka J. noted, the law has drawn a distinction between passive and active euthanasia. In Sopinka J.'s opinion, there was no general societal consensus that active euthanasia is acceptable. Absent that consensus

---

28   Above note 18.
29   *Ibid.* at 588 (S.C.R.).

and given the value placed on human life, the majority of the Court held that it should not find the assisted-suicide prohibition in violation of the principles of fundamental justice.

McLachlin J., who wrote one of the three dissenting opinions, held that the law did not accord with the principles of fundamental justice, because it was arbitrary in its application to individuals such as Ms. Rodriguez. In her view, Parliament has not taken a consistent attitude with respect to decisions to terminate life — for example, it does not prohibit passive euthanasia or suicide. Therefore, she found it arbitrary to deny access to suicide to an individual like Rodriguez who was able to make a free and informed decision about the continuation of her life.[30]

Rodriguez illustrates the difficulty facing judges in determining the scope of the principles of fundamental justice. While the early section 7 cases stated that the principles of fundamental justice are found in the basic tenets of the legal system,[31] the Court has found it difficult to identify a similar grounding for the meaning of fundamental justice in cases like *Rodriguez* which raise complex moral issues.

D. PRIVACY, THE FAMILY, AND FUNDAMENTAL PERSONAL CHOICES

As already noted, in the view of some, the ambit of protection accorded by section 7 is restricted to situations where the individual claiming the right faces a criminal or similar sanction. Another possibility is to give the guarantee a more generous reach and extend it to protect privacy interests, choices relating to family matters, and, more generally, to matters of fundamental personal concern. This debate has not been finally resolved in the case law. In *Morgentaler* and *Rodriguez*, the Court was dealing with fundamental personal choices, but in the context of a criminal sanction, which meant that the prohibitions at issue affected the right to personal security because of the threat of imprisonment.

In *B. (R.)* v. *Children's Aid Society of Metropolitan Toronto*,[32] four members of the Court held that the right to liberty guaranteed by section 7 must allow an individual "to make decisions that are of fundamental personal importance."[33] In *B. (R.)*, the parents were Jehovah's

---

30 Lamer C.J.C. dissented but relied on the equality right in s. 15 of the *Charter*, rather than s. 7.

31 *Motor Vehicle Act*, above note 2.

32 Above note 10.

33 *Ibid.* at 368 (S.C.R.).

Witnesses who, based upon their religious beliefs, refused medical treatment for their child that would likely have involved a blood transfusion. In the words of La Forest J., "the right to nurture a child, to care for its development, and to make decisions for it in fundamental matters such as medical care, are part of the liberty interest of a parent."[34] In this view, any state intervention to protect a child's interests must be justified as conforming with the principles of fundamental justice.

Lamer C.J.C. took issue with this broad reading of section 7 and reiterated the view he has expressed in other cases limiting the protection of the section:

> The liberty in question must therefore be one that may be limited through the operation of some mechanism that involves and actively engages the principles of fundamental justice. Principles of fundamental justice pertain to the justice system. They are designed to govern both the means by which one may be brought before the judicial system and the conduct of judges and other actors once the individual is brought within it.[35]

Lamer C.J.C. would restrict the scope of section 7 to

> the conduct of the state when the state calls on law enforcement officials to enforce and secure obedience to the law, or invokes the law to deprive a person of liberty through judges, magistrates, ministers, board members, etc.[36]

Sopinka J. found it unnecessary to deal with the point, while the remaining three judges held that the liberty interest in section 7 did not allow a parent to deny necessary medical treatment to a child. In their view, the child's right to life, also guaranteed by section 7, placed limits on the parent's right to liberty.

All members of the Court agreed in the result, however, namely, that the wardship order depriving the parents of the right to decide for their child should be upheld. For the majority, La Forest J. found that the parents' case could not survive the second stage of the section 7 analysis relating to the principles of fundamental justice. He found that the wardship provisions of the provincial child-welfare legislation conformed to the principles of fundmental justice. The parents had received notice of the wardship application, there had been a hearing before a judge, and they had been afforded an opportunity to present their views.

---

34   *Ibid.* at 370 (S.C.R.).
35   *Ibid.* at 340 (S.C.R.).
36   *Ibid.*

While the view that the protection of section 7 extends to fundamental personal choices has not yet secured the support of a majority in any case, *B. (R.)* suggests that the issue remains very much alive.[37] Perhaps the most forceful statement of the proposition that section 7 should be interpreted to protect a general right to personal autonomy and dignity is to be found in the judgments of Wilson J. Although these judgments did not attract the support of other judges at the time, the fact that four judges in *B. (R.)* accepted the proposition that section 7 protects certain fundamental choices is significant. In *Jones* v. *R.*, Wilson J. considered the claim that section 7 includes the right to bring up and educate one's children as one sees fit.[38] Wilson J. wrote that liberty included

> the freedom of the individual to develop and realize his potential to the full, to plan his own life to suit his own character, to make his own choices for good or ill, to be non-conformist, idiosyncratic and even eccentric — to be, in today's parlance, "his own person."[39]

Wilson J. expanded upon this theme in *Morgentaler,* where she described the basic underlying theme of the *Charter* as being "that the state will respect choices made by individuals and, to the greatest extent possible, will avoid subordinating those choices to any one conception of the good life." An aspect of this respect for basic human dignity and personal autonomy, in Wilson J.'s view, is "the right to make fundamental personal decisions without interference from the state." She concluded that "the right to liberty contained in s. 7 guarantees to every individual a degree of personal autonomy over personal decisions intimately affecting their private lives."

Future cases are likely to raise difficult questions about the scope of the personal autonomy and privacy interests protected by section 7. They may arise, for example, with respect to government regulation of medical procedures, such as access to new reproductive technologies or with respect to parental control of children, such as the scope of a parent's right to use corporal punishment.

---

37 See also *Godbout* v. *Longueuil (City)* (1997), 152 D.L.R. (4th) 577, where three judges gave an expansive definition to s. 7 as encompassing fundamental personal choice, while the others found it unnecessary to deal with the issue.

38 [1986] 2 S.C.R. 284, 31 D.L.R. (4th) 569. The majority found it unnecessary to consider the question.

39 *Ibid.* at 318–19 (S.C.R.).

E. ECONOMIC RIGHTS

The extent to which the *Charter* should protect economic rights has been the subject of debate from its inception. The language of section 7 would seem to offer a basis to argue against restrictions on economic activity, since its guarantee of the right to liberty could arguably include a right to economic liberty. The right to security of the person, similarly, could encompass a right to economic security in the form of basic rights to social assistance or public housing. To be weighed against these claims, however, is the legislative history of the *Charter*, for property rights were expressly excluded from section 7 and subsequent efforts to add property rights have failed.

To date, the courts have, for the most part, been unsympathetic to those seeking to vindicate pure economic rights through the *Charter*. There have, however, been some successes in the lower courts. In *Wilson*, the British Columbia Court of Appeal upheld a challenge by doctors to provincial regulation of the number of doctors practising in the province and the location of their practices.[40] The weight of authority, however, is to the effect that section 7 does not protect a right to engage in a particular type of professional activity.[41]

More generally, as Dickson C.J.C. stated, the right to liberty protected by section 7 "is not synonymous with unconstrained freedom" in the economic sphere and does not extend "to an unconstrained right to transact business whenever one wishes."[42] In a similar vein, Dickson C.J.C. wrote that care must be taken lest the *Charter* "become an instrument of better situated individuals to roll back legislation which has as its object the improvement of the condition of less advantaged persons."[43] The Supreme Court has flatly rejected the possibility "that economic rights as generally encompassed by the term 'property,' are not within the perimeters of the s. 7 guarantee," and it has held as well that corporations cannot claim the protection of economic rights under section 7.[44]

---

40   *Wilson v. British Columbia (Medical Services Commission)* (1988), 30 B.C.L.R. (2d) 1 (C.A.), leave to appeal to S.C.C. denied. See also *Mia v. British Columbia (Medical Services Commission)* (1985), 17 D.L.R. (4th) 385 (B.C.S.C.).

41   *Biscotti v. Ontario Securities Commission* (1990), 74 O.R. (2d) 119.

42   *Edwards Books & Art Ltd. v. R.*, [1986] 2 S.C.R. 713 at 785–86, 35 D.L.R. (4th) 1.

43   *Ibid.* at 779 (S.C.R.).

44   *Irwin Toy*, above note 12 at 1003 (S.C.R.). It should be noted, however, that s. 1(a) of the *Canadian Bill of Rights* does protect the right of property. As discussed in chapter 1, the *Bill of Rights* applies only to federal laws.

The claims of welfare recipients under section 7 have, for the most part, been rejected in the lower courts. The Ontario Divisional Court rejected a challenge to provincial cutbacks in the level of social assistance, finding that there was no denial of the right to life, liberty, or security of the person.[45] In doing so, the Court made a distinction between the government's decision to act and its decision not to act, concluding that this was a decision not to provide further benefits and that there was no obligation for them to do so. In addition, the Court indicated a judicial discomfort in entering into a realm of political choice about the appropriate level of social assistance.

The question whether section 7 protects a basic minimum of social assistance is still unresolved.[46] The Supreme Court has not yet had an opportunity to consider the question. In an early decision, Wilson J. noted that the broad language of section 7 might extend to the provision of the basic necessitities, referring to the *Universal Declaration of Human Rights*, which includes a guarantee of "the right to a standard of living adequate for . . . health and well-being . . . including food, clothing, housing and medical care and necessary social services."[47] Interestingly, when rejecting the argument that section 7 includes property rights, the Court gave the following caveat, suggesting that consideration of this question is not altogether foreclosed:

> This is not to declare, however, that no right with an economic component can fall within "security of the person." Lower courts have found that the rubric of "economic rights" embraces a broad spectrum of interests, ranging from such rights, included in various international covenants, as rights to social security, equal pay for equal work, adequate food, clothing and shelter, to traditional property — contract rights. To exclude all of these at this early moment in the history of *Charter* interpretation seems to us precipitous. We do not, at this moment, choose to pronounce upon whether these economic rights fundamental to human life and survival are to be treated as though they are of the same ilk as corporate-commercial economic rights.[48]

---

45   *Masse v. Ontario (Ministry of Community and Social Services)* (1996), 134 D.L.R. (4th) 20 (Ont. Ct. (Gen Div.)).

46   For discussion see: M. Jackman, "The Protection of Welfare Rights under the *Charter*" (1988) 20 Ottawa L. Rev. 257; I. Johnstone, "Section 7 of the *Charter* and Constitutionally Protected Welfare" (1988) 46 U.T. Fac. L. Rev. 1

47   *Singh v. Canada (Minister of Employment & Immigration)*, [1985] 1 S.C.R. 177 at 206–7.

48   *Irwin Toy*, above note 12 at 1003–4 (S.C.R.).

Against these statements, however, must be put the Court's general reluctance to interpret *Charter* guarantees as including economic rights as well as the Court's tendency to defer to legislatures where complex economic and social policy choices are at issue.[49]

Some social-welfare advocates have pressed for constitutional amendments to add a "social charter" with court-enforced economic and social rights. There was a vigorous debate about the merits of such a change in the last major round of constitutional reform, but ultimately it was not included in the 1992 Charlottetown Accord.[50]

F. CONCLUSION

Section 7 gives rise to some of the most difficult issues arising under the *Charter*. The right to life, liberty, and security of the person invites the courts to engage a wide array of difficult moral and ethical issues. The Supreme Court's insistence that the principles of fundamental justice have substantive and not merely procedural content signalled an activist role for the Court. Yet the Court has proceeded cautiously in determining the ambit of section 7. It is a virtual certainty that, in the years to come, the courts will continue to be asked to resolve the conflict between the individual's right to control his or her own body and the broader social interest in the protection of the sanctity of life. These issues have arisen in the past in relation to abortion and assisted suicide and are likely to arise in the future in connection with life-choice and health issues generated by the remarkable scientific advances in genetics. While decisions concerning one's physical integrity fall within the reach of section 7, the Court has not finally resolved the question of the extent to which section 7 protects other fundamental personal choices. The degree to which rights of privacy and decisions concerning family and other personal relations are protected by section 7 has yet to be resolved. The Court has shied away from interpreting the *Charter* to include economic rights, but equally it has refused unequivocally to preclude the protection of a right to basic rights of social assistance and housing.

---

49   See especially chapter 4, "Limitation of *Charter* Rights."
50   P. Macklem & C. Scott, "Constitutional Ropes of Sand or Justiciable Guarantees? Social Rights in a New South African Constitution" (1992) 141 U. of Penn. L. Rev. 1; J. Bakan & D. Schneiderman, eds., *Social Justice and the Constitution: Perspectives on a Social Union for Canada* (Ottawa: Carleton University Press, 1992).

While it might be thought that the uncertain state of the law under section 7 indicates a lack of direction or consistency, a more apt conclusion is that the courts have proceeded with appropriate prudence. Given the range and importance of the issues that arise under section 7, the Supreme Court has quite properly refused to make sweeping pronouncements, preferring a more judicious case-by-case approach and allowing principles to emerge over time from the diverse range of issues presented by litigants.

FURTHER READINGS

BAKAN, J., & D. SCHNEIDERMAN, eds., *Social Justice and the Constitution: Perspectives on a Social Union for Canada* (Ottawa: Carleton University Press, 1992)

BRODIE, J., et al., *The Politics of Abortion* (Don Mills, ON: Oxford University Press, 1992)

COLVIN, E., "Section 7 of the *Charter of Rights and Freedoms*" (1989) 68 Can. Bar Rev. 560

JACKMAN, M., "The Protection of Welfare Rights under the *Charter*" (1988) 20 Ottawa L. Rev. 257

JACKMAN, M., "Poor Rights: Using the Charter to Support Social Welfare Claims" (1993) 19 Queen's L.J. 65

JOHNSTONE, I., "Section 7 of the *Charter* and Constitutionally Protected Welfare" (1988) 46 U.T. Fac. L. Rev. 1

MORTON, F.L., & R. KNOPFF, *Charter Politics* (Scarborough: Nelson, 1992) c. 10

CHAPTER 14

CHARTER RIGHTS IN THE CRIMINAL PROCESS

The *Charter of Rights and Freedoms* has had a profound impact in the area of criminal law. *Charter* claims are routinely asserted in criminal proceedings. There have been thousands of cases decided by the courts involving detailed consideration of investigative techniques, pre-trial procedures, and the trial process itself. We offer here a sampling of some of the most significant issues that are raised by the *Charter*.

In *Criminal Law*, one of the volumes in this series, Professor Kent Roach refers to the work of a leading American scholar of the criminal law identifying two models of the criminal process.[1] The first is the "crime control model" in which the focus of the criminal justice system is to find and punish the guilty through efficient police and prosecutorial work, usually leading to a guilty plea. The second is the "due process" model in which the focus is on controlling the exercise of police powers through an elaborate series of procedural guarantees, violation of which results in the release of the accused regardless of guilt or innocence. The Canadian criminal justice system, in common with the systems of other liberal democracies, has always exhibited features of both models.

Crime control is bound to be a central feature of any system of criminal justice. The fundamental reason for the existence of the criminal law is to protect society from those individuals whose behaviour causes

---

1   H. Packer, *The Limits of the Criminal Sanction* (Stanford: Stanford University Press, 1968).

serious harm. The severe sanction of deprivation of liberty and imprisonment is justified by the criminal's significant departure from the norms of civil society and by the need to punish such conduct in order to protect society from further transgressions.

Our system of criminal justice has always recognized, however, that crime control is achieved through the assertion of coercive state power, which inevitably involves risks of abuse and oppression. To guard against these risks, the criminal process has evolved a range of procedural protections, designed to ensure that individuals suspected of crime are dealt with fairly and humanely. These guarantees, products of both the common law tradition and statutes enacted by Parliament, include such basic rights as the presumption of innocence, the right to silence, *habeas corpus,* and the right to be tried by a jury of one's peers. These procedural norms, identified as elements of the "due process" model, restrain the exercise of coercive power in a significant way. They are designed to protect the innocent and to avoid the risk of wrongful conviction. But they also benefit the guilty, since they ensure that everyone caught up in the criminal process should be treated fairly. A part of our tradition is the principle that it is better that ten guilty persons should go free than one innocent person be convicted. It is not possible to have a scheme of rights that protects only those who are innocent of wrongdoing. Procedural rights often cause consternation when they assist the guilty. Yet, that is a price to be paid in a free society where rights are enjoyed by all individuals.

The criminal justice system is continually striving to strike an appropriate balance between crime control and the protection of society on the one hand, and fairness to accused persons and the prevention of abuse of police powers on the other. The courts have always played an important role in this exercise. However, by entrenching a number of procedural rights in the constitution, the *Charter of Rights and Freedoms* has increased the courts' responsibility to delineate the line between crime control and due process. While the fundamental purpose of the Canadian criminal justice system remains the protection of society, there can be little question that the result of the courts' efforts has been to move Canada closer towards the due-process end of the spectrum.

A. SECTION 7 AND THE PRINCIPLES OF FUNDAMENTAL JUSTICE

1) The Fault Element

As noted in chapter 13, a crucial question that was faced in the early years of the *Charter* was whether the very general language of section 7 permitted the courts to review the substance of laws or whether judicial review was restricted to procedural matters. In *Reference Re s. 94(2) of the Motor Vehicle Act (B.C.)*,[2] the Supreme Court held that "the principles of fundamental justice" are not restricted to procedural values but have substantive content as well. The case involved a fundamental issue in the criminal law, namely, the extent to which moral blameworthiness should be a requirement for conviction. Criminal offences typically require proof of two elements, harm and fault. Ordinarily, the fact that harm has resulted from someone's conduct is not enough to support a conviction. To label someone a criminal, we must also be satisfied that the individual charged is morally blameworthy. The behaviour of the individual accused of a crime must be shown to have fallen short of an expected standard by intending, or at least foreseeing, the forbidden harm. However, the fault requirement is often difficult to prove, and the legislature may judge it to be in the public interest to impose a sanction without proof of fault of the accused. The *Motor Vehicle Act* involved such a law. It imposed a mandatory penalty of imprisonment for driving an automobile while one's licence was under suspension. There were a number of situations that could lead to a licence suspension without the knowledge of the licence-holder. An individual might not have even been aware of a licence suspension, and so the result was that one who had no criminal intent could face a mandatory jail sentence. In the Supreme Court of Canada's view, such a situation violated the principles of fundamental justice:

> A law that has the potential to convict a person who has not really done anything wrong offends the principles of fundamental justice and, if imprisonment is available as a penalty, such a law then violates a person's right to liberty under s. 7 of the *Canadian Charter of Rights and Freedoms*. . . . In other words, absolute liability and imprisonment cannot be combined.[3]

---

2   [1985] 2 S.C.R. 486, 24 D.L.R. (4th) 536 [*Motor Vehicle Act*].
3   *Ibid.* at 492 (S.C.R.), Lamer J.

The Supreme Court has given further consideration to the principles limiting the imposition of no-fault liability in criminal law in a number of situations. The *Criminal Code* "constructive murder" provisions, obviating the need to prove an intent to kill if death is caused in the commission of certain offences or in other specified circumstances, were challenged as violating the principles of fundamental justice. While there is no question that an individual who causes death in the commission of an offence is guilty of manslaughter, itself a serious crime, the issue was whether an accused who did not intend to kill and did not even foresee the possibility that death might result should be convicted of murder. In *R. v. Vaillancourt*,[4] the Court ruled that, absent proof of moral blameworthiness connected to the death, such an individual could not be found guilty of murder, the most serious offence known to the law. At a minimum, said the majority, there must be proof beyond a reasonable doubt of at least objective foreseeability that the conduct could result in death:

> The punishment for murder is the most severe in our society and the stigma that attaches to a conviction for murder is similarly extreme. . . . there must be some special mental element with respect to the death before a culpable homicide can be treated as a murder. That special mental element gives rise to the moral blameworthiness which justifies the stigma and sentence attached to a murder conviction.[5]

At the other end of the spectrum are regulatory offences. They are enacted to enforce non-criminal behaviour with regard to matters that are not inherently unlawful but that require standards to protect an important public interest. These offences do not carry the same moral connotation and have long been regarded as different from traditional criminal law offences. In a 1991 decision,[6] the Supreme Court held that the *Charter* does not require the same degree of moral culpability as a prerequisite for conviction of a regulatory offence. Where such offences carry the possibility of imprisonment, section 7 does require a minimal degree of fault, but that is satisfied by a standard of negligence.

---

4   [1987] 2 S.C.R. 636, 47 D.L.R. (4th) 399 [*Vaillancourt*]; see also *R. v. Martineau*, [1990] 2 S.C.R. 633, 58 C.C.C. (3d) 353.

5   *Vaillancourt*, *ibid.* at 653–54, Lamer J.

6   *R. v. Wholesale Travel Group Inc.*, [1991] 3 S.C.R. 154, 84 D.L.R. (4th) 161.

Between these two extremes are criminal offences less serious than murder but more grave than regulatory offences. In this grey area, the Supreme Court has insisted upon a minimal level of culpability as a prerequisite for conviction, but it has found that standard to be satisfied by conduct judged blameworthy on an objective standard. Thus, offences such as unlawfully causing bodily harm[7] and dangerous driving[8] have been upheld despite the fact that they require proof of fault on an objective rather than a subjective standard, that is, proof of fault based on what a reasonable person might have foreseen rather than what this particular accused foresaw.

2) Procedural Rights

The general language of section 7 has been found by the Supreme Court of Canada to incorporate and require respect for certain procedural rights that are not specifically guaranteed by sections 8 to 14. In a variety of situations, the Court has held that the "principles of fundamental justice" are broader than the specific rights enjoyed at common law or under particular provisions of the *Charter*. This has had significant implications for all stages of the criminal process.

a) Right to Silence
R. v. Hebert[9] dealt with the issue of a statement made by an accused person, detained in custody, to an undercover police officer posing as a fellow prisoner. The accused had received legal advice and indicated that he did not wish to make a statement. The undercover officer engaged the accused in conversation and an incriminating statement was made. The specific right to counsel (section 10(b)) and right against self-incrimination (section 11(c)) conferred by the *Charter* did not apply in these circumstances. The Court held, however, that the principles of fundamental justice implicitly include a broader right to silence. An accused person has the right to choose whether or not to speak to the authorities. The police are permitted to question an accused person, but they are not entitled to use their superior power to override the accused's decision to assert his legal rights. The Court viewed the use of an undercover agent as a trick, designed to deprive the accused of the choice he had made upon legal advice to remain silent in the face of their questions. It found that the accused's right not to be deprived of

---

7   *R. v. DeSousa*, [1992] 2 S.C.R. 944, 95 D.L.R. (4th) 595.
8   *R. v. Hundal*, [1993] 1 S.C.R. 867, 79 C.C.C. (3d) 97.
9   [1990] 2 S.C.R. 151, 57 C.C.C. (3d) 1.

life, liberty, or security of the person except in accordance with the principles of fundamental justice had been denied. A later decision[10] applied this principle where the statement was elicited by a prisoner acting as a police informer since, in the circumstances, the informer was an agent of the state and, but for his intervention, the statement would not have been given by the accused.

b) Right to Disclosure of the Prosecution's Case

In *R. v. Stinchcombe*,[11] the Court interpreted section 7 to impose upon the Crown a duty of disclosure. The Court was clearly influenced by a number of recent Canadian causes célèbres where serious injustices had occurred because the Crown had failed to disclose information important to the defence. It held that, while the defence has no obligation to assist the prosecution, the Crown is obliged to use the information it has in the interests of justice. The Crown, said the Court, must disclose prior to trial any evidence it intends to use and also any evidence that might assist the accused, even if the Crown does not intend to adduce such evidence at trial. The position of Crown counsel, representing the public interest in seeing that justice be done, is not that of an ordinary adversary. Crown counsel are expected to act in the interest of justice, and the fruits of a police investigation must be used in a manner that respects the right of the accused to make full answer and defence, "one of the pillars of criminal justice on which we heavily depend to ensure that the innocent are not convicted."[12] This decision has had a profound effect on the behaviour of both police and Crown counsel. Disclosure to the accused has now become a routine step in pre-trial proceedings.

c) Right to Make Full Answer and Defence

Section 7 has also had a significant impact upon the trial process itself. A *Criminal Code* provision limiting the right of an accused charged with sexual assault to cross-examine a complainant as to prior sexual conduct at the trial of a sexual offence was struck down as being inconsistent with the principles of fundamental justice.[13] While the majority recognized the importance of protecting complainants in sexual assault cases from unjustified and unwarranted inquiry into their personal histories, it concluded that a complete ban on any questions regarding past sexual conduct went too far and might preclude the trial court from hearing a

---

10   *R. v. Broyles*, [1991] 3 S.C.R. 595, 68 C.C.C. (3d) 308.

11   [1991] 3 S.C.R. 326, 68 C.C.C. (3d) 1.

12   *Ibid.* at 336 (S.C.R.), Sopinka J.

13   *R. v. Seaboyer*, [1991] 2 S.C.R. 577, 83 D.L.R. (4th) 193.

legitimate defence. As McLachlin J. explained, eliminating the possibility that the judge and jury might draw unwarranted and inappropriate conclusions based on sexist or stereotypical attitudes carried the risk of convicting the innocent:

> [I]t exacts as a price the real risk that an innocent person may be convicted. The price is too great in relation to the benefit secured, and cannot be tolerated in a society that does not countenance in any form the conviction of the innocent.[14]

The decision was decried by feminist groups that had lobbied for the law and saw it as vital in encouraging women to come forward to the police with complaints. The sting of the judgment was, however, softened by the Court. While the law was struck down, the Court did impose strict guidelines defining the specific circumstances in which such questions would be permitted. The issue was subsequently addressed by legislation.

d) Detention of Those Found Not Guilty by Reason of Insanity

Post-trial proceedings have not escaped the reach of section 7. In *R. v. Swain*,[15] the Court held that the *Criminal Code* provision for the automatic detention of an accused person found not guilty by reason of insanity at "the pleasure of the Lieutenant Governor" violated the principles of fundamental justice. The *Code* made no provision for a hearing or for any other procedural protection, and to hold someone indefinitely without according such rights was found to be inconsistent with the *Charter*. The Court recognized, however, that striking down the section immediately could result in a number of dangerous people being released, and accordingly it declared the law to be valid for a stated period to afford Parliament the opportunity to enact legislation conferring the appropriate procedural protections.

B. UNREASONABLE SEARCH AND SEIZURE

Section 8 of the *Charter* states:

> Everyone has the right to be secure against unreasonable search or seizure.

The right conferred by section 8 is of ancient origin. The common law tradition has long recognized the need to protect the property and privacy of citizens against unwarranted incursions by state agents.

---

14   *Ibid.* at 274 (D.L.R.).
15   [1991] 1 S.C.R. 933, 63 C.C.C. (3d) 481.

This section of the *Charter* has produced a significant volume of case law. Many, if not most, criminal trials involve the introduction of evidence seized by the police, and the propriety of the investigative methods employed by the police in obtaining evidence now comes under close scrutiny. Before the *Charter*, illegally obtained evidence was admissible. Now, under section 24, (discussed in greater detail below), evidence obtained in a manner that violates a *Charter* right "shall be excluded if it is established that, having regard to all the circumstances, the admission of it in the proceedings would bring the administration of justice into disrepute." This provides accused persons with a powerful incentive to raise *Charter* challenges to the manner in which the incriminating evidence was obtained.

While the protection of an individual's right to privacy can be readily understood, that right has to be reconciled with the competing state interest to conduct searches and seize evidence as part of the law-enforcement process. The right conferred by section 8 is, by its very terms, a relative one since the individual is protected only against *unreasonable* searches and seizures. To determine when a search or seizure is unreasonable, it is necessary to consider and balance, on the one hand, the right of the individual to be left alone, and on the other, the legitimate public interest in effective law enforcement.

In one of the Supreme Court's first *Charter* decisions, *Hunter* v. *Southam Inc.*,[16] the Court set out the basic framework for analysis of these issues. It started by interpreting section 8 generously. The section was found to confer a broad and general right to be secure from unreasonable search and seizure. This right extended beyond the protection of property and encompassed the protection of an individual's reasonable expectation of privacy. From that basic purpose of the right, the Court reasoned that certain procedural elements had to be imposed to reconcile the competing values of privacy and law enforcement. The first was the need for prior authorization. The justification for a search should be assessed before it has been conducted. It would be inconsistent with the notion of an individual right to hold that, if the police find something, the search was reasonable, for that is to invite searches on a whim. Protecting individuals against unjustified state intrusion requires preventative measures prior to the search, and hence the Court held that there is a presumption of unreasonableness where a search has been undertaken without a warrant obtained from an officer charged with the duty of acting judicially. The Court added that, to obtain a warrant, the

16   [1984] 2 S.C.R. 145, 11 D.L.R. (4th) 641.

authorities should be required to justify the need for the search by sworn evidence which satisfies an objective standard. The Court recognized that there could be "exigent" circumstances where the police had to act quickly and where circumstances did not allow time to obtain a warrant, but those cases, said the Court, were very much the exception to the general rule that a warrant is required.

A number of subsequent search-and-seizure cases have turned upon what constitutes a "reasonable" expectation of privacy in particular circumstances. In *R. v. Dersch*,[17] for example, the acquisition of blood samples by police, initially taken by physicians for medical purposes while the accused was unconscious in hospital, was found to constitute an unreasonable search and seizure under section 8. The accused was found to have a reasonable expectation that such information would be kept confidential. In a number of cases,[18] the Court has dealt with non-consensual taking of bodily substances. It has taken a tough line on this issue, holding that the individual's right to bodily integrity must take priority and that the police have no right to require suspects to give such samples. Legislation has been enacted authorizing the police to obtain a warrant to take bodily substances without the consent of the suspect. The constitutional validity of these measures has yet to be considered by the Supreme Court.

The validity of the *Criminal Code* provisions authorizing wire-taps in certain specified circumstances has been upheld.[19] However, the Supreme Court has not hesitated to limit police investigative techniques. In *R. v. Duarte*,[20] the Court found that surreptitiously recording a communication the originator expects will not be intercepted by anyone other than the intended recipient violates section 8 unless authorized by warrant. The police had used the familiar technique of equipping an informer with a body-pack recorder to tape a conversation with a suspect. No warrant had been obtained since it was thought that the procedure was legal where one party, here the informer, consented. The Court decided that a reasonable expectation of privacy demanded that the police obtain a warrant authorizing such procedures. Similarly in *R. v. Wong*,[21] the Court held that surreptitious video surveillance consti-

---

17   [1993] 3 S.C.R. 768, 85 C.C.C. (3d) 1.
18   *R. v. Dyment*, [1988] 2 S.C.R. 417, 45 C.C.C. (3d) 244; *R. v. Pohoretsky*, [1987] 1 S.C.R. 945, 33 C.C.C. (3d) 398; *R. v. Stillman*, [1997] 1 S.C.R. 607, 144 D.L.R. (4th) 193 [*Stillman*].
19   *R. v. Finlay* (1985), 23 D.L.R. (4th) 532 (Ont. C.A.), leave to appeal to S.C.C. refused, [1986] 1 S.C.R. ix; *R. v. Garofoli*, [1990] 2 S.C.R. 1421, 60 C.C.C. 161.
20   [1990] 1 S.C.R. 30, 65 D.L.R. (4th) 240.
21   [1990] 3 S.C.R. 36, 60 C.C.C. (3d) 460.

tutes a search and seizure requiring prior judicial authorization when conducted in circumstances in which the suspect had a reasonable expectation of privacy. In that case, individuals engaged in illegal gambling in a hotel room were found to have a reasonable expectation of privacy. In *R. v. Kokesch*,[22] the Court found that a warrantless "perimeter search," during which the police trespassed on the accused's property and peered into his windows to confirm a suspicion that he was cultivating marijuana, constituted a violation of section 8. The Court has also upheld the individual's privacy interest in a dwelling-house by finding that the police violate section 8 by forcible entry to make a warrantless arrest absent circumstances of "hot pursuit" of a fleeing suspect.[23]

A distinction has been drawn between personal information, which is protected against unreasonable search and seizure, and routine commercial records, which are not. In *R. v. Plant*,[24] the police used information regarding electricity consumption, obtained in the course of a drug investigation from the utility commission, to incriminate the accused who was charged with cultivating marijuana. No warrant had been issued to obtain the records, but the seizure was not found to trigger a section 8 violation. Since these commercial records were not of a personal and confidential nature and did not reveal intimate details of the accused's lifestyle or personal choices, there was not a reasonable expectation that they would be protected from state surveillance. In another complex case,[25] the Court was deeply split, but in the result the majority found that compelled production of documents pursuant to anti-combines legislation did not constitute a seizure within the meaning of section 8. This result was confirmed in a subsequent case holding that demands for information and documents pursuant to the *Income Tax Act* do not constitute seizures under section 8.[26]

C. ARBITRARY DETENTION AND IMPRISONMENT

Section 9 of the *Charter* guarantees:

Everyone has the right not to be arbitrarily detained or imprisoned.

---

22 [1990] 3 S.C.R. 3, 61 C.C.C. (3d) 207.

23 *R. v. Feeney* (1997), 146 D.L.R. (4th) 609.

24 [1993] 3 S.C.R. 281, 84 C.C.C. (3d) 203.

25 *Thomson Newspapers Ltd. v. Canada (Director of Investigation & Research)*, [1990] 1 S.C.R. 425, 54 C.C.C. (3d) 417.

26 *R. v. McKinlay Transport Ltd.*, [1990] 1 S.C.R. 627, 55 C.C.C. (3d) 530.

The meaning of "detention," a term crucial to both sections 9 and 10, was first considered in the context of section 10. In *R. v. Therens*,[27] an impaired-driving case, the issue of the accused's right to retain and instruct counsel depended upon whether he was "detained" within the meaning of section 10 when asked to go to the police station to give a breath sample. Rejecting the notion of detention as limited to instances of physical constraint, the Court instead defined the term as including any occasion when a police officer, by some form of compulsion or coercion, "assumes control over the movement of a person by a demand or direction which may have significant legal consequence . . ."[28] The Court found that, even where the individual was not subjected to physical force or to a legally enforceable demand, "psychological compulsion, in the form of a reasonable perception of suspension of freedom of choice"[29] could result in detention within the meaning of the *Charter*.

By its very terms, the right section 9 secures is a relative one. There are clearly situations where the authorities must have the power to detain or imprison individuals, and the *Charter* right is engaged only where denial of freedom is arbitrary. Yet the Supreme Court has interpreted "arbitrarily" in a manner that favours individual liberty. The Court has recognized the danger posed by giving the police unfettered discretion to detain. There must be some objective standard, defined by the law, governing the power. *R. v. Hufsky*,[30] and *R. v. Ladouceur*[31] dealt with provincial legislation authorizing random "spot checks" for impaired drivers. The Court found that stopping a motorist amounted to a detention under section 9 and that such a detention was arbitrary. The selection of which cars would be stopped was at the absolute discretion of the individual officer, and when establishing the program, the authorities had failed to provide any criteria for the exercise of this discretion, leaving it subject to the whim of each officer. The Court went on to consider whether a random stop of a driver could be justified under section 1. In view of the importance of highway safety and the deterrent function served by these stops, legislation authorizing random spot checks was found to be a reasonable limit on the right conferred by section 9. In a later decision,[32] the Court limited the powers of the police conducting random spot checks under this legislation. In the absence of

---

27   [1985] 1 S.C.R. 613, 18 D.L.R. (4th) 655.
28   *Ibid.* at 642 (S.C.R.).
29   *Ibid.* 644 (S.C.R.).
30   [1988] 1 S.C.R. 621, 40 C.C.C. (3d) 398.
31   [1990] 1 S.C.R. 1257, 56 C.C.C. (3d) 22.
32   *R. v. Mellenthin*, [1992] 3 S.C.R. 615, 76 C.C.C. (3d) 481.

reasonable and probable grounds for a more intrusive investigation, questioning by the police, when acting under this legislation, is constitutionally restricted to checking the driver's licence and insurance, the driver's sobriety, and the mechanical fitness of the vehicle.

The power to arrest and detain a suspect without a warrant is defined by the *Criminal Code* and requires that the officer have reasonable grounds to believe that the person has committed an offence. Detention without reasonable grounds will be arbitrary and in breach of section 9. In *R. v. Charley*,[33] the Ontario Court of Appeal held that the arrest of a black suspect near the scene of a robbery could not be justified as reasonable when based on the following description of the individual suspected of the robbery: "'male, black, 5'8" to 5'11", with a short afro, wearing a dark jacket, armed with a knife and a gun.'" This description was too general in nature and could be used to identify any number of individuals in a large city. In *R. v. Simpson*,[34] the Ontario Court of Appeal suggested that there may be common law power, broader than the *Criminal Code* power of arrest, to detain a suspect for questioning on some "articulable cause," but it found that such grounds did not exist on the basis of an educated "hunch." In that case, the Court found it was a *Charter* violation for the police to detain for questioning an individual who had entered and left a residence suspected to be a "crack house."

Detention following a conviction will not be arbitrary, but in *R. v. Lyons*[35] it was argued that the dangerous-offender provision, which allows a judge to impose a sentence of indefinite imprisonment where certain stated criteria were met and where the convicted person posed a serious threat to public safety, was arbitrary. The Court rejected this argument, finding that Parliament had adequately defined the class of offenders subject to this sentence. Similarly, the Court has upheld the *Criminal Code* provisions providing for minimum periods of imprisonment for first-degree murder without eligibility for parole.[36]

D. RIGHTS ON DETENTION AND ARREST

Section 10 confers certain specific rights that apply upon arrest or detention. As noted above, "detention" has been given a broad interpretation

---

33   (1993), 22 C.R. (4th) 297 (Ont. C.A.).
34   (1993), 79 C.C.C. (3d) 482 (Ont. C.A.).
35   [1987] 2 S.C.R. 309, 37 C.C.C. (3d) 1 [*Lyons*].
36   *R. v. Luxton*, [1990] 2 S.C.R. 711, 58 C.C.C. (3d) 449 [*Luxton*].

so that the rights conferred under this section may be invoked in circumstances well short of incarceration. Section 10 provides as follows:

> Everyone has the right on arrest or detention
> (a) to be informed promptly of the reasons therefor;
> (b) to retain and instruct counsel without delay and to be informed of that right; and
> (c) to have the validity of the detention determined by way of *habeas corpus* and to be released if the detention is not lawful.

1) Right to Be Informed of the Reasons for Arrest or Detention

Under our system of criminal justice, police powers are limited by law, and before the police interfere with the liberty of an individual, they must be able to justify their actions. Arrest and detention represent a serious interference with personal liberty, and it is a basic right of the individual arrested or detained to know the reason. Requiring the authorities to state promptly the reasons for an arrest or detention permits the person arrested or detained to assess the situation and to decide upon an appropriate response, including submitting to the arrest, seeking counsel, and responding to police questions.

The right to be advised of the reasons arises upon arrest, but it may arise again if the reason for the arrest changes. For example, in *R. v. Borden*,[37] the accused was told that he had been arrested for one sexual assault that did not involve intercourse; on this occasion, he agreed to provide a blood sample. He was not told that the police wanted the sample in relation to another sexual assault of which he was also suspected. The Supreme Court held that the accused's section 10(a) right to be informed of the reason for his detention had been violated. Similarly, in *R. v. Black*,[38] the accused was arrested for attempted murder. The victim died while she was in custody. The accused was told that she was now charged with murder, but she was not told again of her right to counsel under section 10(b). The Court held that section 10(a) and (b) required that the police fully advise her of rights again when the reason for the arrest changed. On the other hand, in *R. v. Evans*,[39] the Court held that, although the police did not specifically inform an individual arrested on a drug charge that he was also suspected of two murders, it was clear to

---

37   [1994] 3 S.C.R. 145, 119 D.L.R. (4th) 74.
38   [1989] 2 S.C.R. 138, 50 C.C.C. (3d) 1.
39   [1991] 1 S.C.R. 869, 63 C.C.C. (3d) 289.

the accused from the nature of the questions being asked that he was being held for the murders as well.

2) Right to Retain and Instruct Counsel and to Be Informed of That Right

The courts have been vigilant in upholding the right to counsel. The rationale for this right is the need to ensure that every one who is detained has the opportunity to learn immediately of his or her rights and obligations under the law. An individual in police custody is in a vulnerable situation and is entitled to the assistance of someone knowledgeable in the law and independent of the state:

> [W]hen an individual is detained by state authorities, he or she is put in a position of disadvantage relative to the state. Not only has this person suffered a deprivation of liberty, but also this person may be at risk of incriminating him- or herself.[40]

Section 10(b) affords not only the right to counsel but also the right to be informed of that right. In *R. v. Manninen*,[41] it was made clear that this is more than a formal or hollow right. There, the Supreme Court held that the police must provide the accused with a reasonable opportunity to exercise the right to consult counsel, and they must desist from questioning the accused or attempting to elicit information until he or she has had an opportunity to confer with counsel. Another case, *R. v. Brydges*,[42] dealt with the situation of an accused who could not afford counsel. The Court held that, where it appeared to the police that the accused wished to consult a lawyer but thought that his inability to afford legal counsel would prevent him from exercising the right, it was incumbent upon the police to advise the accused of the availability of legal aid and duty counsel provided under the legal aid scheme.

While *Brydges* required police to inform a detainee of the availability of free legal advice where it is provided, the Court did not go so far as mandating the legislative enactment of such a system. In *R. v. Matheson*[43] and *R. v. Prosper*,[44] the Court rejected the suggestion that section 10(b) imposes a positive obligation on governments to provide free preliminary legal advice through a duty-counsel system. The police instead

---

40 *R. v. Bartle*, [1994] 3 S.C.R. 173 at 191, 92 C.C.C. (3d) 289, Lamer C.J.C.
41 [1987] 1 S.C.R. 1233, 34 C.C.C. (3d) 385.
42 [1990] 1 S.C.R. 190, 53 C.C.C. (3d) 330 [*Brydges*].
43 [1994] 3 S.C.R. 328, 118 D.L.R. (4th) 323.
44 [1994] 3 S.C.R. 236, 118 D.L.R. (4th) 154.

have a twofold duty to inform detainees of legal services actually available in the jurisdiction and then to "hold-off" questioning until a detainee has had a reasonable opportunity to consult counsel. It has also been held that a detained person must be reasonably diligent in attempting to seek the advice of counsel, failing which the police are entitled to proceed with questioning the suspect.[45]

The right to counsel guaranteed under section 10(b) continues to check police conduct after the initial charges have been laid. In *R. v. Burlingham*,[46] police impropriety in the plea-bargaining process was found to violate the accused's right to counsel. The police belittled the defence counsel with the express purpose of undermining the relationship between the accused and his lawyer, and they then pressured the accused, in the absence of counsel, to accept a plea bargain. Both aspects of their conduct were found to violate the section 10(b) right to counsel.

3) Right to *Habeas Corpus*

Habeas corpus is a common law remedy against unlawful detention. It is of ancient origin and permits anyone who is detained to require the person having custody to bring the detainee immediately before a court and to provide legal justification for the detention. If the jailer is unable to satisfy the judge that the detention is lawful, the subject has the right to immediate release. The rights secured by this common law remedy are guaranteed by other *Charter* provisions: the right to be secure from arbitrary arrest and detention, the right to a speedy trial, and the right not to be denied reasonable bail. The effect of section 10(c) is to reinforce the common law remedy and to require that any legislative curtailment of the remedy satisfy the exacting standards of section 1.

E. RIGHTS OF PERSONS CHARGED WITH AN OFFENCE

Section 11 deals with the rights of persons charged with an offence. This section applies only to criminal or quasi-criminal proceedings and proceedings that give rise to penal consequences. Accordingly, it does apply to prosecutions for criminal offences proper, as well as to prosecutions under provincial legislation. Professional and other similar disciplinary

---

45   *R. v. Tremblay*, [1987] 2 S.C.R. 435, 37 C.C.C. (3d) 565.
46   [1995] 2 S.C.R. 206, 124 D.L.R. (4th) 7.

proceedings will be caught only where the consequences are truly penal in nature, reflecting an attempt to redress a wrong done to society as a whole.[47] Section 11 reads:

> Any person charged with an offence has the right
> (a) to be informed without unreasonable delay of the specific offence;
> (b) to be tried within a reasonable time;
> (c) not to be compelled to be a witness in proceedings against that person in respect of the offence;
> (d) to be presumed innocent until proven guilty according to law in a fair and public hearing by an independent and impartial tribunal;
> (e) not to be denied reasonable bail without just cause;
> (f) except in the case of an offence under military law tried before a military tribunal, to the benefit of trial by jury where the maximum punishment for the offence is imprisonment for five years or a more severe punishment;
> (g) not to be found guilty on account of any act or omission unless, at the time of the act or omission, it constituted an offence under Canadian or international law or was criminal according to the general principles of law recognized by the community of nations;
> (h) if finally acquitted of the offence, not to be tried for it again and, if finally found guilty and punished for the offence, not to be tried or punished for it again; and
> (i) if found guilty of the offence and if the punishment for the offence has been varied between the time of commission and the time of sentencing, to the benefit of the lesser punishment.

1) Right to Be Informed without Unreasonable Delay of the Specific Offence

An accused person needs to know the precise nature of the charges he or she faces for a number of reasons. Identification of the specific offence will enable the accused to challenge the proceedings if they are unlawful or to prepare a defence if they are not. The right to be informed of the offence without unreasonable delay also defines and narrows the proceedings, thereby limiting the scope of the prosecution and the powers of the police.

---

47   *R. v. Wigglesworth*, [1987] 2 S.C.R. 541, 45 D.L.R. (4th) 235 [*Wigglesworth*].

2) Right to Be Tried without Unreasonable Delay

It has often been said that "justice delayed is justice denied." Delay in prosecution may result in unfairness to the accused since it may well become more difficult to defend oneself after the passage of time. Quite apart from the unfairness, all parties — victims, accused persons, and society at large — have an obvious interest in speedy justice.

Delay in bringing criminal charges to trial has been the subject of a number of controversial decisions of the courts. The most significant was *R. v. Askov*,[48] where the Supreme Court considered a case that had taken twenty-four months to come to trial and where the cause of the delay was no more than the product of an overburdened system. The Court ruled that systemic delay could trigger a section 11(b) claim. While the Court indicated that it was mindful that the allocation of resources was a matter for political decision, the right to a speedy trial was vital to both the accused and the community at large, and solutions to systemic delay had to be found. The Court found that in the circumstances of the case, which arose in one of the busiest and most congested judicial districts in Canada, a two-year delay between committal and trial was unacceptable and in violation of the *Charter*'s guarantee. The impact of the decision was enormous. Thousands of criminal charges were either dropped or stayed and the entire issue of court delay and the allocation of judicial resources has come under intense scrutiny. Though the Court softened its approach somewhat in a subsequent case,[49] the effects of *Askov* continue to be felt, and the risk of having a prosecution stayed for want of speedy trial acts as a powerful incentive for the authorities to bring prosecutions forward to trial on a timely basis.

A distinction has been drawn, however, between pre- and post-charge delay. In Canada, there is no statute of limitations for serious criminal offences. In recent years, significant numbers of sexual-assault charges have been laid years after the occurrence of the alleged offence. The Supreme Court has stated that delay in bringing charges will only rarely be relevant to the right to be tried without unreasonable delay,[50] although, in certain circumstances, unexplained or unjustified delay in initiating proceedings may give rise to a section 7 claim.[51]

---

48   [1990] 2 S.C.R. 1199, 59 C.C.C. (3d) 449 [*Askov*].
49   *R. v. Morin*, [1992] 1 S.C.R. 771, 71 C.C.C. (3d) 1.
50   *R. v. Mills*, [1986] 1 S.C.R. 863, 29 D.L.R. (4th) 161; *R. v. Carter*, [1986] 1 S.C.R. 981, 26 C.C.C. (3d) 572.
51   *R. v. Kalanj*, [1989] 1 S.C.R. 1594, 48 C.C.C. (3d) 459.

3) Right against Self-Incrimination

The right against self-incrimination is protected in a variety of ways under the *Charter*. This right has already been mentioned under section 7. It is also embodied in section 13 of the *Charter*, discussed below, which protects a witness from having incriminating evidence used in subsequent proceedings. The right conferred by section 11(c) relates specifically to the trial of the accused and protects the accused from having to testify.

Silence of an accused cannot, by statute, be the subject of comment by counsel or by the judge. Yet, while an accused person does not have to testify, to what extent does section 11(c) protect the accused who elects to remain silent from having the judge or jury draw an adverse inference from his or her silence? In a 1994 decision,[52] the Supreme Court suggested that it would be a violation of the right against self-incrimination to draw an adverse inference where the prosecution has failed to make out any case against the accused. But where there is "a case to meet," the accused who fails to answer must risk the possibility that his failure to testify may lead the judge or jury to convict.

The Supreme Court has held that a corporation is not entitled to claim the protection of section 11(c), and that an officer of an accused corporation can be compelled to testify,[53] a decision that corresponds to the Court's general tendency to avoid applying the *Charter* to protect purely commercial or corporate interests.

4) Presumption of Innocence and Right to a Fair Hearing by an Independent and Impartial Tribunal

a) Presumption of Innocence

The presumption of innocence has long been an important common law principle in Canada. The accused does not have to prove anything. It is for the prosecution to prove the guilt of the accused beyond a reasonable doubt, failing which the accused is entitled to an acquittal. However, before the *Charter*, this principle was subject to legislation overriding the presumption and Parliament frequently enacted reverse-onus provisions. A "reverse-onus" provision alters the usual rule and requires the accused to prove innocence. A significant body of case law challenging legislation of this kind has now developed under the *Charter*.

---

52 *R. v. P. (M.B.)*, [1994] 1 S.C.R. 555, 89 C.C.C. (3d) 289.
53 *R. v. Amway Corp.*, [1989] 1 S.C.R. 21, 56 D.L.R. (4th) 309.

The case of *R.* v. *Oakes*,[54] better known for its articulation of the proportionality test under section 1, provides an example. Narcotics legislation provided that where, on a charge of possession for the purposes
of trafficking, it was shown that an accused person was in possession of
a prohibited drug, the burden shifted to the accused to prove that he or
she was not in possession of the drug for the purposes of trafficking.
Describing the presumption of innocence as "essential in a society committed to fairness and social justice," the Court held that the presumption
of innocence was violated and that the violation could not be sustained
under section 1. The reverse-onus provision applied even where an
accused was in possession of very small quantities of narcotic, and in
light of the lack of a rational connection between the proved fact, possession, and the presumed fact, trafficking, the provision was found to
create an unjustifiable risk of conviction without proof of guilt and an
unwarranted limitation on the presumption of innocence.

However, many reverse-onus provisions have survived as reasonable limits under section 1. For example, the Supreme Court upheld as
a reasonable limit the presumption applicable to drinking and driving
cases that, where the accused is found behind the wheel of a car, care
and control of the vehicle, an essential element of the offence, shall be
presumed absent proof to the contrary.[55] Similarly, the Court upheld as
a reasonable limit the presumption that an accused lives off the avails of
prostitution if the fact is proved that he lives with or is habitually in the
company of prostitutes.[56]

In some situations, a reverse-onus provision may be part of a package
that benefits the accused and that would not be made available without
the reverse-onus provision. Parliament may be willing to establish a
defence but require the accused to prove it. An example is the anti-hate
law, which makes truth a defence but which requires the accused to
make out the defence of truth. The Supreme Court found this to be justifiable under section 1.[57] In the Court's opinion, Parliament was not
required to afford the defence of truth. It had done so as a concession to
the value of freedom of expression. As Dickson C.J.C. explained:

> Parliament has used the reverse onus provision to strike a balance
> between two legitimate concerns. Requiring the accused to prove on

---

54   *R.* v. *Oakes*, [1986] 1 S.C.R. 103, 26 D.L.R. (4th) 200, also discussed at length in
     chapter 4.
55   *R.* v. *Whyte*, [1988] 2 S.C.R. 3, 51 D.L.R. (4th) 481.
56   *R.* v. *Downey*, [1992] 2 S.C.R. 10, 90 D.L.R. (4th) 449.
57   *R.* v. *Keegstra* [1990] 3 S.C.R. 697, 61 C.C.C. (3d) 1.

the civil standard that his or her statements are true is an integral part of this balance, and any less onerous burden would severely skew the equilibrium.[58]

The effect of striking down such a reverse-onus clause might well be to make matters worse for the accused since Parliament would be entitled to remove the defence altogether.

One of the most significant cases upholding a reverse-onus provision dealt with the insanity defence.[59] Information regarding the state of the mental health of the accused is a matter particularly within the control of the accused. Without the cooperation of the accused, the prosecution would have great difficulty in proving sanity. The Supreme Court found that it would be virtually impossible for the Crown to secure convictions if it had to bear the onus of proving sanity. While the Court accepted that there were a variety of measures that might have been enacted to alleviate the problem, in the end, it found that the adoption of the traditional common law presumption of sanity was justifiable.

b) Right to a Fair Hearing by an Independent and Impartial Tribunal
Though the right to trial by "an independent and impartial tribunal" is conferred upon an accused person, it indirectly guarantees the independence of the judges who preside in criminal cases. In a 1985 decision,[60] the Supreme Court of Canada identified the three essential attributes of judicial independence. First, independence requires tenure of office and that judges be removable only for a cause related to their capacity to perform a judicial function. Secondly, independence requires financial security so that judges need not fear diminution in their salary or benefits because of judgments that are unpopular or unfavourable to the government. Third, the Court held that institutional independence in relation to the administration of the courts is a necessary element, in particular, the assignment of judges to particular cases and the establishment of court lists.

5) Right to Reasonable Bail

The judicial interim-release provisions of the *Criminal Code* strongly favour affording accused persons bail pending their trial, but one element

---

58 *Ibid.* at 70–71 (C.C.C.).
59 *R. v. Chaulk,* [1990] 3 S.C.R. 1303, 62 C.C.C. (3d) 193.
60 *Valente v. R.* [1985] 2 S.C.R. 673, 24 D.L.R. (4th) 161. See also *Reference Re Public Sector Pay Reduction Act (P.E.I.), s. 10* (1997), 150 D.L.R. (4th) 577 (S.C.C.).

of the *Code*'s package was found wanting in *R. v. Morales*.[61] The *Code* provided as a secondary ground for refusing judicial interim release that the detention of the accused "is necessary in the public interest." This was held to be unacceptably vague and imprecise. It imposed a "standardless sweep" that was found to infringe section 11(e) and could not be saved under the section 1 proportionality test.

6) Right to Jury Trial

The *Criminal Code* confers the right to a jury trial in virtually all serious offences. *R. v. Lee*[62] dealt with an exception. The accused had initially failed to appear for trial, and the *Criminal Code* provided that, as a consequence, he lost his right to be tried by a jury as a consequence. The Court found that the provision violated section 11(f) but could be upheld as a reasonable limit under section 1. Parliament was entitled to protect the integrity of the criminal process from delay, inconvenience, and expense. Denying the right to a jury trial in such circumstances was held to be proportional to this legitimate governmental objective.

An individual is not required to take advantage of his or her constitutional rights and ordinarily those rights may be waived. In *R. v. Turpin*,[63] the accused was charged with murder, an offence that is required by the *Criminal Code* to be tried by jury. The accused argued that the right to a jury trial implicitly carried with it the right to waive trial by jury and be tried by a judge alone. The Supreme Court did not agree and held that there was no inconsistency between the right to be tried by jury and the statutory requirement that certain offences must be tried by jury.

7) *Ex Post Facto* Laws

While the section 11(g) requirement that an act or omission constitute an offence at the time it was committed is an important right, it has not been the subject of substantial litigation since attempts to prosecute individuals for offences created after the fact are extremely rare. The issue was raised, however, in the complex case of *R. v. Finta*,[64] which dealt with war crimes relating to the Nazi occupation of Hungary. The accused, a captain in the Royal Hungarian Gendarmerie during the Sec-

---

61   [1992] 3 S.C.R. 711, 77 C.C.C. (3d) 91.
62   [1989] 2 S.C.R. 1384, 52 C.C.C. 289.
63   [1989] 1 S.C.R. 1296, 48 C.C.C. (3d) 8.
64   [1994] 1 S.C.R. 701, 112 D.L.R. (4th) 513.

ond World War, was charged with war crimes and crimes against humanity for allegedly participating in the unlawful confinement, kidnapping, robbery, and in some cases manslaughter of over 8,000 people. The Court rejected the accused's claim under section 11(g). It stated that justice required the retroactive punishment of those who committed acts that were internationally illegal and known to be morally objectionable, regardless of the fact that the acts were not formally criminal under positive law at the time. The accused was acquitted at trial on other grounds, however, and the Crown's appeals were rejected.

8) Double Jeopardy

Though much of the law on double jeopardy is governed by pre-*Charter* jurisprudence, there have been some significant cases under section 11(h). In *R. v. Wigglesworth*,[65] an RCMP officer, having been convicted under the *Royal Canadian Mounted Police Act* for assaulting a prisoner, was then charged with criminal assault for the same incident. The Court allowed the second set of proceedings to continue, noting a "double aspect" to the wrongful conduct. That is to say, while the accused had already answered to his profession through the private sanctions of internal discipline, he must still be made to account to society at large for his actions. The word "offence" in section 11(h) was thus defined narrowly so as to include only truly criminal or penal offences. This approach was applied and affirmed in *R. v. Shubley*,[66] a case involving a charge of criminal assault where the accused had already been subject to prison discipline in relation to the same incident. Applying the two-stage test from *Wigglesworth*, the court found that, since the prison discipline was neither by its nature criminal nor did it impose true penal consequences, no violation of section 11(h) had occurred.

9) Benefit of Lesser Punishment

This guarantee confirms a pre-*Charter* common law principle similar to the preclusion of conviction for matters that were not an offence at the time the act was committed (section 11(g)). The guarantee rests on a fundamental principle of legality, namely, that an individual's conduct is to be assessed on the basis of the law in force at the time and that it would be unfair to impose penalties not then provided for by law.

---

65   Above note 47.
66   [1990] 1 S.C.R. 3, 65 D.L.R. (4th) 193.

F.   CRUEL AND UNUSUAL PUNISHMENT

Section 12 of the *Charter* provides:

> Everyone has the right not to be subject to any cruel and unusual treat-
> ment or punishment

Laws requiring minimum sentences for specified offences are the exception rather than the rule in Canadian criminal law. In *Smith* v. *R.*,[67] the
Court struck down a minimum punishment of seven years' imprisonment for importing narcotics. Too wide a range of activities was caught
by the prohibition against importing drugs, from large-scale trafficking
of dangerous drugs by organized crime to the importation of a small
quantity of marijuana for personal consumption. While the Court did
not settle on a precise definition of "cruel and unusual," a majority
found that imposing a minimum sentence of such length would, in
many instances, be so grossly disproportionate to the gravity of the
offence committed by the accused as to outrage standards of decency
and thus offend the guarantee. The Court was not willing to trust the
matter to prosecutorial discretion to charge minor offenders with simple possession since that would amount to an unacceptable delegation
of decision-making authority in a situation where a fundamental right
was at issue.

Less severe minimum sentences have been upheld by the Court,[68] as
have *Criminal Code* provisions providing for the indefinite detention of
dangerous offenders[69] and the statutory minimum sentence of life imprisonment for murder without eligibility for parole for stated periods.[70]
However, in *Steele* v. *Mountain Institution (Warden)*,[71] the Court found
that the continued detention after thirty-five years incarceration of a sexual psychopath could no longer be justified in light of the evidence of
experts as to his present state. The Parole Board was charged with responsibility for assessing such cases, but there had been serious procedural
and substantive flaws in the Parole Board's proceedings. The Court held
that detention of the prisoner had become so grossly disproportionate to
the circumstances of his case as to constitute cruel and unusual punishment, and it ordered that he be released on a *habeas corpus* application.

---

67   [1987] 1 S.C.R. 1045, 34 C.C.C. (3d) 97.
68   See, for example, *R. v. Goltz*, [1991] 3 S.C.R. 485, 67 C.C.C. (3d) 481 (seven days
     for driving under suspension).
69   *Lyons*, above note 35.
70   *Luxton*, above note 36.
71   [1990] 2 S.C.R. 1385, 60 C.C.C. (3d) 1.

Capital punishment has been abolished in Canada, and thus the courts have not been confronted with the issue of whether the death penalty constitutes cruel and unusual punishment. The Supreme Court did, however, uphold the extradition of an offender to the United States where he faced a serious risk of capital punishment. The Court refused to impose, as a condition on his surrender, an undertaking from the receiving jurisdiction not to impose the penalty.[72] It is clear that the decision was based upon the view that, since the punishment would not be applied by Canadian authorities, section 12 did not apply.

G. RIGHT AGAINST SELF-INCRIMINATION

The right against self-incrimination is dealt with under a variety of *Charter* provisions. As already noted, aspects of the right against self-incrimination may be invoked under section 7. Under section 11(c), an accused person cannot be required to testify at his or her own trial. Section 13 of the *Charter* provides as follows:

> A witness who testifies in any proceeding has the right not to have any incriminating evidence so given used to incriminate that witness in any other proceedings, except in a prosecution for perjury or for the giving of contradictory evidence.

The right against self-incrimination is narrower in Canadian law than it is under the common law or under the Fifth Amendment of the American constitution. In Canada, there is no right to refuse to give evidence in a proceeding in which the witness is not the accused.[73] The right conferred by section 13 of the *Charter* is restricted to not having that evidence used against the witness in a subsequent proceeding.

In *R. v. Dubois*,[74] this protection was extended to an accused who had testified at his trial, was convicted, appealed, and was given a new trial. The Supreme Court of Canada held that the testimony given at the first trial could not be used at the new trial. The guarantee was further extended in *R. v. Mannion*[75] where, in similar circumstances, the Court held that the previous testimony could not even be used to cross-examine the accused at his subsequent trial. However, in a later ruling,[76] the

---

72 *Kindler v. Canada (Minister of Justice)*, [1991] 2 S.C.R. 779, 84 D.L.R. (4th) 438.

73 *Canada Evidence Act*, R.S.C. 1985, c. C-5, s. 5 (2).

74 [1985] 2 S.C.R. 350, 22 C.C.C. (3d) 513.

75 [1986] 2 S.C.R. 272, 28 C.C.C. (3d) 544.

76 *R. v. Kuldip*, [1990] 3 S.C.R. 618, 61 C.C.C. (3d) 385.

Court held that evidence given at a previous trial could be used to cross-examine as to credibility of the accused as distinct from the use of such evidence to prove guilt.

H. RIGHT TO AN INTERPRETER

Section 14 of the *Charter* guarantees parties and witnesses the right to an interpreter:

> A party or witness in any proceeding who does not understand or speak the language in which the proceedings are conducted or who is deaf has the right to the assistance of an interpreter.

The *Charter* also contains English- and French-language guarantees that apply to criminal proceedings in certain provinces, as discussed in chapter 16.

The leading case on the section 14 right to an interpreter is *R. v. Tran*.[77] Convicted of sexual assault, the accused's interpreter at trial failed to translate much of the key testimony in full and instead merely summarized the evidence. Embracing a "liberal interpretation and principled application" of the right to an interpreter, the Court allowed the accused's appeal and ordered a new trial. Grounded in the basic requirement that a person charged with a criminal offence has the right to hear the case against him or her and to be given a full opportunity to answer it, the Court stated section 14 guarantees that those who need an interpreter must be given assistance that is continuous, precise, impartial, competent, and contemporaneous. Not every deviation from perfection will constitute a violation of section 14, however. The claimant must establish that the lapse in interpretation involved procedure, evidence, or law and not merely some collateral or extrinsic matter.

I. REMEDIES IN THE CRIMINAL PROCESS

One of the most difficult issues the courts face is determining the appropriate remedy for a *Charter* breach. Typically, *Charter* rights are asserted by accused persons because the police have obtained incriminating evidence as a result of the conduct that forms the basis for the *Charter* claim. A judicial decision that a *Charter* right has been infringed will have a declaratory effect. The authorities may be expected to abide by court rulings and alter their practices and procedures to comply with

---

77   [1994] 2 S.C.R. 951, 117 D.L.R. (4th) 7.

the dictates of the *Charter* in subsequent cases. But what of the individual who is before the court and whose rights have been infringed? A decision that merely declares that his or her rights have been infringed will ring hollow if no further action is taken. Can a system of justice premised on respect for certain fundamental rights countenance continuation of the proceedings or reliance on evidence obtained in violation of those rights? On the other hand, if the evidence obtained as a result of the *Charter* breach is not accepted by the court, relevant facts are excluded and the search for the truth is inhibited. As a result, a guilty person may go free. Is exclusion of evidence acceptable in these circumstances? Is this an appropriate way to control police behaviour?

Chapter 17 considers remedial issues in general, while the specific issues of stay of proceedings and exclusion of evidence in criminal proceedings is dealt with here. Section 24 of the *Charter* provides as follows:

(1)   Anyone whose rights or freedoms, as guaranteed by this *Charter*, have been infringed or denied may apply to a court of competent jurisdiction to obtain such remedy as the court considers appropriate and just in the circumstances.

(2)   Where, in proceedings under subsection (1), a court concludes that evidence was obtained in a manner that infringed or denied any rights or freedoms guaranteed by this *Charter*, the evidence shall be excluded if it is established that, having regard to all the circumstances, the admission of it in the proceedings would bring the administration of justice into disrepute.

1) Stay of Proceedings

In certain cases, a prosecution may be so tainted by the *Charter* breach that a stay of proceedings is appropriate. A stay of proceedings is an order that forbids the prosecutor from taking any further steps against the accused on the charges before the court. It is obviously a drastic remedy. Before the *Charter*, stays were available in cases where the court found that a prosecution amounted to an abuse of the court's process. Since the *Charter*'s enactment, the common law stay has been assimilated and adapted as a *Charter* remedy. The Supreme Court had made it clear that, given its severity, the remedy of a stay should be granted only

> . . . "in the clearest of cases," where the prejudice to the accused's right to make full answer and defence cannot be remedied or where irreparable prejudice would be caused to the integrity of the judicial system if the prosecution were continued.[78]

---

78   *R. v. O'Connor* (1995), 103 C.C.C. (3d) 1 at 43, L'Heureux-Dubé J.

2) Exclusion of Evidence

The most commonly ordered remedy for breach of *Charter* rights in the criminal process is exclusion of evidence. Prior to the enactment of the *Charter*, illegally obtained evidence was admissible, even where it was obtained in a manner that violated a right guaranteed by the *Canadian Bill of Rights*.[79] Section 24(2) alters that rule but stops short of a presumptive exclusionary rule.

The first question is whether the "evidence was obtained in a manner that infringed or denied any rights or freedoms guaranteed by this *Charter*." The issue here is the extent to which it must be shown that there was a causal link between the *Charter* breach and obtaining the evidence. Evidence found following an unreasonable search may well have been uncovered in any event. Was it obtained "in a manner which violated" a *Charter* right? The Supreme Court has interpreted these words of section 24(2) not to require a strict causal connection. In *R. v. Strachan*,[80] Dickson C.J.C. stated that the inquiry should focus on the "entire chain of events" and that, ordinarily, a temporal link between the *Charter* breach and discovery of the evidence will be sufficient. The case involved a search and arrest at the home of the accused. The police refused to allow the accused to telephone his lawyer and proceeded to find drugs. Despite the tenuous causal connection between the *Charter* breach of denial of counsel and the discovery of the drugs, the Court found that section 24(2) was engaged. In the end, the majority held that drugs could be admitted into evidence, but the case stands for the proposition that a strict causal relationship between the *Charter* breach and the discovery of the evidence is not required.

If this initial hurdle is satisfied, the Court must turn to a second issue and the central component of section 24(2), namely, whether admission of the evidence "would bring the administration of justice into disrepute." A significant body of case law has developed on the admissibility of evidence where a *Charter* right has been infringed. The basic framework for analysis was set out in the Supreme Court of Canada's 1987 decision in *R. v. Collins*[81] and confirmed by later decisions.[82]

In *Collins*, the Court stated that the purpose of section 24(2) was not to control the conduct of the police but rather to protect the integ-

---

79   *Hogan v. R.*, [1975] 2 S.C.R. 574, 48 D.L.R. (3d) 427.
80   [1988] 2 S.C.R. 980, 46 C.C.C. (3d) 479.
81   [1987] 1 S.C.R. 265, 33 C.C.C. (3d) 1 [*Collins*].
82   *R. v. Genest*, [1989] 1 S.C.R. 59, 45 C.C.C. (3d) 385; *R. v. Jacoy* (1988), [1989] 2 S.C.R. 548, 45 C.C.C. (3d) 46; *R. v. Simmons*, [1988] 2 S.C.R. 495, 45 C.C.C. (3d) 296.

rity of the judicial system. Lamer J. identified as relevant the "disrepute that will result from the admission of the evidence that would deprive the accused of a fair hearing, or from judicial condonation of unacceptable conduct by the investigatory and prosecutorial agencies."[83] The Court rejected the suggestion that disrepute should be assessed on the basis of public opinion or shock to the community. That, said Lamer J., would be contrary to the very purpose of the *Charter*, to protect the individual from the majority. The question of bringing the administration of justice into disrepute is, accordingly, to be assessed on a judicial and dispassionate basis. The relevant question is: "[W]ould the admission of the evidence bring the administration of justice into disrepute in the eyes of a reasonable man, dispassionate and fully apprised of the circumstances of the case?"[84] Very often, those who assert *Charter* claims and seek to exclude evidence as a result are undeserving of public sympathy, but *Charter* protections apply to all. As Iacobucci J. explained:

> [W]e should never lose sight of the fact that even a person accused of the most heinous crimes, and no matter the likelihood that he actually committed those crimes, is entitled to the full protection of the *Charter*. Short-cutting or short-circuiting those rights affects not only the accused, but also the entire reputation of the criminal justice system. It must be emphasized that the goals of preserving the integrity of the criminal justice system, as well as promoting the decency of investigatory techniques, are of fundamental importance in applying s. 24 (2).[85]

Collins sets out a three-step test for the determination of whether the admission of the evidence would bring the administration of justice into disrepute. The first set of factors to be considered is the way the evidence affects the fairness of the trial. If the Court concludes that admission of the evidence would adversely affect the fairness of the trial, the evidence will almost always be excluded. A 1997 decision of the Supreme Court draws a distinction between "conscriptive" and "nonconscriptive" evidence.[86] Conscriptive evidence is obtained when, in

---

83 Above note 81 at 16–17 (C.C.C.).
84 *Ibid.* at 18 (C.C.C.).
85 *R. v. Burlingham*, [1995] 2 S.C.R. 206, 124 D.L.R. (4th) 7 at 31. See also *R. v. Feeney* (1997), 146 D.L.R. (4th) 609 at 651, Sopinka J.: "If the exclusion of this evidence is likely to result in an acquittal of the accused as suggested by L'Heureux-Dubé J. in her reasons, then the Crown is deprived of a conviction based on illegally obtained evidence. Any price to society occasioned by the loss of such a conviction is fully justified in a free and democratic society which is governed by the rule of law."
86 *Stillman,* above note 18.

violation of *Charter* rights, an accused "is compelled to incriminate him-self at the behest of the state by means of a statement, the use of the body, or the production of bodily samples."[87] "Non-conscriptive" evidence is that which is obtained by the state without the accused's participation or which existed independently of any *Charter* breach. Conscriptive evidence will ordinarily be excluded without considering any other factors, unless the prosecutor can show that it would have been discovered by non-conscripted means. Conscriptive evidence does not exist prior to the *Charter* violation and, in the view of the Supreme Court, its admission would strike at a fundamental tenet of a fair trial, the right against self-incrimination. Statements obtained following denial of the right to counsel have frequently been excluded.[88] The notion of evidence emanating from the accused has been extended to exclude evidence obtained as a result of a police line-up following the denial of the right to counsel since such evidence could be obtained only through the participation of the accused.[89] Similarly, body samples obtained as a result of a *Charter* breach have been considered conscriptive evidence.[90]

On the other hand, non-conscriptive evidence — in other words, tangible evidence that exists independently of the accused (such as a weapon or drugs) — will ordinarily not render the trial unfair. To determine whether such evidence should be admitted, it is necessary to proceed to consider the next two steps.

The second set of factors is the seriousness of the *Charter* breach and the reasons for it. Technical or minor violations do not attract the same censure as serious ones. A distinction has been drawn between situations where the police have acted in good faith, relying on what is believed to be the existing state of the law, and cases where the police intentionally or carelessly abuse the rights of the accused.[91] In the latter category of case, evidence has often been excluded, while, in the former, the good faith of the police will be a factor favouring admissibility.

The third set of considerations involves weighing the effect of excluding the evidence against the effect of admitting it. Disrepute to the administration of justice could result if evidence were excluded because of a trivial breach. The seriousness of the charge is also a factor to be considered.

---

87   *Ibid.* at 655 (S.C.R.), Cory J.
88   See, for example, *Clarkson v. R.*, [1986] 1 S.C.R. 383, 26 D.L.R. (4th) 493; *R. v. Brydges*, [1990] 1 S.C.R. 190, 53 C.C.C. (3d) 330.
89   *R. v. Leclair*, [1989] 1 S.C.R. 3, 46 C.C.C. (3d) 129.
90   *Stillman*, above note 18.
91   *Collins*, above note 81.

This catalogue of factors falls well short of a precise test, and there is considerable room for case-by-case judgment and discretion. Fairness of the trial is clearly an important factor, but evidence may be excluded even where fairness is not at issue. In cases where the other two considerations favour exclusion, the courts have not hesitated to grant the remedy. In *R. v. Genest*,[92] the Court noted that, while the purpose of section 24(2) is not to prevent convicting the guilty, it must be available even in cases where it will have that effect. Evidence of weapons found on the accused's premises following an unauthorized, quasi-military police raid was excluded. In other cases, tangible evidence has been excluded where the breach of *Charter* rights has been considerably less serious. For example, in *R. v. Mellenthin*,[93] the Court held that evidence of narcotics in the possession of the accused should be excluded where it had been obtained following a random vehicle spot check. The officer had no reason to believe that the accused was in possession of drugs but had asked the accused to reveal the contents of a gym bag on the seat. The bag was found to contain cannabis resin. The Court found that the accused was detained when stopped, but that absent reasonable grounds the officer had no right to question the accused or search the vehicle. It could not be said that the accused had waived his rights since there was an inference of compulsion in the circumstances.

J. CONCLUSION

It will be evident from this brief survey that Canadian criminal law has been significantly affected by the *Charter of Rights and Freedoms* and that the judges have assumed an important law-making role. Not surprisingly, *Charter* decisions have provoked debate concerning both the substantive content of fundamental rights and freedoms and the appropriateness of judicial review as a way of protecting rights.

There are two core principles to be considered here. First is the issue of the legitimacy of judicial review, a matter considered more broadly in chapter 2. Judicial review qualifies majority rule, and it is evident from the cases considered in this chapter that Canadian judges have not hesitated to exercise the power to strike down laws they consider violate *Charter* guarantees. One point to be noted, however, particularly in the realm of the criminal law, is that more often than not,

---

92 Above note 82.
93 Above note 32.

what is at issue is not the solemn pronouncement of Parliament but rather the action of a police officer or prosecutor. The number of cases challenging the constitutionality of police conduct or that of other unelected state officials far exceeds the number of cases challenging the constitutionality of laws enacted by the representatives of the people. Judicial review of the propriety of the conduct of law-enforcement officials is considerably less controversial and very much more in keeping with the common law tradition. Control of the exercise of power by state officials through judicial review is a cornerstone of the rule of law, and subjecting the actions of police and other state officials to judicial scrutiny is one of the hallmarks of a civilized society. The *Charter* bolsters judicial powers in this area and, in so doing, does not conflict with democratic principles.

The second tension concerns the competing conceptions of the appropriate focus of the criminal law, identified at the beginning of this chapter, crime control and due process. Crime control is a matter of paramount concern in most modern societies and Canada is no exception. Condemning anti-social behaviour, convicting the guilty, and punishing wrongdoers for their transgressions represent central and important purposes of the criminal law. At the same time, however, the criminal law involves the assertion of state power over citizens, and the tradition of liberal democracy requires that coercive powers be limited by law and that those who assert power comply with specified standards. Due-process standards are designed to ensure that the state respects the human dignity of all citizens, even those accused of serious wrongdoing. The *Charter of Rights and Freedoms*, as interpreted and applied by our courts, pushes Canada decidedly in the due-process direction. It has to be recognized, however, that the imposition of limits on the authority of state officials and the extension of procedural protections to persons accused of crime not only benefits the innocent but also makes it more difficult to convict the guilty.

FURTHER READINGS

ATRENS, J., *The Charter and Criminal Procedure: The Application of Sections 7 and 11* (Toronto: Butterworths, 1989)

CAMERON, J., ed., *The Charter's Impact on the Criminal Justice System* (Toronto: Carswell, 1996)

MORTON, J.C., & S. HUTCHISON, *The Presumption of Innocence* (Toronto: Carswell, 1987)

PACIOCCO, D.M., *Charter Principles and Proof in Criminal Cases* (Toronto: Carswell, 1987)

STUART, D., *Charter Justice in Canadian Criminal Law*, 2d ed. (Toronto: Carswell, 1996)

CHAPTER 15

EQUALITY

Equality is a fundamental value in a democratic society and yet its precise meaning is elusive in political and legal discourse. As a legal concept, it includes the notion that every individual is entitled to dignity and respect and that the law should apply to all in an even-handed manner. Equality thus involves comparisons between individuals or groups but there is considerable debate about proper comparisons — who should be equal to whom, and what constitutes equal treatment? Should there be absolute equality, with everyone treated identically? Should differences be taken into account? Some theories of equality emphasize equal opportunity; others emphasize equality of outcomes.[1] As we shall see in this chapter, the Canadian courts have had to struggle with these difficult issues and the search for appropriate responses continues.

A. EQUALITY UNDER THE *CANADIAN BILL OF RIGHTS*

In order to understand the scope of the *Charter's* equality guarantee, it is useful to consider briefly the Supreme Court of Canada's treatment of

---

1   For further discussion of the debate about equality, see M. Schwarzschild, "Constitutional Law and Equality" in D. Patterson, ed., *A Companion to Philosophy of Law and Legal Theory* (Cambridge: Blackwell, 1996) at 156; W. Black & L. Smith, "The Equality Rights" in G.A. Beaudoin & E. Mendes, eds., *The Canadian Charter of Rights and Freedoms*, 3d ed. (Toronto: Carswell, 1996) at 14-17 to 14-29.

equality under section 1(b) of the *Canadian Bill of Rights*, which guaranteed "the right to equality before the law and the protection of the law." As noted in chapter 1, the Court's performance under the *Bill of Rights* was generally regarded as a disappointment. The most expansive interpretation of the equality guarantee was reached in *R. v. Drybones*,[2] the 1969 decision where the Court found inoperative a section of the *Indian Act* that made it an offence for an Indian to be intoxicated off a reserve. The *Indian Act* provision was held by the Court to deny racial equality because it imposed more onerous constraints on Aboriginals than did the general liquor ordinance of the Northwest Territories, which merely prohibited drunkenness in a public place.

While *Drybones* was widely applauded as an important affirmation of the equality principle, the Court quickly retreated. In *Lavell*,[3] the Court upheld a provision of the *Indian Act* depriving of status an Indian woman who married a non-Indian while not imposing a similar disability on Indian men who married non-Indian wives. Despite the blatantly discriminatory nature of this law, a majority refused to find that it violated the equality guarantee of the *Bill of Rights*. Similarly, in *Canard*,[4] the Court upheld a provision preventing an Indian from acting as the administrator of the estate of a deceased Indian, leaving that role to a federal official. In the Court's view, this was not a form of racial discrimination. In *Bliss*,[5] the Court upheld limitations on the rights of pregnant women to unemployment-insurance benefits, finding that discrimination on the basis of pregnancy was not sex discrimination and holding that since the legislation conferred a benefit, it could not be challenged. In these and other cases, the Court used a variety of rationales to uphold legislation — describing the law as designed to meet a valid federal objective, characterizing it as beneficial rather than burdensome, and focusing narrowly on the question whether the law was equally applied in the courts without regard to its substantive effect.[6]

---

2   (1969), [1970] S.C.R. 282, 9 D.L.R. (3d) 473 [*Drybones*].

3   *Canada (A.G.) v. Lavell* (1973), [1974] S.C.R. 1349, 38 D.L.R. (3d) 481 [*Lavell*].

4   *Canard v. Canada (A.G.)*, [1976] 1 S.C.R. 170, 52 D.L.R. (3d) 548 [*Canard*].

5   *Bliss v. Canada (A.G.)*, [1979] 1 S.C.R. 183, 92 D.L.R. (3d) 417 [*Bliss*]. The benefit lay in the fact that pregnant women, unlike other unemployment-insurance claimants, did not have to prove they were available for work.

6   A good overview is found in W.S. Tarnopolsky, *The Canadian Bill of Rights*, 2d rev. ed. (Toronto: McClelland and Stewart, 1975) c. 8.

B. DRAFTING THE *CHARTER'S* EQUALITY GUARANTEE

In the debates about the appropriate wording of the equality provision of the *Canadian Charter of Rights and Freedoms,* there was a significant lobbying effort to strengthen the guarantee so as to prevent a repetition of the experience under the *Canadian Bill of Rights.* Section 15 of the *Charter,* the equality guarantee, reads:

(1) Every individual is equal before and under the law and has the right to the equal protection and equal benefit of the law without discrimination and, in particular, without discrimination based on race, national or ethnic origin, colour, religion, sex, age or mental or physical disability.

(2) Subsection (1) does not preclude any law, program or activity that has as its object the amelioration of conditions of disadvantaged individuals or groups including those that are disadvantaged because of race, national or ethnic origin, colour, religion, sex, age or mental or physical disability.

The insistence in the careful wording in section 15 that the guarantee includes equality *before* and *under* the law, as well as *equal protection* and *equal benefit* of the law, was meant to signal to the courts that section 15 was intended to be a much more powerful instrument of protection than its predecessor. In particular, the reference to "equal protection" echoed the Fourteenth Amendment to the United States' constitution which had proved to be a powerful tool in the fight against racial discrimination. The reference to "equal benefit" was a signal that the reasoning in *Bliss,* distinguishing benefits and burdens, was no longer acceptable. Similarly, the explicit protection in section 15(2) of programs designed to ameliorate the conditions of disadvantaged individuals and groups is intended to ensure that legislatures will not be discouraged from taking affirmative measures to enhance equality.

The message that the promise of equality was to be meaningful was reinforced by the addition of section 28 of the *Charter,* which contained a further statement about gender equality:

28. Notwithstanding anything in this Charter, the rights and freedoms referred to in it are guaranteed equally to male and female persons.

This was also a signal to the courts of the importance attached by the drafters of the *Charter* to the commitment to gender equality. At a minimum, it seems to prevent the use of the override in section 33 to permit laws that are discriminatory on the basis of sex.

C. THE SCOPE OF THE EQUALITY GUARANTEE

While section 15 of the *Charter* was clearly a departure from section 1(b) of the *Bill of Rights*, its precise meaning was far from clear. The early cases had to confront questions about the scope of the guarantee, particularly the issue of who could claim its protection. As well, there was debate (which continues to the present) about the appropriate method of interpreting section 15 and its interrelation with section 1.[7]

Section 15 contains a list of characteristics which should not be the basis for discriminatory treatment. That list incorporates the most common grounds for discrimination found in human rights codes: race, national or ethnic origin, sex, age, religion, and physical or mental disability.[8] Although the original draft of section 15 treated that list as more limited in its coverage, the final wording that was adopted makes it clear that the list of prohibited grounds of discrimination is not exhaustive and that further grounds may be added by the courts.

Not surprisingly, many early cases dealt with laws challenged on grounds not included in the "enumerated" grounds in section 15. These cases involved challenges to laws setting shorter limitation periods for suing municipalities, regulatory provisions of various kinds including the ban on actions in tort for work-related accidents covered by workers' compensation legislation, and regulations prohibiting the use of aluminum cans in order to protect the steel industry from competition. The courts were required to consider the purpose underlying section 15 to decide whether to allow these claims. Since all laws make distinctions between individuals and groups, it is almost always possible to say that a law discriminates in that it imposes burdens or confers benefits on some but not others. Was section 15 meant to give the courts a mandate to oversee the general rationality of the legislative process? Did it forbid different treatment of individuals unless there could be shown in a court of law to be a reasonable basis for doing so? Or did the words "without discrimination" signal a narrower purpose, namely, that the section was meant only to address the adverse treatment of certain groups on the basis of characteristics like those listed, which have led to prejudice, stereotype, and unjust disadvantage in many societies, including our own?[9]

---

7   Section 15 came into effect three years after the rest of the *Charter* (on 17 April 1985), in order to allow governments time to bring their statutes into line with the section.

8   The first draft of the *Charter* was more limited in its coverage, listing only race, national or ethnic origin, colour, religion, age, and sex.

9   Section 15 guarantees equality to "individuals," which has been interpreted to mean that people, not corporations, can invoke its protection.

Initially, some lower courts adopted the broader approach and were prepared to consider reviewing a wide range of laws under section 15. This was a cause for concern among advocacy groups, in particular, those representing women and those with disabilities. They feared that, if section 15 were to be applied to such a wide range of laws, it might well lead the judiciary to adopt a relaxed interpretation of section 1, in order to avoid frequent second-guessing of legislatures' decisions.

A related concern arose in connection with the use of the "similarly situated" test, reminiscent of certain undesirable aspects of American equal-protection jurisprudence. This test has venerable roots in the teachings of Aristotle, who stated that "those who are alike should be treated alike." The test is deceptively simple and superficially attractive.[10] For example, in applications for admission to university, one might argue that anyone receiving a certain grade on a standardized test should be admitted and that no other distinctions should be made. But problems quickly emerge from a mechanical application of this concept of equality. What if there was no oral or braille examination available so that a blind individual could not apply? Is it really consistent with a commitment to equality to ignore visual disability and treat that individual in precisely the same way as sighted individuals? May it not be necessary to look beyond the formal legal rule to ask whether there is equality in substance?

The determination of similarity and difference can be made only in relation to some criterion, which is often the purpose behind the rule or the law. Critics of the similarly situated test argue that this makes the test inherently unreliable because determining the purpose is uncertain and subject to manipulation. The *Bliss* decision, finding that pregnant women could be treated differently from other unemployment-insurance claimants since they were not generally available for work, is often cited as an example of the perils of the similarly situated approach.

It was argued that, if the promise of equality is to be meaningful, the formal "similarly situated" test had to be abandoned and the emphasis placed on a search for "substantive equality" that emphasizes consideration of the impact of laws on members of groups subject to stereotyping and historic disadvantage.[11] This approach was reflected by the

---

10   This approach is sometimes called formal equality, sometimes equality of process. See, for example, K. Crenshaw, "Race, Reform and Retrenchment: Transformation and Legitimation in Anti-Discrimination Law" (1988) 101 Harv. L. Rev. 1331.

11   An early example of this type of writing is G. Brodksy & S. Day, *Canadian Charter Equality Rights for Women: One Step Forward or Two Steps Back?* (Ottawa: Canadian Advisory Council on Status of Women, 1989).

jurisprudence developed in the interpretation of Canadian human rights codes which seemed much concerned about the actual impact of rules on groups. For example, the Supreme Court found rules requiring everyone to work Saturday in a retail store to be discriminatory. While seemingly grounded in a valid business purpose and not obviously treating anyone differently on the basis of religion, such rules do have an adverse impact on those for whom Saturday is a day of worship. Saturday observers are required to sacrifice their religious beliefs or their job.[12] Similarly, the failure to move furniture in an office to give space for a wheelchair to pass, while seemingly inoffensive, might have the effect of denying access to employment to a person with physical disabilities. The human rights jurisprudence had determined that "adverse-effects" discrimination of this sort gave rise to a duty to accommodate the group adversely affected unless such accommodation would produce undue hardship.[13]

D. THE SUPREME COURT SPEAKS: *ANDREWS* v. *LAW SOCIETY OF BRITISH COLUMBIA*

Andrews,[14] the first equality case to reach the Supreme Court of Canada, was acknowledged to be of fundamental importance in charting the future direction of section 15 interpretation. A number of intervenors made submissions, including the Women's Legal Education and Action Fund (LEAF) and the Coalition of Provincial Organizations of the Handicapped (COPOH). The case involved a challenge to the citizenship requirement for admission to the Law Society of British Columbia. The Court held, in a four to two decision, that this violated section 15, and was not justified under section 1 of the *Charter*.

The most significant aspect of the case was the Court's conceptualization of section 15. It soundly rejected the formalism of the similarly situated test and emphasized that the purpose behind section 15 was to protect vulnerable groups from discrimination. In the Court's view, this meant that section 15 could not be used to challenge every differential

---

12 *Simpsons Sears* v. *Ontario (Human Rights Commission)*, [1985] 2 S.C.R. 536, 23 D.L.R. (4th) 321; *Central Alberta Dairy Pool* v. *Alberta (Human Rights Commission)*, [1990] 2 S.C.R. 489, 72 D.L.R. (4th) 417.

13 This jurisprudence is discussed in greater detail in K.E. Swinton, "Accommodating Equality in the Unionized Workplace" (1995) 33 Osgoode Hall L.J. 703.

14 *Andrews* v. *Law Society (British Columbia)*, [1989] 1 S.C.R. 143, 56 D.L.R.(4th) 1 [*Andrews*].

treatment created by a law. To succeed in a section 15 claim, a litigant would have to show, first, that there had been a denial of one of the four equality provisions in section 15 — equality before or under the law or equal benefit or protection of the law — and second, that this differential treatment was discriminatory on the basis of a personal characteristic constituting an enumerated or analogous ground within section 15.

The Court made it clear that there was a threshold requirement for those invoking section 15: there must be discrimination on an enumerated or analogous ground. The enumerated grounds were described as "the most common and probably the most socially destructive and historically practised bases of discrimination."[15] No attempt was made to define "analogous grounds" precisely at this point. McIntyre J. noted that "[t]he enumerated grounds in s. 15(1) are not exclusive and the limits, if any on grounds for discrimination which may be established in future cases await definition."[16]

The insistence on enumerated or analogous grounds significantly restricted the reach of section 15 and closed the door on attempts to use the equality guarantee to review all legislative distinctions.[17] The Court insisted, however, that the restriction of section 15 to discrimination on enumerated and analogous grounds was required to ensure that when it did apply, the guarantee could be given a vigorous interpretation and afford effective protection to members of disadvantaged groups.

Discrimination was described by McIntyre J. in the following manner:

> . . . a distinction, whether intentional or not but based on grounds relating to personal characteristics of the individual or group, which has the effect of imposing burdens, obligations, or disadvantages on such individual or group not imposed upon others, or which withholds or limits access to opportunities, benefits, and advantages available to other members of society. Distinctions based on personal characteristics attributed to an individual solely on the basis of association with a group will rarely escape the charge of discrimination, while those based on an individual's merits and capacities will rarely be so classed.[18]

Thus, in deciding whether discrimination has occurred, the Court indicated that it would look at the legislature's purpose — for example, whether it acted out of prejudice against a group or on the basis of unjustified stereotypes about its members' capacity. But it would go further and

---

15   *Ibid.* at 175 (S.C.R.)
16   *Ibid.*
17   See, for example, *Reference Re Workers' Compensation Act, 1983 (Newfoundland)*, [1989] 1 S.C.R. 922, 56 D.L.R. (4th) 765.
18   *Andrews*, above note 14 at 175 (S.C.R.).

consider as well the impact of laws on a group claiming section 15 protection. This willingness to look at both purpose and effects signalled that the Court would take the same approach under section 15 as it had taken in the interpretation of other *Charter* rights and human rights codes.

Finally, the Court remained true to past *Charter* cases in drawing a sharp line between the consideration of whether a right was violated and whether that infringement was justified under section 1. Some of the lower court cases, including the British Columbia Court of Appeal's decision in *Andrews*, had dealt with the justification for differential treatment within section 15 itself. This seemed to put the onus on the rights claimant to show that the differential treatment was not justified — an approach that the Supreme Court rejected in *Andrews*. McIntyre J. emphasized that the justification for discriminatory treatment under section 1 should be on the government.

In applying this structure to the facts in *Andrews*, all members of the Court agreed that section 15 had been violated. The law drew a distinction between citizens and non-citizens, and citizenship was held to be an analogous ground within section 15, for reasons discussed below. Discrimination resulted from the burden placed on the non-citizen's ability to practise law until citizenship was acquired. A majority of the Court held that the law was not justified under section 1, because there were other ways to address the Law Society's justifiable concerns about a lawyer's competence and familiarity with Canadian institutions than through a citizenship requirement — for example, by testing or the requirement of a Canadian law degree.

E. ANALOGOUS GROUNDS

In *Andrews*, there is little discussion of why citizenship is an analogous ground under section 15. Both McIntyre and Wilson JJ. made reference to the American terminology of "discrete and insular minorities," a term derived from an American case involving the Equal Protection clause.[19] The use of American jurisprudence here is unusual, given the Court's general reluctance to adopt American approaches. Reference was made to the relevance of the lack of political power of non-citizens, while La Forest J. also noted that citizenship was an "immutable" characteristic, in the sense that it is not within the individual's control — it was "not alterable by conscious action and in some cases not alterable except on

---

19 *United States v. Carolene Products Co.*, 304 U.S. 144 (1938) at 152–53, footnote 4.

the basis of unacceptable costs."[20] Wilson J. emphasized that the determination "must not be made only in the context of the law which is subject to challenge but rather in the context of the place of the group in the entire social, political and legal fabric of our society."[21]

This notion was reiterated in *Turpin,* where Wilson J. explained: "A finding that there is discrimination will, I think, in most but perhaps not all cases, necessarily entail a search for disadvantage that exists apart from and independent of the particular legal distinction being challenged."[22] In *Turpin,* Wilson J. described the purpose of section 15 as "remedying or preventing discrimination against groups suffering social, political and legal disadvantage in our society." The indicia of discrimination, stated Wilson J., are "stereotyping, historical disadvantage or vulnerability to political and social prejudice." With reference to the "discrete and insular minority" categorization, she stated that it "is not an end in itself but merely one of the analytical tools which are of assistance in determining whether the interest advanced by a particular claimant is the kind of interest s. 15 of the *Charter* is designed to protect."[23]

The Court revisited the inquiry into analogous grounds in two later cases, *Miron* v. *Trudel*[24] and *Egan* v. *Canada.*[25] In *Miron,* McLachlin J. stated that "the fundamental consideration is whether the characteristic may serve as an irrelevant basis of exclusion and a denial of essential human dignity in the human rights tradition." For her, the "unifying principle" is

> . . . the avoidance of stereotypical reasoning and the creation of legal distinctions which violate the dignity and freedom of the individual, on the basis of some preconceived perception about the attributed characteristics of a group rather than the true capacity, worth or circumstances of the individual."[26]

To help make that determination, she listed a number of factors to consider: whether the group seeking protection had suffered historical disadvantage, whether it was a discrete and insular minority, whether the

---

20   *Andrews,* above note 14 at 195 (S.C.R.).
21   *Ibid.* at 152 (S.C.R.).
22   *R. v. Turpin,* [1989] 1 S.C.R. 1296 at 1332, 48 C.C.C. (3d) 8 [*Turpin*].
23   *Ibid.* at 1333 (S.C.R.).
24   [1995] 2 S.C.R. 418, 124 D.L.R. (4th) 693 [*Miron*].
25   [1995] 2 S.C.R. 513, 124 D.L.R. (4th) 609 [*Egan*].
26   Above note 24 at 748 (D.L.R.).

personal characteristic was immutable, and whether the characteristic bears some similarity to those enumerated.[27]

In *Miron* the Court concluded that marital status was analogous to the grounds protected under section 15, while in *Egan* all members of the Court agreed that sexual orientation was also an analogous ground.[28] While La Forest J. continued to focus on the immutability of the characteristic in determining whether it is an analogous ground,[29] the majority in the Court seem more concerned with the disadvantages facing the group seeking protection within our society.

The Court, then, has not offered a precise test that will identify an analogous ground. As noted, citizenship, marital status, and sexual orientation have been accepted as analogous grounds. Province of residence was rejected in the context of special procedural rules for criminal cases but not ruled out altogether for other situations.[30] The Court has, on the other side, consistently rejected equality claims made by those not identified by any personal characteristic enumerated in section 15(1) or analogous thereto.[31] While the Court has not identified a precise test, there appear to be certain guiding principles. First is the basic point, articulated in *Andrews*, that section 15 does not permit courts to review all legislative distinctions. The second and related point is that the focus of section 15(1) is upon discrimination that denies human dignity by granting or withholding benefits based upon certain personal

27   In *Egan*, above note 25, Cory J. wrote (at 673 (S.C.R.)): "Since one of the aims of s. 15(1) is to prevent discrimination against groups which suffer from a social or political disadvantage it follows that it may be helpful to see if there is any indication that the group in question has suffered discrimination arising from stereotyping, historical disadvantage or vulnerability to political and social prejudice."

28   See also *Vriend v. Alberta*, [1998] S.C.J. No. 29.

29   In *Egan*, above note 25, La Forest J. (writing for himself and three others) stated that sexual orientation (at 619 (S.C.R.)) "is a deeply personal characteristic that is either unchangeable or changeable only at unacceptable personal costs. . . ."

30   *Turpin*, above note 22.

31   See *Reference Re Workers' Compensation Act, 1983 (Newfoundland)*, above note 17 at 924 (S.C.R.), La Forest J. rejecting the claim of victims of work-related accidents : "The situation of the workers and dependants here is in no way analogous to those listed in s. 15(1), as a majority in *Andrews* stated was required to permit recourse to s. 15(1)"; *Rudolf Wolff & Co. v. Canada*, [1990] 1 S.C.R. 695 at 702, rejecting the claim of those seeking relief against the federal Crown and challenging the statutory requirement that they sue in the Federal Court of Canada: "[I]t cannot be said that individuals claiming relief against the Federal Crown are . . . a 'discrete and insular minority' or a 'disadvantaged group in Canadian society within the contemplation of s. 15.' Rather, they are a disparate group with the sole common interest of seeking to bring a claim against the Crown before a court."

traits or characteristics. Traits and characteristics that fall into this category may be identified in a number of ways but broadly tend to be matters that history and experience show to have been the subject of stereotypical application of presumed group characteristics that deny individual human dignity.

F. AGE DISCRIMINATION

McKinney,[32] the first significant case after *Andrews*, dealt with a constitutional challenge to the mandatory retirement at age sixty-five years of university professors employed at a number of Ontario institutions. Two companion cases, *Harrison* and *Stoffman*, dealt with mandatory retirement in British Columbia universities and hospitals.[33] In each of these cases, there was a preliminary issue of whether the *Charter* applied directly to universities and hospitals so as to allow a *Charter* challenge to their employment policies, as discussed earlier in chapter 6. The majority of the Supreme Court of Canada held that the *Charter* did not apply but nevertheless proceeded to deal with the constitutionality of the mandatory-retirement policies. In *McKinney* and *Harrison*, the provincial human rights codes were also challenged, since both protected against discrimination in employment on the basis of age but then defined age with an upper limit of sixty-five years, thereby precluding complaints by workers faced with mandatory retirement at age sixty-five. If that cap on the definition was impermissible under the *Charter*, mandatory retirement could be challenged through a human rights complaint, and past cases involving mandatory retirement at ages caught by the human rights codes had succeeded.[34]

Speaking for the majority in *McKinney*, La Forest J. noted that age, as a ground of discrimination, differed from other enumerated grounds in section 15, in that "[t]here is a general relationship between advancing age and declining ability." While courts should protect against age-based discrimination resulting from unfounded assumptions or stereotypes about the capacity of older individuals, courts should also be

---

32   *McKinney v. University of Guelph*, [1990] 3 S.C.R. 229, 76 D.L.R. (4th) 545 [*McKinney*].

33   *Harrison v. University of British Columbia*, [1990] 3 S.C.R. 451, [1991] 77 D.L.R. (4th) 55 [*Harrison*]; *Stoffman v. Vancouver General Hospital*, [1990] 3 S.C.R. 483, 76 D.L.R. (4th) 700 [*Stoffman*].

34   For example, *Ontario (Human Rights Commission) v. Etobicoke (Borough)*, [1982] 1 (S.C.R.) 202, 132 D.L.R. (3d) 14.

conscious of the justification for granting or withholding certain social benefits on the basis of age. La Forest J. found that both mandatory retirement and the cap on age in the human rights codes violated section 15 because of the burden imposed on older workers, but he then went on to apply a relaxed test under section 1 of the *Charter*. In so doing, he stressed the complexity of mandatory-retirement schemes which also protected older workers through deferred-compensation arrangements and by allowing departure from the workplace in dignity without unpleasant merit reviews. As well, mandatory retirement served the need for renewal through hiring younger workers with different skills and qualities. Moreover, with respect to the human rights codes' protection for existing mandatory-retirement schemes, La Forest J. noted that their widespread use in the private sector was generally beneficial in nature. This justified the legislative action, which provided a reasonable balance of competing social values. Finally, with respect to the human rights codes, La Forest J. noted that a legislature should be permitted to proceed incrementally in enacting legislation addressing the problems of discrimination, provided that there was a reasonable basis for its cut-off point, as there was here.

Both Wilson and L'Heureux-Dubé JJ. dissented. In their view, the legislation and the mandatory-retirement policies could not be justified under section 1 since there were other ways to meet the concerns for productivity and employment turnover that would allow a more individualized treatment of older workers.

In a later case, the Supreme Court unanimously concluded that there was age discrimination in the *Unemployment Insurance Act* provision preventing those over sixty-five from receiving insurance benefits and restricting them to a lump-sum payment equivalent to three weeks' benefits. This restriction could not be justified, said the Court, because it denied access to benefits to those over sixty-five who needed to continue to work because of inadequate pension entitlements.[35]

G. DISABILITY

In *Swain*,[36] the Court upheld a common law rule allowing the Crown to raise the issue of the accused's insanity in a criminal trial, either after conviction or if the accused led evidence that put his capacity for crim-

---

35 *Canada (Employment and Immigration Commission)* v. *Tétreault-Gadoury*, [1991] 2 S.C.R. 22, 81 D.L.R. (4th) 358.

36 *R.* v. *Swain*, [1991] 1 S.C.R. 933, 63 C.C.C. (3d) 481 [*Swain*].

inal intent in question. Even though this rule drew a distinction on the basis of mental disability, there was no discrimination within section 15, said Lamer C.J.C., because the rule did not impose a burden or disadvantage on those with mental disabilities. In his words, "it is a principle of fundamental justice that the criminal justice system not convict a person who was insane at the time of the offence."[37] This case raised the question whether the determination of burdens and disadvantages should be made from the perspective of the rights claimant or from a more objective standpoint. From Swain's perspective, it might well seem burdensome to allow the Crown to raise the issue of his insanity, if the outcome was an acquittal by reason of insanity that would lead to indeterminate detention because of his mental state. In contrast, and more beneficial from his perspective, a conviction might have resulted in a fixed sentence, perhaps without incarceration.

The question of perspective was raised again in *Eaton*,[38] a case involving a challenge to the special-education provisions in Ontario under which a child with cerebral palsy had been assigned to a special-education class after three years in an integrated classroom. Her counsel argued that the decision contravened section 15, because it discriminated on the basis of physical disability. The Supreme Court of Canada disagreed, concluding that while integrated classes might benefit some with disabilities, it might be a burden to others. A special-education tribunal, after considering extensive evidence about the child's abilities and needs, had concluded that a special classroom was in her best interests. Therefore, said the Court, there was no discrimination in that there was no burden or disadvantage placed on the child, nor was she denied a benefit.

While *Eaton* was a disappointment to many advocates of the rights of those with disabilities, the Court's subsequent decision in *Eldridge*[39] was greeted with delight. In that case, individuals with hearing disabilities successfully argued that the failure to provide them with sign-language interpreters when they receive medical services violated section 15 and was not justified under section 1. This was a case of adverse-effects discrimination, said the Supreme Court, which essentially adopted the same approach here as has been used in the interpretation of human rights codes. In the words of La Forest J., sign-language interpretation "is the means by which deaf persons may receive the same quality of medical care as the

---

37   *Ibid.* at 509 (C.C.C.).
38   *Eaton v. Brant County*, [1997] 1 S.C.R. 241 [*Eaton*].
39   *Eldridge v. British Columbia (A.G.)*, [1997] 3 S.C.R. 624, 151 D.L.R. (4th) 577 [*Eldridge*].

hearing population."[40] He then went on to say that the *Charter* includes a duty to make reasonable accommodation, up to the point of undue hardship, for those adversely affected by a rule — a principle that he concluded should be addressed under section 1.[41] Clearly, cost would be a relevant consideration, since governments have to make difficult decisions about the appropriate allocation of limited public resources.

H. SEX DISCRIMINATION

In several cases coming before the Supreme Court, section 15 claims have alleged discrimination on the basis of sex, but none has succeeded. In *Hess*,[42] the accused challenged the statutory-rape provisions of the *Criminal Code*, which made it an offence for a male over fourteen years to have sexual intercourse with a female under that age. The accused argued that this was sex discrimination, because only men could be charged with the crime and only females could be the victims. Wilson J. held that there was no violation of section 15 here, since biological reality determined that only men could commit the offence: "[W]e are therefore dealing with an offence that involves an act that as a matter of biological fact only men over a certain age are capable of committing."[43] Because men and women are different in their ability to commit the offence, she held there to be no discrimination.

But what of the fact that a woman might have intercourse with a young male under fourteen and escape punishment? Does this not demonstrate that the law is non-inclusive on grounds of gender in its coverage of sexual offences against the young? Wilson J.'s response was similar to that of the majority in *McKinney* — it is up to the legislature to decide whether questions of morality and social disapprobation warrant criminalizing such conduct, and there is no discrimination involved in the legislature proceeding part-way, prohibiting only some sexual misconduct.

In contrast, McLachlin J., with Gonthier J. concurring, would have found a section 15 violation here, both because of the burden that the offence placed on men but not women and because of the protection provided for young females but not for young males. However, she upheld the legislation as justifiable under section 1, since it protected a particularly vulnerable group, young women.

---

40   *Ibid.* at 620 (D.L.R.).
41   *Ibid.* at 624 (D.L.R.).
42   *R. v. Hess*, [1990] 2 S.C.R. 906, 59 C.C.C. (3d) 161 [*Hess*].
43   *Ibid.* at 930 (S.C.R.).

Wilson J.'s approach in this case was troubling to some, because she rejected the claim within section 15 itself. Her holding that the differential treatment was, in effect, justified and non-discriminatory because of the nature of the offence and the biological difference between men and women seemed to import into section 15 itself the issues of justification, which were usually left to the state to bring forward under section 1.

Despite these concerns, a majority of the Court followed the same approach in *Conway*.[44] This case rejected a challenge to the practice in the prison system whereby male prisoners could be "frisk-searched" and have their cell areas patrolled by female guards, while the practice in the women's penitentiary was to have women guards perform these duties, except in emergency situations. In an unusually short judgment, La Forest J. stated that it was "doubtful" that section 15 was violated, "given the historical, biological and sociological differences between men and women." More precisely, because of the history of violence of men against women, cross-gender searching is "different and more threatening for women than for men."[45] Thus, the issue of justification seemed to enter into the finding of discrimination. In contrast, earlier cases had suggested that, if the rights claimant felt burdened or disadvantaged by the rule because of sex, the justification would be discussed under section 1 with the government bearing the onus.

However, the Court went on to say that, even if there were discrimination here, the differential treatment was justified under section 1, because of the benefits from the presence in male prisons of women guards, who are said to have a "humanizing effect." As well, their employment promotes Parliament's objective of employment equity for women.

In *Symes* v. *Canada*,[46] the Court was asked to determine whether the provisions in the *Income Tax Act* limiting the amount that a taxpayer can deduct for childcare expenses violated section 15. This was a difficult case because it required the application of an adverse-effects approach to section 15. On its face, there was no indication of sex discrimination in section 63 of the *Income Tax Act*, which allowed a childcare deduction of a fixed amount to taxpayers while requiring that in families with two supporting parents, the deduction be taken by the lower-income earner. However, the claimant, a self-employed female lawyer, argued that the effect of the legislation was discriminatory against women. It limited her deduction to an amount less than the actual cost that she paid for childcare and prevented her from taking childcare as a business deduction

---

44   *Conway* v. *R.* (1993), 105 D.L.R. (4th) 210 [*Conway*].
45   *Ibid.* at 214.
46   [1993] 4 S.C.R. 695, 110 D.L.R. (4th) 470.

elsewhere in the Act. She argued that this was sex discrimination, because women disproportionately bear the cost of childcare. The denial of a full deduction for childcare, while allowing full deductions for other items that disproportionately benefited businessmen, was said to violate section 15.

The majority in the Supreme Court, in reasons written by Iacobucci J., concluded that sex discrimination was not established. Even if the evidence showed that women disproportionately bear the burden of childcare in Canadian society, there was no evidence that they disproportionately bear the *cost* of childcare. In fact, the law requires both parents to provide support and care for their children. While Symes and her husband had made an agreement that she would pay for childcare, this did not change the situation: the cost of childcare is borne by families, not just women. Iacobucci J. went on to discuss the difficulties of proving adverse-effects discrimination. In particular, he noted that there are potential problems when a law has adverse effects on both men and women, implying that it will be difficult to conclude that there is sex discrimination where both men and women are burdened and benefited by legislation.

I. A DIVIDED COURT: THE 1995 TRILOGY

While the *Andrews* analysis remains the starting point, it is clear that judges of the Supreme Court are not united in their understanding of discrimination within section 15. Three equality decisions, issued at the same time in the spring of 1995, signalled a Court divided on the proper approach to section 15. *Egan*[47] dealt with a challenge to the spousal allowance under the *Old Age Security Act*, which provided a benefit for the spouse of a pensioner who was between sixty and sixty-five when the couple's combined income fell below a certain level. "Spouse" was defined as a person of the opposite sex to whom the pensioner was married or with whom he or she lived in a common-law relationship as husband and wife. Egan was a gay man, whose partner, Norris, applied for the spousal benefit and was turned down because he was not a spouse as defined by the Act. He argued that this amounted to discrimination on the basis of sexual orientation. *Miron*[48] involved a challenge to a provision of the Ontario *Insurance Act*, which at the time provided accident

---

47   Above note 25.
48   Above note 24.

benefits for uninsured motorist claims under the standard automobile-insurance policy prescribed by the Act when the loss of income or damages was incurred by married spouses, but not common-law spouses. Miron, injured in a car accident by an uninsured motorist, sought benefits under his common-law spouse's insurance policy, arguing that the law was discriminatory on the basis of marital status and not justified under section 1. Finally, *Thibaudeau*[49] involved a challenge to a provision of the *Income Tax Act* which provided that child-support payments are taxable to the recipient and deductible to the payor. It was argued that this scheme disproportionately burdened women, who were much more likely to be the custodial parent while the payors were more likely to be male.

The decisions in these cases reveal three distinct approaches to section 15. Four judges (La Forest, Gonthier, Major JJ., and Lamer C.J.C.) used what can be called an "internal-relevance" approach that builds on earlier cases like *Conway* and *Hess*. Four others (McLachlin, Cory, Iacobucci, and Sopinka JJ.) continued to use the *Andrews* approach, while L'Heureux-Dubé J. adopted her own distinctive approach.

The judges adopting the internal-relevance approach stated that there is no discrimination within section 15 if the distinction drawn between two groups by legislation is relevant "to the functional values underlying the legislation,"[50] even though the distinction is made on the basis of an enumerated or analogous ground. Support for considering the relevance of the distinction is drawn from earlier cases, including *Andrews*, where the Court had noted that not all distinctions constitute discrimination. Therefore, according to Gonthier J. in *Miron*, one must decide whether a distinction is relevant to "some objective physical or biological reality, or fundamental value,"[51]

In both *Miron* and *Egan*, the judges adopting the internal-relevance approach held that the legislative scheme was designed to support the institution of marriage, an institution of fundamental and long-standing importance in Canadian society. In *Miron*, Gonthier J. concluded that the legislature had no obligation to confer all the benefits of marriage on common-law couples. Indeed, to do so "would interfere directly with the individual's freedom to voluntarily choose whether to enter the institution of marriage by imposing consequences on cohabitation without any regard to the will of the parties."[52] Similarly, in *Egan*, marriage was described by La Forest J. as "by nature heterosexual" and, given its societal importance, Parliament should be able to give it special support:

---

49   *Thibaudeau v. Canada*, [1995] 2 S.C.R. 627, 124 D.L.R. 449 [*Thibaudeau*].
50   *Miron*, above note 24 at 436 (S.C.R.), Gonthier J.
51   *Ibid.* at 446 (S.C.R.).
52   *Ibid.* at 463 (S.C.R.).

Neither in its purpose or effect does the legislation constitute an infringement of the fundamental values sought to be protected by the Charter. None of the couples excluded from benefits under the Act are capable of meeting the fundamental social objectives thereby sought to be promoted by Parliament. These couples undoubtedly provide mutual support for one another, and that, no doubt, is of some benefit to society. They may, it is true, occasionally adopt or bring up children, but this is exceptional and in no way affects the general picture. I fail to see how homosexuals differ from other excluded couples in terms of the fundamental social reasons for which Parliament has sought to favour heterosexuals who live as married couples . . .[53]

In contrast, another group of four judges, represented by McLachlin J. in *Miron* and Cory J. in *Egan*, rejected the internal-relevance approach as unjustifiably narrow. As McLachlin J. stated in *Miron*:

If the basis of the distinction on an enumerated or analogous ground is clearly irrelevant to the functional values of the legislation, then the distinction will be discriminatory. However, it does not follow from a finding that a group characteristic is relevant to the legislative aim, that the legislator has employed that characteristic in a manner which does not perpetuate limitations, burdens and disadvantages in violation of s. 15(1). This can be ascertained only by examining the effect of the distinction in the social and economic context of the legislation and the lives of the individuals it touches.[54]

McLachlin J. here echoes the insistence in Wilson J.'s opinions in *Andrews* and *Turpin* that comparisons between groups in relation to a particular law are not determinative of inequality. Rather, one must look at the impact of the law and the distinctions it draws within the larger historical and social context. The purpose of section 15, McLachlin J. wrote, is "the avoidance of stereotypical reasoning and the creation of legal distinctions which violate the dignity and freedom of the individual, on the basis of some preconceived perception about the attributed characteristics of a group rather than the true capacity, worth or circumstances of the individual."[55] While past cases indicated that some distinctions on an enumerated or analogous ground might not constitute discrimination within section 15, that situation would be rare — arising where "the distinction may be found not to engage the purpose

---

53   Above note 25 at 538 (S.C.R.).
54   Above note 24 at 742 (D.L.R.).
55   *Ibid.* at 748 (D.L.R.).

202 THE *CHARTER OF RIGHTS AND FREEDOMS*

of the Charter guarantee" or where the effect of the law is not to impose a real disadvantage, given the larger social and political context.

Applying this approach in *Miron*, McLachlin J. found the distinction between married and common-law couples in eligibility for accident-insurance benefits was discriminatory on the basis of marital status. This infringement was not justified under section 1, given that common-law couples, like married couples, could suffer economic disloca-tion if one member was injured in an accident, and there was no reason to bar them from benefits.

In *Egan*, Cory J. similarly concluded that the distinction drawn between homosexual couples and heterosexual couples living in a com-mon-law relationship was discriminatory. Noting that discrimination is to be determined from the perspective of the individual claiming a *Char-ter* violation, he said:

> The definition of "spouse" as someone of the opposite sex reinforces the stereotype that homosexuals cannot and do not form lasting, car-ing, mutually supportive relationships with economic interdepen-dence in the same manner as heterosexual couples. The appellants' relationship vividly demonstrates the error of that approach. The dis-criminatory impact can hardly be deemed trivial when the legislation reinforces prejudicial attitudes based on such faulty stereotypes. The effect of the impugned provision is clearly contrary to s. 15's aim of protecting human dignity . . .[56]

L'Heureux-Dubé J. took a distinctive position, critical of the "cate-gorical" approach of her colleagues, arguing that the inquiry in section 15 cases should turn on the nature of the group adversely affected by a distinction and the nature of the interest adversely affected.

The trilogy of cases demonstrated that the Court was seriously divided with respect to section 15, giving rise to the concern that the promise in *Andrews* of vigorous protection for disadvantaged groups is in danger. This fear is heightened when one adds into consideration the discussion of sec-tion 1 in *Egan*. Even though five of the judges found a violation of section 15, the legislation was upheld under section 1 because Sopinka J. joined the four judges who had found that section 15 was not violated. The latter group, in brief reasons by La Forest J., stated that the legislation was a rea-sonable limit under section 1, both because of the justifiability of support-ing the institution of marriage and also because a deferential approach to section 1 was deemed appropriate. Sopinka J. elaborated the argument in his own reasons, adopting an extremely deferential approach to legislative

---

56   Above note 25 at 604 (S.C.R.).

decision making, partly because he felt that Parliament should be allowed to move incrementally in providing financial assistance to the needy by acting first to benefit those most in need. He also noted that the recognition of sexual orientation as a ground of prohibited discrimination was relatively recent in Canadian human rights laws, and, therefore, Parliament's inaction with respect to this "novel concept" was not fatal.[57]

In the section 15 cases that have followed, the Court has dealt with this basic disagreement about section 15, by referring to the two approaches and then justifying the result under both. The current state of the law and the debate between various members of the Court were summarized by La Forest J. in *Eldridge:*

> While this Court has not adopted a uniform approach to s.15(1), there is broad agreement on the general analytic framework; see *Eaton v. Brant County Board of Education*, [1997] 1 S.C.R. 241, at para. 62, *Miron, supra* and *Egan, supra*. A person claiming a violation of s.15 (1) must first establish that, because of a distinction drawn between the claimant and others, the claimant has been denied "equal protection" or "equal benefit" of the law. Secondly, the claimant must show that the denial constitutes discrimination on the basis of one of the enumerated grounds listed in s. 15(1) or one analogous thereto. Before concluding that a distinction is discriminatory, some members of this Court have held that it must be shown to be based on an irrelevant personal characteristic; see *Miron, supra (per* Gonthier J.), and *Egan, supra (per* La Forest J.). Under this view, s. 15(1) will not be infringed unless the distinguished personal characteristic is irrelevant to the functional values underlying the law, provided that those values are not themselves discriminatory. Others have suggested that relevance is only one factor to be considered in determining whether a distinction based on an enumerated or analogous ground is discriminatory; see *Miron, supra (per* McLachlin J.), and *Thibaudeau v. Canada*, [1995] 2 S.C.R. 627 *(per* Cory and Iacobucci JJ.)[58]

Again in *Benner*, the Court openly acknowledged the three approaches.[59] In *Eaton*, Sopinka J. declared that there was agreement among members of the Court on certain principles, noting that the majority in

---

57   *Ibid.* at 576 (S.C.R.).

58   Above note 39 at 614 (D.L.R.).

59   In *Benner v. Canada (Secretary of State)*, [1997] 1 S.C.R. 358, 143 D.L.R. (4th) 577 [*Benner*], the Court struck down a provision in the *Citizenship Act* which imposed more onerous requirements for the acquisition of Canadian citizenship for the children of women who married non-Canadians at a given period than for men who married non-citizens.

Miron (the McLachlin view) had agreed with the internal-relevance approach to the extent that it was acknowledged that, in rare cases, distinctions on an enumerated or analogous ground might not constitute discrimination.[60] While in none of these cases is the split significant to the outcome, the difference could well be decisive in future cases, especially those dealing with discrimination on the basis of sexual orientation and marital status.[61]

J. SECTION 15(2)

Section 15(2) of the *Charter* has received little judicial notice to date, and it is unclear how it will be interpreted. Some argue that it was included in the *Charter* to prevent claims of "reverse discrimination" by more privileged groups in our society, ensuring that Canadian courts did not emulate the hostility of the American Supreme Court to programs that accord preferences to members of disadvantaged groups.[62] For example, it could protect a program designed to compensate for the effects of past discrimination (as in the case of Aboriginal peoples)[63] Specific measures designed to break down barriers to the participation of certain groups may be justified, for instance, by creating role models for a group or by ensuring that a critical mass of their numbers is present in an institution so as to break down stereotypical attitudes.[64] Others argue that section 15(2) should not be an automatic defence to all affirmative-action programs but should merely signal that preferential treatment can sometimes be justified. There may still be room for judicial scrutiny of such special programs to determine that the group benefited is one that has suffered disadvantage and that the means chosen to redress this disadvantage do not put an undue burden on those excluded.[65]

---

60   *Eaton*, above note 38 at 271.
61   For example, *M. v. H.* (1997), 25 R.F.L. (4th) 116 (Ont. C.A.), in which a majority of the Ontario Court of Appeal found the provisions of the family-support regime unconstitutional in their treatment of lesbian couples.
62   *Roberts v. Ontario* (1994), 117 D.L.R. (4th) 297 (Ont. C.A.).
63   *Athabasca Tribal Council v. Amoco Canada Petroleum Co.*, [1981] 1 S.C.R. 699, 124 D.L.R. (3d) 1.
64   *Canadian National Railway v. Canada (Human Rights Commission)*, [1987] 1 S.C.R. 1114, 40 D.L.R. (4th) 193.
65   See C. Sheppard, *Study Paper on Litigating and the Relationship between Equity and Equality* (Toronto: Ontario Law Reform Commission, 1993); *Apsit v. Manitoba (Human Rights Commission)* (1985), 37 Man. R. (2d) 50, 23 D.L.R. (4th) 277 (Q.B.), additional reasons at [1988] 1 W.W.R. 629, reversed in part (1988), [1989] 1 W.W.R. 481 (C.A.); A. Drumbl & J. Craig, "Affirmative Action in Question: A Coherent Theory for Section 15(2)" (1997) 4 Rev. Const. Stud. 124.

K. CONCLUSION

Equality is a powerful yet illusive concept. It is apparent from this review that, while certain broad lines have been drawn by the courts in the definition of the meaning of equality under the *Charter*, many questions remain. In one important respect, the Supreme Court has given section 15 a restricted meaning, requiring a claimant to show discrimination on a prohibited or analogous ground and thereby precluding wholesale review of all laws that create burdens or confer benefits on some but not others. This has disappointed those who saw section 15 as a charter of social rights capable of remedying injustice on a more general scale. However, it coincides with the Supreme Court's general inclination under the *Charter* to defer to legislative judgment on questions of distributive justice. It may be seen as consistent with the Court's cautious approach to the interpretation of freedom of association and "life, liberty and security of the person" in section 7 and its refusal to recognize property rights as protected under the *Charter*.

On the other hand, where discrimination has been shown on a prohibited or analogous ground, the Court has adopted a rigorous approach designed to ensure that the promise of equality will be respected. The Court has insisted that the equality guarantee mandates substantive review, avoiding a formalistic approach that would fail to take into account social reality. The Court has rejected the idea that a discriminatory intention must be shown, and it has proved willing to find a denial of the guarantee from circumstances of actual disadvantage.

Section 15 has yielded significant gains for gays and lesbians, in this area, where the most recent decision of the Supreme Court can be applauded for leading public opinion. Until recently, the lot of the disabled had not been significantly improved by virtue of section 15, but the Supreme Court has now signalled a willingness to impose significant burdens on governments to ensure access to health services.[66] While women's groups were among the most active in lobbying for a powerful equality guarantee, the gains to women from equality litigation have been modest. On the other hand, there can be little doubt that general public acceptance of and respect for gender equality has been enhanced by the *Charter*.

It is also apparent, however, that the Supreme Court continues to struggle with important aspects of the equality guarantee and that a full *Charter* picture of equality is yet to be drawn. The Court has found itself

---

66   *Eldridge*, above note 39.

seriously divided on a significant element of section 15 analysis. As with section 7, another broadly worded guarantee, it is perhaps unrealistic to expect the Court to deliver sweeping and definitive answers at a stroke. The judicial method is inherently more gradual and incremental. The Court can deal with the issues only in the context of specific cases as they arise. Moreover, the precise implementation of a fundamental concept such as equality is bound to evolve with changing social conditions and attitudes.

FURTHER READINGS

BLACK, W., & L.A. SMITH, "The Equality Rights" in G.A. Beaudoin & E. Mendes, eds., *The Canadian Charter of Rights and Freedoms*, 3d ed. (Toronto: Carswell, 1996)

GIBSON, D., *The Law of the Charter: Equality Rights* (Toronto: Carswell, 1990)

JACKMAN, M., "Constitutional Contact with the Disparities in the World: Poverty as a Prohibited Ground of Discrimination under the Canadian *Charter* and Human Rights Law" (1994) 2 Rev. Const. Stud. 76

LEPOFSKY, M.D., "A Report Card on the Charter's Guarantee of Equality to Persons with Disabilities after 10 Years — What Progress? What Prospects? (1997) 7 N.J.C.L. 263

SHEPPARD, C., *Study Paper on Litigating and the Relationship between Equity and Equality* (Toronto: Ontario Law Reform Commission, 1993)

CHAPTER 16

LANGUAGE RIGHTS

The appropriate status of the French and English languages has been an ongoing source of debate throughout Canadian history, both in the political and in the legal sphere. For some, particularly French-speaking Quebeckers, Canada is a compact of two founding nations, French and English. This implies a special place for the English and French languages of these historic communities. Many other Canadians, while conceding the historic importance of French and English, insist on recognition for other communities and forms of identity as well. These debates have affected the place of language in the constitution and the legal interpretation afforded constitutional guarantees.

A. THE NATURE OF LANGUAGE RIGHTS

There is a range of options to protect ethnic communities, including those who share a common language. One possibility is to provide a degree of self-government for an ethnic or language community, giving it the powers to preserve and promote a distinct identity. In a federation, a language group may form the majority in a province while representing a minority in the country as a whole. Another option is to provide specific rights that permit groups to use their language or express their culture. Examples are separate-school rights, access to broadcasting outlets, or guarantees that government services will be provided in a certain language. Yet another device is protection against discrimination on the basis of language or culture, preventing the majority from disadvantaging the minority because of language or cultural practice. As will be seen, all of these options have been resorted to in the Canadian constitution.

The territorial principle, adopted in countries such as Belgium and Switzerland, leaves the determination of language rights to each province or territorial unit. The result is linguistic uniformity in most territorial units. While Canada's federal structure, with a francophone majority in Quebec and anglophone majorities in the other provinces, contains elements of the territorial principle, important elements of the Canadian constitution see language as an element of the individual's personality which is to be respected wherever one lives in Canada. Even though francophones are a small minority in most provinces, and anglophones are a minority in Quebec, both groups are given constitutional rights that limit the ability of provinces to impose linguistic uniformity.

Language rights in Canada are distinctive because they are "positive" in nature. They entitle an individual to certain action on the part of government, such as funding for schools, printing of bilingual statutes, and service from government offices in one's chosen official language. They are different from most other rights in the *Charter*, which constrain government from acting but do not require positive action. For example, the guarantee of freedom of expression does not, as a general rule, require the government to ensure equality of access to funds to ensure that one's voice is heard.[1]

B. THE *CONSTITUTION ACT, 1867*

The original Confederation bargain in 1867 was shaped very much by Canadian dualism — that is, by the desires and needs of French- and English-speaking communities to express and protect their identities. For the French-speaking population of Quebec, federalism was the primary method to protect its interests. Federalism ensured that the French-speaking majority in that province would have the powers necessary for cultural preservation — notably, education and civil law.

"Language" was not expressly mentioned as a subject of either federal or provincial legislative jurisdiction in sections 91 and 92 of the *Constitution Act, 1867*, the sections that distribute legislative powers between federal and provincial governments. Accordingly, it is treated as an

---

1   *Native Women's Association of Canada* v. *Canada*, [1994] 3 S.C.R. 627, 119 D.L.R. (4th) 224.

"ancillary" matter — that is, either government can legislate with respect to language when acting within other assigned legislative fields. For example, Parliament has enacted the *Official Languages Act*, which regulates bilingualism in the federal public service.[2] Similarly, Quebec has the authority to require that French be used as the language of business in the province and to regulate the use of English in signs (although these laws are now subject to the *Charter* rights described below).[3]

In addition, the *Constitution Act, 1867*, contained limited positive rights protecting the use of the French and English languages in certain federal and Quebec institutions. Section 133 provides as follows:

> Either the English or French Language may be used by any Person in the Debates of the Houses of Parliament of Canada and of the House of the Legislature of Quebec; and both those Languages shall be used in the respective Records and Journals of those Houses; and either of those Languages may be used by any Person in any Pleading or Process issuing from any Court of Canada established under this Act, and in or from all or any of the Courts of Quebec.

This provision was duplicated in section 23 of the *Manitoba Act* upon Manitoba entering Confederation in 1870,[4] while the provinces of Saskatchewan and Alberta were required to comply with similar obligations by section 110 of the *North-West Territories Act*.[5] Those obligations continued after they became provinces in 1905 because of sections 16(1) of their constituent Acts.[6] However, these language rights were not entrenched and could be changed by legislation, and both provinces have since done so.[7]

The Supreme Court has held that these provisions provide a floor of guaranteed rights but that this does not prevent Parliament or the provincial legislatures from expanding on them.[8] Equally, however, prior to the *Charter*, section 133 did not prevent provinces from restricting the use of minority languages in areas other than those mentioned in the constitution. For example, the courts upheld the right of Ontario to

---

2   R.S.C. 1985, c. O-3. The constitutionality of this Act was determined in *Jones* v. *New Brunswick (A.G.)*, [1975] 2 S.C.R. 182, 45 D.L.R. (3d) 583 [*Jones*].

3   *Devine* v. *Quebec (A.G.)*, [1988] 2 S.C.R. 790, 55 D.L.R. (4th) 641.

4   *Manitoba Act, 1870*, S.C. 1870, c. 3, s. 23.

5   R.S.C. 1886, c. 50, s. 110, as amended S.C. 1891, c. 22, s. 18.

6   *Saskatchewan Act*, S.C. 1905, c. 42.

7   The state of language rights in these provinces was discussed by the Supreme Court of Canada in *R.* v. *Mercure*, [1988] 1 S.C.R., 48 D.L.R. (4th) 1.

8   See *Jones*, above note 2.

abolish French-language instruction in Roman Catholic separate schools in 1912,[9] holding that language of instruction was not protected as an aspect of the denominational school rights conferred by section 93 of the *Constitution Act, 1867.*

C. LANGUAGE RIGHTS AND THE *CHARTER*

With the *Charter of Rights* came new protection for language rights. The language provisions in sections 16 to 23 of the *Charter* were a key component of the 1982 constitutional amendments. The government of Prime Minister Pierre Trudeau saw the *Charter* as a whole, and the language rights in particular, as a way to strengthen Canadians' attachment to their country.[10] The language rights expanded on section 133 of the 1867 constitution, affirming in section 16 that French and English are the two official languages of Canada. To emphasize their importance, sections 16 through 23 were not made subject to the legislative override in section 33 of the *Charter*. The clear message was that French and English minority-language communities were to be supported and fostered throughout the country.

After declaring that English and French are the official languages of Canada and New Brunswick, section 16(1) goes on to say that these languages have "equality of status and equal rights and privileges as to their use in all institutions of the Parliament and government of Canada," while section 16(2) makes a similar statement with respect to the institutions of the legislature and government of New Brunswick.[11]

Sections 17 to 20 affirm and expand on the former section 133. Section 17 guarantees the right to use English or French in debates and other proceedings of Parliament and the New Brunswick legislature, while section 18 guarantees that the statutes, records, and journals of the federal Parliament and the New Brunswick legislature must be in both languages and that both versions are of equal legal authority. Section 19 guarantees the right to use either French or English in pleadings or processes of federally established courts and those of New Brunswick. Finally, section 20 gives a right for the public to communicate in

---

9   This was upheld in *Ottawa Roman Catholic Separate School Board* v. *Mackell,* [1917] A.C. 62, 32 D.L.R. 1 (P.C.) and *Ottawa Roman Catholic Separate School Board* v. *Ottawa (City)*, [1917] A.C. 76, 32 D.L.R. 10 (P.C.).

10 P.H. Russell, "The Political Purposes of the *Canadian Charter of Rights and Freedoms*" (1983) 61 Can. Bar Rev. 30.

11 The term "Canada" here refers to the federal level of government.

either language with the head or central office of an institution of the Parliament or government of Canada or any office of an institution of New Brunswick's government or legislature. An individual has a right to communicate with other Canadian government offices if there is "significant demand for communications with and services from that office" in French or English, or "due to the nature of the office, it is reasonable that communications with and services from that office" be available in both languages.

In addition to these "institutional bilingualism" provisions, there is a right to publicly funded minority-language education in section 23. This section gives a right to education in the minority language of a province to two groups of children: those of Canadian citizens whose first language learned is that of the French or English minority in the province in which they reside,[12] and children of citizens educated in primary school in Canada in the language of the minority of the province in which they reside. Where some children of a family are receiving education in the minority-language because of this section, all children in the family have the same entitlement. This right is qualified by the requirement that the numbers of children warrant receiving public funding for minority-language instruction (section 23(3)(a)). Where the number warrants, the right extends to instruction in minority-language educational facilities (section 23(3)(a)).

D. FREEDOM OF EXPRESSION AND LANGUAGE

In *Ford*, the Supreme Court of Canada held that the guarantee of freedom of expression in section 2(b) includes the right to speak in the language of one's choice.[13] Accordingly, section 2(b) provides a check on government action designed to restrict the use of certain languages or to compel expression in a particular language. In effect, this interpretation of section 2(b) protects linguistic minorities against state discrimination and demands tolerance with respect to the use of their languages. Unlike the specific language rights of sections 16 to 23, section 2(b) protects all languages.

---

12 This clause is not in force in Quebec because of s. 59 of the *Constitution Act, 1982*. Section 59 responds to Quebec concerns about immigrants' refusal to assimilate into the francophone community.

13 *Ford* v. *Quebec (A.G.)*, [1988] 2 S.C.R. 712, 54 D.L.R. (4th) 577 [*Ford*], discussed in greater detail in chapter 9, "Freedom of Expression."

Ford, as we have seen, arose out of a challenge to Quebec's language legislation prohibiting the use of any language other than French on commercial signs or firm names. The Court rejected the argument that the constitution's specific language rights were a complete code that belied constitutional protection for any other languages. Instead, the Court quoted from an earlier decision involving the Manitoba language guarantees, where it had stated:

> The importance of language rights is grounded in the essential role that language plays in human existence, development and dignity. It is through language that we are able to form concepts; to structure and order the world around us. Language bridges the gap between isolation and community, allowing humans to delineate the rights and duties they hold in respect of one another, and thus to live in society.[14]

The Court went on to say:

> Language is so intimately related to the form and content of expression that there cannot be true freedom of expression by means of language if one is prohibited from using the language of one's choice. Language is not merely a means or medium of expression; it colours the content and meaning of expression.[15]

Language is a central way in which a group expresses its cultural identity and individuals express their personal identity. It follows that laws restricting the use of one's language will infringe section 2(b) and have to be justified under section 1.

It was acknowledged that Quebec had a pressing and substantial objective in enacting the legislation, given the vulnerable position of French in Quebec because of declining birth rates among francophones, a tendency for new immigrants to gravitate to the anglophone community in Quebec, and a predominance of English in the more important economic sectors. The Court accepted that the attempt to assure Quebeckers that the "visage linguistique" of Quebec reflected the predominance of French was a serious and legitimate objective. However, the Court was not satisfied that the achievement of this objective required the suppression of all other languages on public signs and in firm names. Rather, the judges concluded that a law requiring the predomi-

---

14   *Reference Re Language Rights under s. 23 of Manitoba Act, 1870 and s. 133 of Constitution Act, 1867*, [1985] 1 S.C.R. 721, (*sub nom Reference Re Manitoba Language Rights*) 19 D.L.R. (4th) 1 at 19 [*Reference Re Manitoba Language Rights*].

15   Above note 13 at 604 (D.L.R.).

nance of French on a sign, while still allowing other communities to use their language, would be more consistent with *Charter* rights.

Although the language rights guaranteed by sections 16 to 23 are not subject to the override, the "signs" law was found to violate freedom of expression. As described in chapter 5, the aftermath was that the Quebec government invoked section 33 of the *Charter* in new legislation limiting the use of English in public signs. This law was then the subject of a successful complaint to the United Nations Human Rights Committee under the *International Covenant on Civil and Political Rights*. The Committee's reasons echo those of the Supreme Court in *Ford*, stating that the law was an unreasonable limitation on freedom of expression.[16]

E. INTERPRETING LANGUAGE RIGHTS

1) Institutional Bilingualism

The Supreme Court has not been entirely consistent in its approach to the interpretation of language rights. In early cases involving section 133 of the *Constitution Act, 1867*, the Court took an expansive view. In *Blaikie (No. 1)*,[17] the Court held that, in deciding which institutions were covered by section 133, the words of the constitution should be given a progressive interpretation, taking into account the changing nature of courts and government since 1867. Although section 133 required that "laws" be in both French and English, the Court found that the guarantee should encompass regulations and delegated legislation, not just statutes, given the proliferation of this type of law making today. In addition, the term "courts" was interpreted to include adjudicative tribunals, like labour relations boards or human rights tribunals, since many legal disputes are now determined by these bodies.

This generous view of language rights was evident again in *Reference Re Manitoba Language Rights*.[18] In an earlier decision, *Manitoba (A.G.)* v.

---

16   *Ballantyne, Davidson & McIntyre* v. *Canada*, Communications Nos. 359/1989 and 385/1989, UN Doc. CCPR/C/47/D/359/1989 and 385/1989/Rev. 1 (1993). In para. 11.4, the Committee stated: "A State may choose one or more official languages, but it may not exclude, outside the spheres of public life, the freedom to express oneself in a language of one's choice."

17   *Quebec (A.G.)* v. *Blaikie (No. 1)*, [1979] 2 S.C.R. 1016, 101 D.L.R. (3d) 394. In *Quebec (A.G.)* v. *Blaikie (No. 2)*, [1981] 1 S.C.R. 312, 123 D.L.R. (3d) 15, the Court expanded on the earlier holding. A more recent application of these cases is found in *Sinclair* v. *Quebec (A.G.)*, [1992] 1 S.C.R. 579, 89 D.L.R. (4th) 500.

18   Above note 14.

Forest, the Court had found that legislation enacted by Manitoba in 1890 purporting to repeal the bilingualism requirement in section 23 of the *Manitoba Act, 1870*, was unconstitutional.[19] A reference was then launched to determine the effect of almost one hundred years of non-compliance with section 23. The Court held that the requirement was mandatory, so that all laws passed only in English were invalid. If the Court had stopped here, a large component of Manitoba law would have been invalid and the legislature would have been improperly elected under an English-only law. Recognizing the need to prevent a "legislative vacuum" and to preserve the rule of law, the Supreme Court suspended the effect of its declaration of invalidity for a period that allowed Manitoba to translate and re-enact its laws — this time, in both official languages.

In contrast, the Supreme Court seemed much less willing to embrace an expansive view of language rights in relation to court proceedings. In cases decided under both section 133 of the *Constitution Act, 1867*, and section 19(2) of the *Charter*, a majority of the Court accepted the argument that the right to use French or English in proceedings of the courts entitles an individual to no more than that — a right to speak in either language. The individual cannot demand that the Court proceedings be conducted in the language of his or her choice, nor that the judge understand that language. The right to use French or English in court proceedings extended not only to the litigant but also to the court staff and the judges. In *MacDonald* v. *Montreal (City)*,[20] the use of a unilingual French summons was found to be acceptable, while in *Société des Acadiens*, the Court held that a francophone litigant in New Brunswick could not demand a French-speaking judge.[21] In both cases, Beetz J., writing for the majority, emphasized that language rights were different from most others in the *Charter*. In his view, they were the result of a historic political compromise and should be interpreted more narrowly, with an attitude of judicial restraint.[22] In contrast, legal rights were described as "seminal in nature because they are rooted in principle."[23] It should be noted, however, that in *Société des Acadiens*, Beetz J. emphasized that the rules of natural justice or procedural fairness would require that any individual who did not understand proceedings be given access to an interpreter.

---

19   (1979), 101 D.L.R. (3d) 385.
20   [1986] 1 S.C.R. 460 at 483–84, 27 D.L.R. (4th) 321.
21   *Société des Acadiens du Nouveau-Brunswick* v. *Association of Parents for Fairness in Education*, [1986] 1 S.C.R. 549, 27 D.L.R. (4th) 406 [*Société des Acadiens*].
22   Above note 20 at 496–97 (S.C.R.).
23   Above note 21 at 578 (S.C.R.).

In contrast, the dissenting reasons of Dickson C.J.C. and Wilson J. emphasized that the right to use one's language included the notion of being understood. Neither stated definitively what this would mean. Dickson C.J.C. stated that this might encompass the use of interpreters or simultaneous translation, although on the facts of the case it had not been shown that the judges did not understand French. Wilson J. felt that section 19(2) of the *Charter* was evolving towards a requirement of a bilingual judiciary.

2) Minority-Language Education Rights

Despite the restrictive treatment of language rights in relation to the courts, minority-language education rights in section 23 of the Charter have been generously interpreted. While subsequent cases have paid lip-service to Beetz J.'s views on the nature of language rights, the Court still managed to give section 23 a creative interpretation. The first major section 23 case to come before the Supreme Court was *Mahé* from Alberta, which examined the degree to which minority-language groups could demand management and control of their education system.[24] Dickson C.J.C., writing for the Court, emphasized that the minority-language education guarantee had two purposes. First, education in one's language provides an important way to preserve and promote the minority group's language and culture. As well, educational institutions can provide a centre for the community, which helps promote the minority culture. Dickson C.J.C. also noted the strong remedial component to section 23: the section was designed to protect the French and English minorities from assimilation and to give recognition and encouragement to the two official language groups in Canada.[25] In sum, section 23 represented, for him, the "linchpin in this nation's commitment to the values of bilingualism and biculturalism."[26]

In interpreting the scope of section 23(3), Dickson C.J.C. refused to set out a numerical formula whereby a certain number of students would entitle a group to minority-language *instruction* while a larger number would ensure that this instruction then be given in separate educational

---

24   *Mahé v. Alberta*, [1990] 1 S.C.R. 342, 68 D.L.R. (4th) 69 [*Mahé*]. An earlier case from Quebec, *Quebec (A.G.) v. Quebec Association of Protestant School Boards*, [1984] 2 S.C.R. 66, 10 D.L.R. (4th) 321 had struck down Quebec's attempts to narrow the group who could assert s. 23 rights. The Court described this as an attempt to abrogate s. 23 that could not be characterized as a "reasonable limitation" on rights under s. 1.

25   *Mahé*, above note 24 at 362–63 (S.C.R.).

26   *Ibid.* at 350 (S.C.R.).

facilities. Rather, he concluded that the section imposed a "sliding scale requirement": "[S]ection 23 guarantees whatever type and level of rights and services is appropriate in order to provide minority language instruction for the particular number of students involved."[27]

With respect to section 23(3)(b) and the guarantee of separate educational facilities, Dickson C.J.C. concluded that this mandated a measure of management and control for the minority group. In some cases, this would require the establishment of an independent minority-language school board; in other cases, guaranteed representation and certain exclusive authority within the majority board would be sufficient.[28] In deciding what level of service is required, a province should consider actual and potential numbers of students.

In *Mahé* and in subsequent cases, the courts had to confront the question of how closely involved judges should become in the design and management of school facilities. To date, the courts have acted in a restrained manner, preferring to state principles and leave implementation to the appropriate authorities. This sets up a dialogue between legislatures and the courts as to the appropriate application of the principles established in particular situations.[29] Only over time will it become clear as to the way in which section 23 will operate in various settings throughout the country.

F. CONCLUSION

Language continues to be an issue, at least indirectly, in the discussions on constitutional reform which have occurred over the last decade. While there has been no proposal for explicit change to language rights or legislative powers concerning language rights, in both the 1987 Meech Lake Accord and the 1992 Charlottetown Accord a clause was proposed that would recognize Quebec as a "distinct society." In each case, this clause was part of a larger provision that would be used in interpreting the constitution.

Some feared that this would result in new powers for Quebec — for example, tipping the balance to allow Quebec to win in a case like *Ford*, the signs case described earlier. Others argued that this clause only echoed what the Supreme Court had acknowledged in *Ford* — that Quebec, the

---

27   *Ibid.* at 366 (S.C.R.).

28   *Ibid.* at 371–73 (S.C.R.). Further discussion of s. 23 is found in *Reference Re Public Schools Act (Manitoba) s. 79(3), (4) and (7)*, [1993] 1 S.C.R. 839, 100 D.L.R. (4th) 723.

29   This approach is further discussed in chapter 17, "Remedies."

home of a French-speaking minority in North America, might justifiably act to protect the French language, but not through the suppression of other languages.[30]

While the proposals were never entrenched in the constitution, the federal Parliament has since passed a resolution recognizing Quebec as a distinct society and encouraged all government actors to be guided by this fact. The 1997 "Calgary Declaration" of the premiers of all provinces except Quebec calls for recognition of Quebec as a "unique society." It remains to be seen whether these efforts to confer constitutional recognition on Quebec's important role to preserve and enhance the French fact in North America will come to fruition.

FURTHER READINGS

BASTARACHE, M., ed., *Language Rights in Canada* (Montreal: Yvon Blais, 1987)

GREEN, L.C., & D. RÉAUME, "Second-Class Rights? Principle and Compromise in the Charter" (1990) 13 Dal. L.J. 565

MAGNET, J.E., *Official Languages of Canada* (Cowansville, PQ: Yvon Blais, 1995)

RÉAUME, D., & L.C. GREEN, "Education and Linguistic Security in the Charter" (1989) 34 McGill L.J. 777

SCHNEIDERMAN, D., ed., *Language and the State: The Law and Politics of Identity* (Cowansville, PQ: Yvon Blais, 1991)

---

30 For discussion, see K. Swinton, "Federalism, the Charter, and the Courts: Rethinking Constitutional Dialogue in Canada" in K.E. Swinton, S. Ostry, et al, eds., *Rethinking Federalism: Citizens, Markets, and Governments in a Changing World* (Vancouver: U.B.C. Press, 1995).

CHAPTER 17

REMEDIES

One of the most significant guarantees in the *Charter of Rights and Freedoms* is that of an effective remedy where a right has been violated. Section 24 of the *Charter* provides:

> 24 (1) Anyone whose rights or freedoms, as guaranteed by this *Charter*, have been infringed or denied may apply to a court of competent jurisdiction to obtain such remedy as the court considers appropriate and just in the circumstances.

> (2) Where, in proceedings under subsection (1), a court concludes that evidence was obtained in a manner that infringed or denied any rights or freedoms guaranteed by this *Charter*, the evidence shall be excluded if it is established that, having regard to all the circumstances, the admission of it in the proceedings would bring the administration of justice into disrepute.

As noted in chapters 3 and 4, the first stage in any *Charter* case is the consideration of whether a right or freedom has been infringed or denied. If the court finds that there has been a *Charter* violation, it then passes to the second stage to consider whether the violation can be justified as a reasonable limit under section 1. If a violation cannot be justified, the court must then decide what practical measures should be taken in view of the infringement. It has long been a principle of our law that there can be no right without an effective remedy. A remedy is the operative element of a court's order which translates the right into concrete form. There are a variety of possible remedial options. Section 24(1) assures the individual whose rights have been violated that he or she will be given "such remedy as the court considers appropriate and just in the circumstances." The remedies of stay of proceeding and exclusion of evidence under section 24(2) in criminal cases has been considered in chapter 14. This chapter will review remedies available under section 24(1).

A. DECLARATORY RELIEF

In some cases, the rights claimant may seek no more than a declaration from the court of the *Charter* right at issue. In the common law tradition, courts tend to avoid making hollow pronouncements of law removed from any concrete order. There is, however, a well-established jurisdiction to award declarations of right in appropriate cases. In constitutional law, the declaration has proved to be an important remedy because of its flexibility. By declaring the right and going no further, the court defines the respective legal rights and obligations of the parties but leaves to them the task of implementing the demands of the constitution. From an institutional perspective, it may not be desirable for the court to become too involved in the details of implementation unless absolutely necessary.

Litigation involving minority-language education rights serves as an example of the effective use of the remedy of declaration. As seen in chapter 16, section 23 of the *Charter* guarantees parents the right to have their children educated in English or French in certain circumstances. While the courts are able to determine when section 23 rights arise, it is quite another matter to determine the institutional arrangements appropriate to fulfil those rights. The demands of the *Charter* will be one important consideration in the design of a minority-language education facility, but there will be many other matters to be taken into account that have nothing to do with constitutional law. Furthermore, there may be a variety of ways to design a school system that respects the demands of section 23. Courts and judges are not experts in schools or education. Courts do not have the competence to raise resources or allocate public funds among competing claims and demands. In view of this, it may be in the public interest as well as in the interest of the litigants for the court simply to declare the right and leave it to the litigants and the appropriate public authorities to work out the practical arrangements. In *Mahé* v. *Alberta*,[1] the Supreme Court of Canada upheld the section 23 claim of a group of French-speaking parents and granted a

---

1   [1990] 1 S.C.R. 342, 68 D.L.R. (4th) 69.

declaration of their rights but stopped short of determining the details of school administration. Dickson C.J.C. explained:

> . . . I think it best if the court restricts itself in this appeal to making a declaration in respect of the concrete rights which are due to the minority language parents in Edmonton under s. 23. Such a declaration will ensure that the appellant's rights are realized while, at the same time, leaving the government with the flexibility necessary to fashion a response which is suited to the circumstances . . . [T]he government should have the widest possible discretion in selecting the institutional means by which its s. 23 obligations are to be met; the courts should be loath to interfere and impose what will be necessarily procrustean standards, unless that discretion is not exercised at all, or is exercised in such a way as to deny a constitutional right.[2]

We will return below, under the heading "Injunctions," to the question of the appropriate remedial response should the government fail to implement the rights so declared.

B. DAMAGES

In ordinary civil litigation, the most common remedy is damages, a money award designed to compensate the injured party for the wrong suffered. The aim of compensatory damages is, to the extent possible, to put the innocent party in the position he or she would have been in but for the wrong. A commercial case may lend itself readily to monetary assessment of the wrong, but in other cases damages are a less than perfect remedy. It can be extremely difficult to measure in money terms the amount appropriate to compensate the plaintiff for physical injuries or for damage to reputation, dignity, or privacy. Translating into money the extent of the injury amounts to little more than sophisticated guesswork. In many cases, the damage suffered as a result of a *Charter* violation will fall into this intangible category. The rights and freedoms guaranteed by the *Charter* are abstract and intangible and thus assessment of the extent of the injury in monetary terms will often be difficult.

On the other hand, there seems no reason in principle why compensatory damages should not be available where the injured party can establish a loss, capable of measurement in money terms, that was caused by the *Charter* breach.[3] In a few cases, damages have been

---

2   *Ibid.* at 393 (S.C.R.).
3   See the statement of Lamer C.J.C. in *R. v. Delaronde* (1997), 115 C.C.C. (3d) 355 at 371.

awarded by the courts for *Charter* violations, typically in situations where the wrong is closely analogous to a recognized common law wrong such as assault or false imprisonment.[4]

Some scholars argue that damages should be available in a broad range of cases to remedy *Charter* breaches.[5] It has been suggested that damages should be used as a means of controlling or disciplining inappropriate behaviour. There are, however, a number of hurdles in the way. Most *Charter* claims are advanced in criminal proceedings, and a criminal court lacks jurisdiction to make a damages award.[6] The result is that a separate civil proceeding is required. In civil proceedings, compensatory damages ordinarily must be proved to have been directly caused by the wrong. Fault must be brought home to an individual or organization capable of being sued. While the courts have removed the protection of common law immunity applicable to certain public officials, including crown prosecutors, it may still be necessary to prove malice in order to succeed.[7]

In certain cases, punitive damages are available in civil proceedings. An award of punitive damages serves to sanction wrongful behaviour and the amount awarded serves, in effect, as a penalty or fine rather than as an attempt to compensate. In a few cases, judges have found it appropriate to award punitive damages in addition to compensatory damages. The Quebec courts have made significant punitive damage awards under the Quebec *Charter of Human Rights and Freedoms*. In *Patenaude* v. *Roy*,[8] the Quebec Court of Appeal found that there had been a "planned and deliberate violation of *Charter* provisions leading to a calamity."[9] A police SWAT team, acting without a warrant, had used a battering ram to enter a suspect's apartment and then fired twenty-five shots. The suspect died in the hail of bullets. The court awarded $100,000 in exemplary damages.[10]

Despite the infrequency of damages as *Charter* remedy, court orders in *Charter* cases often have significant financial consequences. A finding

---

4   See, for example, *Crossman v. R.* (1984), 9 D.L.R. (4th) 588 (F.C.T.D.); *Persaud v. Ottawa (City) Police* (1995), 130 D.L.R. (4th) 701 (Ont. Ct. (Gen. Div.)).

5   See especially, K.D. Cooper-Stephenson, *Charter Damage Claims* (Calgary: Carswell, 1990).

6   *R. v. Mills*, [1986] 1 S.C.R. 863, 29 D.L.R. (4th) 161.

7   *Nelles v. Ontario*, [1989] 2 S.C.R. 170, 60 D.L.R. (4th) 609.

8   (1994), 123 D.L.R. (4th) 78.

9   *Ibid.* at 91, Tyndale J.A.

10 See also *Québec v. Syndicat National des Employés de l'Hôpital St. Ferdinand* (1996), 138 D.L.R. (4th) 577 (S.C.C.) awarding $200,000 punitive damages to a group of mental patients denied essential services during an illegal strike.

that procedural guarantees must be respected may require the state to create expensive administrative measures.[11] Rulings in equality cases that a benefit has been wrongfully denied will require the state to spend money.[12] An injunction requiring the state to take, or refrain from, certain action may result in the expenditure of significant sums of public funds.[13] However, in each of these cases, while the remedy will have the effect of requiring money to be spent, the court is not quantifying the harm and requiring the wrongdoer to pay compensation to the party whose right was infringed.

C. INJUNCTIONS

An injunction is an order of the court requiring a party to act in a manner specified by the order. In its usual form, the injunction is a negative order that forbids a party from doing something that infringes the rights of another. It is also possible, however, for the court to give a mandatory injunction that requires the wrongdoer to take positive steps required to respect the rights of the other party. In ordinary civil litigation, injunctions are seen as exceptional remedies, available only where damages are an inadequate remedy for the wrong. In constitutional litigation, as just noted, damages are not commonly awarded, and while the courts still consider injunctions to be exceptional remedies, they may be given where appropriate to remedy a constitutional wrong.

The most difficult issue faced in connection with injunctions as a *Charter* remedy arises where the court is asked to grant an injunction that requires ongoing supervision or judicial involvement. *Charter* litigation often involves the operation of complex public institutions. Granting an injunction requiring that an institution take certain steps implies that the court is willing to enforce its order. If the public institution willingly complies, there is no problem. But what happens if there is resistance to the court's order?

American experience with constitutional injunctions is instructive. In litigation involving desegregation of schools and conditions of prisons, American judges evolved what came to be known as the "structural" or "civil rights" injunction whereby courts became involved in the detailed

---

11   *Singh v. Canada (Minister of Employment and Immigration)*, [1985] 1 S.C.R. 177, 17 D.L.R. (4th) 422.
12   See, for example, *Eldridge v. British Columbia (A.G.)* (1997), 3 S.C.R. 624, 151 D.L.R. (4th) 577, requiring hospitals to provide sign-language interpreters for deaf patients.
13   See below, under "Injunctions."

management of a scheme required to bring the school system or prison into compliance with the constitution.[14] American judges did not rush into making these orders; they did so only when their directives as to desegregation or improvement of prison conditions were not obeyed.

As noted in the earlier discussion of declarations as a *Charter* remedy, Canadian courts have been overtly conscious of the need for judicial restraint when making orders requiring complicated changes to public institutions. In the case of minority-language education rights, the courts' first step was to grant a declaratory order, stating the requirements of the *Charter*, but leaving the task of implementation to the school authorities. While it is to be hoped, and expected, that those authorities will comply, there is every indication that should they fail to do so, the courts will not sit idly by and fail to insist upon respect for the rights protected by the *Charter* as interpreted by the courts. In an Ontario case, a judge granted a mandatory order requiring a local school board "to provide the facilities and funding necessary to achieve . . . the provision of instruction and facilities equivalent to those provided to English language secondary schools."[15] In a subsequent ruling, the court reviewed the plans submitted by the school board to assess their adequacy.[16] More recently, another Ontario judge declared that a long-delayed school construction project for a minority-language facility should be exempted from a ministry moratorium on capital projects on the ground that "the open-ended delay in funding the construction . . . after seven years of temporary and inadequate facilities does constitute an infringement of the applicant's rights under s. 23 of the *Charter*."[17]

D. REMEDIES AFFECTING LEGISLATION

Section 24 of the *Charter* guarantees an appropriate remedy to an individual whose rights have been infringed. This provision must be read with the broader terms of section 52 of the *Constitution Act, 1982*, the "supremacy clause":

> 52. (1) The Constitution of Canada is the supreme law of Canada, and any law that is inconsistent with the provisions of the Constitution is, to the extent of the inconsistency, of no force or effect.

---

14   See O.M. Fiss, *The Civil Rights Injunction* (Bloomington: Indiana University Press, 1978).

15   *Marchand v. Simcoe County Board of Education* (1986), 29 D.L.R. (4th) 596.

16   *Marchand v. Simcoe County Board of Education* (1987), 44 D.L.R. (4th) 171.

17   *Conseil des écoles séparées catholique romaines de Dufferin & Peel v. Ontario (Ministre de l'education & de la formation)* (1996), 30 O.R. 681 at 685, Hawkins J.

The supremacy clause confirms the established doctrine of judicial review in Canadian constitutional law. The constitution is a law unlike all others, and its provisions, including the rights and freedoms guaranteed by the *Charter*, take priority over other laws. Should Parliament, a provincial legislature, or other law-making body enact a law which is inconsistent with the *Charter*, that law cannot stand.

The courts have evolved a variety of remedial techniques to carry out the mandate conferred by the supremacy clause and those techniques are considered below.

1) Striking Down

Before the *Charter*, the most common constitutional remedy for legislation that did not respect the limits of the constitution was for the court to strike down, or nullify, the law in its entirety. When the constitutionality of a statute is challenged on the ground that the enacting body, Parliament or a legislature, has transgressed the limits of its authority under the division of powers between the federal and provincial governments, the emphasis is upon the essential purpose, or the "pith and substance," of the law. While the effects of a law may serve as a measure of the law's purpose, the established constitutional doctrine in federalism review is to concentrate upon purpose rather than effects. The result is that the courts tend to regard federalism review as an "all or nothing" proposition. As a general rule, the law either falls in its entirety or it is saved in its entirety. If it is upheld, incidental effects it may have in an area of jurisdiction reserved to the other level of government will be tolerated.

By contrast, under the *Charter of Rights and Freedoms*, the focus tends to be upon unconstitutional effects. It is, after all, uncommon for Parliament or a legislature to enact a law that has as its purpose the violation of some fundamental right or freedom.[18] More frequent is the incidence of a law that, although valid in its purpose, has in its operation an unacceptable impact or effect upon some fundamental freedom. For this reason, the range of constitutional remedies is much more varied and innovative in *Charter* cases than in federalism review. While

---

18   Perhaps the leading example is the decision of the Supreme Court of Canada striking down the nineteenth-century Lord's Day Act, which required Sunday observance. This measure was found to be in violation of the guarantee of freedom of religion. See *R. v. Big M Drug Mart Ltd.*, [1985] 1 S.C.R. 295, 18 D.L.R. (4th) 321, discussed in detail in chapter 9.

nullification remains a frequently granted remedy in *Charter* cases, the courts have also developed a range of other remedies.[19]

2) Severance and Partial Invalidity

The most common alternative to striking down an entire statute is severance and a declaration of partial invalidity. This results in the nullification of only the unconstitutional portion of the law. This technique is readily employed where the specific provision challenged represents a discrete and identifiable measure that can be excised without altering the overall structure or operation of the law in which it is contained. It had been used frequently, for example, to strike down provisions of the *Criminal Code*. It has never been suggested that the entire *Criminal Code* should be nullified because one of its provisions violates the *Charter*.

At times, however, the remedy of severance may approach judicial drafting of a statute and become more controversial. For example, one case[20] dealt with a provision of the *Criminal Code*, discussed in chapter 15, making it an offence for a male person to have sexual relations with a female person under the age of fourteen. The offence included the words "whether or not he believes that she is fourteen years of age or more." The Court found that Parliament was entitled to prohibit this conduct but that, as drafted, the section imposed criminal liability on a no-fault basis contrary to section 7 of the *Charter*. Rather than strike out the entire section and thereby leave unprotected a class of persons deemed by Parliament to be in need of protection, the Court "rewrote" the section by striking out the words "whether or not he believes that she is fourteen years of age or more."[21]

The technique of severance has also been employed in the case of "under-inclusive" laws. An under-inclusive law is one that is valid so far as it goes but constitutionally defective because it does not go far enough. Severance only works where the law is drafted to apply generally but then, in a specific exception provision, improperly excludes certain individuals or groups from the benefit. Where the exclusion of those individuals or class of individuals is contrary to a constitutional provision, the courts have held that the specific exclusion may be severed, thus leaving intact the provision granting the benefit to the larger

---

19   The most comprehensive judicial discussion of these remedies is to be found in *Schachter v. Canada*, [1992] 2 S.C.R. 679, 93 D.L.R. (4th) 1 [*Schachter*].

20   *R. v. Hess*, [1990] 2 S.C.R. 906, 59 C.C.C. (3d) 161.

21   For another example, see *R. v. Lucas*, [1998] S.C.J. No. 28, excising certain words from the *Code's* defamatory libel section.

class. An example is the decision that a provision excluding those over sixty-five years of age from entitlement to unemployment-insurance benefits should be severed and struck down as discriminatory, leaving unqualified the general provision conferring the entitlement to the general class of unemployed workers.[22] Severance in cases of this kind has the effect of extending a benefit and is discussed in greater detail below under the heading "Reading In and Extension of Benefits."

3) Reading Down

An "over-inclusive" law is one that has, at its core, a constitutional purpose and application but that, as drafted, casts too wide a net and infringes constitutional rights in some situations. In such cases, the Canadian courts have frequently resorted to the technique known as "reading down" or giving the law a sufficiently narrow interpretation to bring it into line with the demands of the constitution. A good example is the Supreme Court's decision in a case challenging Canada's obscenity law.[23] This provision of the *Criminal Code* was drafted in extremely broad terms that, if applied literally, would have had an unconstitutional effect upon freedom of expression. While the Court did not explicitly describe its judgment as an exercise of the power to "read down" the law, that was the effect. The Court held that the provision had to be interpreted more narrowly so as to catch only certain forms of pornography. The Court's interpretation of the law reads like a statute, setting out point by point the elements to be established for a conviction and thereby significantly curtailing the reach of the general words enacted by Parliament. So interpreted, the obscenity law survived *Charter* scrutiny.

4) Reading In and Extension of Benefits

A more controversial interpretive technique is known as "reading in." Here, the problem is that the statute is under-inclusive and fails to extend its reach to those who have a constitutional claim to its protection. In such cases, nullification is unsatisfactory since it would deprive those who are otherwise entitled to the protection of the law and it would fail to satisfy the constitutional claim of those who ask to be included. On occasion, the courts have decided that the better course is to fill the gap by judicially "reading in" those who have a constitutional

---

22 *Canada (Employment and Immigration Commission)* v. *Tétreault-Gadoury*, [1991] 2 S.C.R. 22, 81 D.L.R. (4th) 358.

23 *R.* v. *Butler*, [1992] 1 S.C.R. 452, 89 D.L.R.(4th) 449, discussed in detail in chapter 9.

claim to the protection of the law, thereby adding to the list of those protected. Perhaps the best example is the decision of the Supreme Court of Canada dealing with the Alberta's *Individual's Rights Protection Act*, a general anti-discrimination statute, which prohibits discrimination on certain specific prohibited grounds.[24] Sexual orientation was not a prohibited ground. The Court found that the Act was constitutionally defective in failing to extend the benefit of anti-discrimination protection to gays and lesbians who were entitled to claim the benefit of the protection of the law pursuant to the *Charter* guarantee of equality. Rather than strike the law down and deprive the other specified groups of its protection, the Court found that the appropriate remedy was to add "sexual orientation" to the list of prohibited grounds.

Reading in is a controversial technique as the Court appears to be exercising a legislative role. However, given the alternative of striking down the law in its entirety, it seems inevitable that reading in should be permitted in certain situations. To strike down an entire statute because it fails to extend its benefit to a group that is relatively small in relation to the overall purpose and application of the statute would seem to constitute an even more serious interference by the judiciary with legislative choice.

Probably the most controversial examples of reading in involve statutes that extend monetary benefits. In a Nova Scotia case, a single father challenged a welfare statute that granted monetary benefits to single mothers.[25] He argued that failure to extend the same benefits to single fathers amounted to discrimination on grounds of sex contrary to the *Charter*'s section 15 guarantee of equal benefit of the law. A trial court in Nova Scotia agreed with his substantive claim but stumbled on the remedy. The Court found that it was not possible for a judge to order the legislature to expend the money and hence that the only available remedy was to strike down the entire statute, thereby depriving single mothers as well as single fathers of its benefit. The result was unsatisfactory to all. The single father would plainly be disappointed by the result. He did not get the benefit for himself and he had no interest in denying the benefit to single mothers. The legislature was clearly entitled to create the benefit scheme provided it acted with an even hand.

---

24 *Vriend v. Alberta*, [1998] S.C.J. No. 29. The Ontario Court of Appeal came to the same conclusion with respect to the *Canadian Human Rights Code* six years earlier: *Haig v. Canada* (1992), 94 D.L.R. (4th) 1 (Ont. C.A.).

25 *Phillips v. Nova Scotia (Social Assistance Appeal Board)* (1986), 27 D.L.R. (4th) 156 (N.S.S.C.T.D.), aff'd (1986), 34 D.L.R. (4th) 633 (C.A.) (*sub nom. Attorney General of Nova Scotia v. Phillips*).

In *Schachter*,[26] the Supreme Court of Canada carefully considered, in the context of extending benefits, the remedies of severance and reading in. The Court suggested that the Nova Scotia decision was wrong in that, where the class of persons to be added is relatively small in relation to those already in receipt of the benefit, a court may order that monetary benefits be extended to those not originally contemplated by the legislation.

Lamer C.J.C. outlined the approach courts are to take. The first element to be considered is the extent of the inconsistency with the *Charter*. The courts will not rewrite a law if the constitutional defect is fundamental. In such cases, the law should be struck down. It is only where the law is invalid because it fails to pass the minimal-impairment test that reading in or severance should be considered. Second, severance or reading in will be available only where the legislative objective is obvious, extending the reach of the law would be consistent with that objective, and extension would constitute a lesser interference with that objective than would striking down the law in its entirety. Third, these remedies are appropriate only where the legislature's choice of means is clear and severance or reading in would not intrude into the legislative domain. Particular care must be exercised where the remedy has budgetary effects. Remedies that are so substantial as to alter the legislative scheme are to be avoided.

5) Constitutional Exemptions

Another remedy, infrequently used but significant nonetheless, is granting a "constitutional exemption." Here, the law remains valid for all purposes save that a particular individual is exempted from its application. A good example is a decision of the Yukon Territory Court of Appeal in a case dealing with a Native person convicted of a weapons offence.[27] The *Criminal Code* provided that, upon conviction for the offence, there was a mandatory order prohibiting the convicted party from possessing a weapon for five years. The convicted Native person established that it was necessary for him to possess a firearm to maintain his traditional lifestyle and to provide for himself and his family. The court found that to deprive him of the right to possess a weapon would, in the circumstances, constitute cruel and unusual treatment, contrary to section 12 of the *Charter*. However, the Court also recognized that

---

26   Above note 19.
27   *R. v. Chief* (1989), 51 C.C.C. (3d) 265 (Y.T.C.A.).

the law was valid in almost every other conceivable application and that it would therefore be undesirable to strike it down. The Court's solution was to hold that the particular litigant before it was to be exempted from the application of the law. A similar result was reached in the *Latimer* case[28] where the accused was found to have killed his seriously disabled daughter because he thought she should not suffer more pain. Despite a prior ruling by the Saskatchewan Court of Appeal, following an earlier trial against the same individual for the same crime, rejecting the argument,[29] the trial judge found that on the specific facts before him, including a favourable recommendation from the jury, the mandatory penalty of life imprisonment without eligibility for parole for ten years would amount to cruel and unusual punishment.

The Supreme Court of Canada has yet to pronounce definitively on constitutional exemptions. The *Seaboyer* case[30] involved an attack on *Criminal Code* provisions precluding an accused charged with sexual assualt from cross-examining a complainant on prior sexual behaviour. Writing for the majority, McLachlin J. found that exempting those situations where the questioning was necessary to ensure the accused's right to a fair trial would be inappropriate, and that the section had to be struck down in its entirety. Granting an exemption would have the effect of giving the trial judge a discretion, the very result Parliament sought to avoid, and would also leave the law in an uncertain state. However, McLachlin J. specifically added that she did not foreclose the possibility that an exemption may be appropriate in some other case. Constitutional exemptions were also discussed in a dissenting judgment of the Supreme Court of Canada in *Rodriguez*, the assisted-suicide case mentioned in chapter 13.[31] There, a minority of the Court, led by Lamer C.J.C., found that the prohibition against assisted suicide did violate the constitutional rights of the terminally ill plaintiff. However, Lamer C.J.C. hesitated to strike down the entire statute and ruled that the appropriate remedy would be a constitutional exemption permitting this particular individual, or others like her, to have the benefit of an assisted suicide provided they could bring themselves within a narrowly defined set of criteria laid down in the judgment.

---

28   *R. v. Latimer* (1997), 121 C.C.C. 327 (Sask. Q.B.).
29   *R. v. Latimer* (1995), 99 C.C.C. (3d) 481 (Sask. C.A.).
30   *R. v. Seaboyer*, [1991], 2 S.C.R. 577, 83 D.L.R. (4th) 193.
31   *Rodriguez v. R.*, [1993] 3 S.C.R. 519, 107 D.L.R. (4th) 342.

6) Temporary Suspension of Invalidity

In certain situations, the Supreme Court of Canada has used the technique of temporary suspension of invalidity. In these cases, the Court has found that, although a challenged law is unconstitutional, the immediate nullification of that law could lead to chaos or a serious threat to public safety. To avoid chaos or serious public harm, the Court has delayed the implementation of its order of invalidity to afford Parliament or the legislature the opportunity to repair the constitutional deficiency.

The leading example is the decision of the Supreme Court of Canada in the *Reference Re Manitoba Language Rights*.[32] The Court held that the failure of the legislature of Manitoba to comply with a constitutional provision requiring it to enact all the laws of Manitoba in both English and French meant that all Manitoba legislation was invalid. Clearly, however, an immediate nullification of all the laws of Manitoba would lead to a situation of chaos, and the Court held that the overriding principle of the rule of law justified a temporary suspension of invalidity. The Court's order gave the legislature of Manitoba time to have its law translated and re-enacted in both languages.

Temporary suspension of invalidity has been resorted to in less dramatic circumstances as well. When the Supreme Court held that provisions of the *Criminal Code* providing for the detention of those found not guilty by reason of insanity were invalid, it held that the immediate release of such individuals, most of whom had escaped convictions for murder because of their mental disorders, would result in a serious threat to public safety. Accordingly, the Court held that the declaration of invalidity of the law should be suspended for a stated period of time to afford Parliament the opportunity to reconsider the matter and to enact a revised law in keeping with the requirements of the constitution.[33]

In *Schachter*,[34] the Supreme Court indicated another situation where the remedy of temporary suspension of invalidity may be employed. As already noted, there are cases where laws are constitutionally defective because they are under-inclusive. In some cases, that defect can be repaired by having the court add the excluded class by using the techniques of reading in or severance. However, where the case does not permit extending the law to those not included, and the law is to be

---

32   *Reference Re Language Rights under s. 23 of Manitoba Act, 1870 and s. 133 of Constitution Act, 1867*, [1985] 1 S.C.R. 721, 19 D.L.R. (4th) 1 [*Reference Re Manitoba Language Rights*].

33   *R. v. Swain*, [1991] 1 S.C.R. 933, 63 C.C.C. (3d) 481.

34   Above note 19 at 715–17 (S.C.R.).

struck down, *Schachter* suggests that the court may temporarily suspend the declaration of invalidity to alleviate the harshness of denying the benefit of the law to deserving persons. This gives the legislature a stated period of time to reconsider the scheme in light of the dictates of the constitution without defeating the operation of the valid portion of the law in the interim.

E. CONCLUSION

Some of the most difficult and controversial *Charter* issues concern remedies. Section 24 confers an express mandate on the courts to ensure that violations of *Charter* rights are remedied in an appropriate fashion. In determining remedial issues, the courts have drawn on existing principles but have also had to find new remedial techniques. As with other *Charter* issues, there is a delicate institutional balance to be struck. Remedial choice is governed in part by the need to ensure individuals an appropriate remedy and in part by consideration of the respective roles of courts and legislatures. In determining remedial measures to right particular wrongs, there is choice ranging from declaratory relief, which entails minimal judicial involvement, to injunctions, which may require ongoing judicial supervision. Similarly, with respect to the validity of legislation, the courts may strike down all or parts of a law, mandate affirmative changes to the law through reading in, and perhaps, in certain cases, leave the law in place but exempt individuals from its application. As with other areas of *Charter* jurisprudence, the Supreme Court has not hesitated to break new ground, but at the same time it has attempted to proceed in a relatively cautious, incremental manner, conscious of the limits of the judicial function and the need to respect the role and responsibilities of the democratically elected representatives of the people.

FURTHER READINGS

COOPER-STEPHENSON, K.D., *Charter Damage Claims* (Calgary: Carswell, 1990)

FITZGERALD, O.E., *Understanding Charter Remedies* (Scarborough, ON: Carswell, 1994)

ROACH, K., *Constitutional Remedies in Canada* (Aurora, ON: Canada Law Book, 1994)

CONCLUSION

The *Charter of Rights and Freedoms* is a fundamental and defining element of the modern Canadian state. While it draws upon certain aspects of our democratic and parliamentary tradition, by entrenching certain rights and freedoms as fundamental and by assigning an important law-making role to the courts, it also marks a break with the past. No longer are Parliament and the legislatures supreme.

We have suggested that this shift of institutional responsibility, subjecting the powers of elected bodies to review by the courts under the *Charter,* is supportive of Canada's traditional democratic values. Experience has shown that majorities, unchecked, may fail to respect the dignity of all individuals, tend to shut out annoying and unpopular views, and ignore or even make worse the plight of vulnerable minorities. The *Charter* protects the values of individual dignity, autonomy, and respect. These attributes of citizenship are essential to a healthy democracy and to free and open democratic debate. The *Charter* also protects the rights of vulnerable minorities and reflects the view that a healthy democracy cannot be defined in terms of crude majoritarianism. The *Charter* may be seen as Canada's commitment to the principle that the exercise of power by the many is conditional on respect for the rights of the few. The role of the *Charter,* we suggest, is to facilitate, not frustrate, democracy.

It is apparent that the difficult task of ensuring that *Charter* rights and freedoms are respected inevitably embroils the judiciary in difficult and contentious issues of public concern. The courts have been willing to exercise the power of judicial review with a certain vigour in many areas. Religious minorities have succeeded in attacking measures that required them to observe the religion of the majority. In some cases, freedom of expression has been defended against measures that limited open debate and dissemination of information. The right to "life, liberty and security of the person" has been found to impose significant constraints on the right of the state to criminalize abortion. It may be that the courts will extend the guarantee generally to protect matters of fundamental personal choice. The *Charter* has had a major impact in the area of criminal justice where judges have not hesitated to subject police powers to close scrutiny. Individual rights of privacy and bodily integrity and the rights to counsel and fair trial have been expanded significantly. The equality guarantee has required legislatures to reassess the manner in which minorities are treated. The Supreme Court has insisted upon close scrutiny of virtually all measures that discriminate on the grounds enumerated in section 15 or on analogous grounds, even where the denial of equality is not intended. This radical departure from the disappointing judicial record under the *Canadian Bill of Rights* has been significant in a number of cases. The guarantee of minority-language education rights has also been interpreted in a generous fashion to encourage a dialogue between the legislatures and rights claimants about the design of school systems.

On the other hand, there are areas where the courts have demonstrated a marked deference to legislative judgment. To date, the courts have been very unsympathetic to claims of pure economic rights and have refused to become embroiled in most distributional issues. The courts have refused to imply a right of property from the language of section 7 and have similarly rejected overtures to protect contract rights. The refusal to accord constitutional protection to the right of collective bargaining and the right to strike as aspects of freedom of association is consistent with this trend, reflecting the view that economic and social-policy questions are best left to the legislative arena. The refusal to permit the equality guarantee in section 15 to extend beyond discrimination on prohibited or analogous grounds is, we suggest, also consistent with this general pattern. An open-ended approach to equality would require the courts to review virtually every line drawn by legislation and would divert attention from, and perhaps dilute the protection accorded to, those groups that have been the subjects of particular disadvantage because of specified and analogous personal characteristics.

The Supreme Court's approach to determining acceptable limitations of *Charter* rights and freedoms under section 1 largely coincides with this pattern. The Supreme Court has not taken a uniform approach to section 1, and the level of scrutiny to which challenged legislation is subjected varies. The Court has seen section 1 as a recognition of the institutional role of Parliament and the legislatures to enhance and protect some of the same values that inform judicial review. Legislative initiatives to protect vulnerable groups have often been upheld when such initiatives have been challenged as violating the fundamental freedoms of more powerful interests in society. Similarly, the Court has given legislatures considerable latitude where broad questions of social or economic policy are involved.

After just sixteen years of *Charter* jurisprudence, certain broad outlines have been drawn, but we certainly do not yet have a fully completed picture. It is often suggested, both by *Charter* "believers" and by *Charter* "sceptics," that this reflects an inadequate and uncertain response from the Supreme Court. We suggest that an element of uncertainty is to be expected. First, a constitution is an expression of a society's most fundamental values. It is an enduring document that must allow our public institutions to address the issues of today but also offer the flexibility to meet the unknown challenges of the future. Definitive judicial pronouncements on every detail of the constitution or rigid adherence to what the words of the constitution may mean in one historical context could produce an institutional straightjacket inconsistent with this broader vision. The courts in the era of the *Charter* have quite appropriately remained faithful to the pre-*Charter* metaphor of the constitution as a "living tree" capable of growth and expansion within its natural limits. Second, there are inherent limits in the judicial process. The most obvious is that *Charter* issues are decided in the context of specific cases. The judicial method is necessarily responsive and incremental. While the Supreme Court has some control of the cases it hears through the leave-to-appeal process, it does not have the capacity to set its own agenda but rather must deal with the issues that the litigants bring before it.

Much can be accomplished through litigation, but the democratically elected representatives of the people retain primary responsibility for social and economic policy and for resolving most of the ills that beset our society. While the *Charter* assigns an important role to the courts, it is but one aspect of a constitution that speaks to all who exercise power in our society. We continue to have a strong parliamentary tradition that has always imposed a moral and political duty upon our elected representatives to respect fundamental rights and freedoms. The enhanced power of the courts under the *Charter* should be seen in this light. In this book, we have canvassed the way in which the *Charter* has altered the nature of public debate in Canada. We suggest that, on the whole, experience to date suggests that the *Charter* offers the promise of a stronger and more vibrant Canadian democracy.

GLOSSARY

Absolute liability: an offence for which the accused is guilty once it is proven that the prohibited act was committed and regardless of the existence of any fault, including negligence.

Affirmative action: positive measures intended to benefit a disadvantaged group.

Agency shop provision: provision in a collective agreement compelling payment of dues to a union by non-member employees.

Appellate court: the court which hears appeals from judgments of the trial courts. There are provincial appellate courts to hear appeals from the provincial courts and the provincial superior courts, and a Federal Court of Appeal to hear appeals from the Federal Court, Trial Division.

Attorney general: the member of Cabinet who is the senior legal adviser to the government and who is ultimately accountable for prosecutions.

Civil law: a legal system in which private law is enacted by the legislature and is predominantly contained in a Civil Code. It is in contradistinction to the common law where the basis of private law is judge-made. Quebec has a civil law tradition.

Closed shop provisions: provision in a collective agreement compelling membership in a union.

Commercial expression: expression conveyed for the purpose of earning money, usually in the form of advertising.

Common law: judge-made law, reflected by precedents established by the decisions of the courts, as distinct from statute-law passed by the legislature. In all provinces other than Quebec, the primary source of private law is the common law.

Constitutional convention: an unwritten rule, rather than formal laws, that is enforced through the political process rather than in the courts. The Canadian constitution consists of the written constitutional texts, judicial precedents, and constitutional conventions.

Constitutional exemption: the law remains valid for all purposes, save that the court exempts a particular individual or situation from its application.

Damages: monetary award received by the injured party to compensate for the wrong suffered.

Declaratory proceedings: a suit in which the only relief sought is a statement by the court delineating the ambit of a right or stating that a statute or practice is contrary to the constitution, with no other concrete remedy provided.

Deference: the view that a court order is not the appropriate solution and that the matter should be left to the legislature.

Disclosure: the obligation of the Crown to notify the accused prior to trial of any evidence it intends to use and any evidence that might assist the accused, even if the Crown does not intend to adduce such evidence at trial.

Division of powers: the consitutional allocation of authority between the federal and provincial governments to enact legislation.

Dualism: the conception of Canadian Confederation as being a historical compromise between the French- and English-speaking communities.

Due process: principles of procedural fairness which have evolved through the common law.

Ex parte **injunction:** an injunction issued without notice to the defendant.

Expression: any activity that conveys or attempts to convey meaning.

Federalism: a governmental structure whereby the power to legislate is divided between various levels of government. In Canada, the division of powers is between the Parliament of Canada and the ten provincial legislatures.

Federalism review: judicial consideration of whether Parliament or a provincial legislature has the authority under the division of powers to enact legislation.

Freedom: ". . . embraces both the absence of coercion and constraint, and the right to manifest beliefs and practices." *R. v. Big M Drug Mart* (1985), 18 D.L.R. (4th) 321 at 354.

Gerrymandering: term connoting the exercise of self-interest on the part of political incumbents in control of the process of drawing electoral boundary lines.

Habeas corpus: a common law remedy, permitting anyone who is detained to require the person having custody to bring the detainee immediately before a court and to provide legal justification.

Injunction: an order of the court requiring a party to perform some act or refrain from some conduct so as to respect the rights of another.

Judicial activism: an inclination by the court to be fairly bold about striking down laws and policies that contravene the constitution.

Judicial Committee of the Privy Council: during the British Empire, the Privy Council was the final court of appeal for the colonies. The right of appeal from the Supreme Court of Canada to the Privy Council was abolished in 1949.

Judicial interim release: the release of an accused person pending trial, formerly referred to as bail.

Judicial review: the power of the courts to determine the constitutionality of legislation enacted by the people's elected representatives. It is a consequence of having a written constitution that is the supreme law of the land.

Judicial restraint: an inclination by the court to be more cautious about overturning government laws and policies.

Jurisdiction: legal authority to decide.

Legislative override: section 33 of the *Charter of Rights and Freedoms* permits a legislature to declare, for a period of five years, that a law shall operate "notwithstanding a provision included in section 2 or sections 7 to 15" of the *Charter*.

Natural justice: procedural rights evolved by the common law which apply when a decision affecting one's legal rights is taken, including the right to be heard by an impartial tribunal.

Negative right: a right to be left alone, therefore precluding Parliament or a legislature from interfering.

Notwithstanding clause: see "Legislative override."

Oakes **test:** the method described by the Supreme Court of Canada for determining whether a law that violates a fundamental right or freedom should be saved as a reasonable limit under section 1.

Override: see "Legislative override."

Parliamentary supremacy: the principle that the elected representatives of the people, assembled in Parliament, have unlimited power to make the law, the one exception being that Parliament cannot bind its successors.

Positive right: a right to be accorded some privilege or benefit, therefore requiring action on the part of Parliament or a legislature.

Presumption of constitutionality: the presumption that evolved under federalism that legislation enacted by Parliament or a legislature does not violate the constitution.

Presumption of innocence: the principle, now protected by section 11(d) of the Charter, that everyone accused of a crime is presumed to be innocent until the Crown has proven the accused's guilt beyond a reasonable doubt to the satisfaction of a judge or jury.

Prima facie: a case of sufficient weight presented by the party having the burden of proof to warrant judgment in that party's favour absent a response from the other side.

Private action: acts by individuals or corporations not subject to the direct control of government.

Proportionality: the central element of the *Oakes* test under section 1, weighing the breach of *Charter* rights against the government interest advanced by a challenged law.

Provincial court: a court consisting of judges appointed by a provincial government which deals with criminal cases not tried by jury, family matters, and small civil claims.

Punitive damages: monetary award to an injured party designed to punish the wrongdoer and deter others from taking the same course of conduct, rather than to compensate the injured party.

Purposive approach: a method of interpretation based upon delving into the fundamental and underlying reason for a law or constitutional guarantee.

Reading down: where the Court gives an over-inclusive statute a sufficiently narrow interpretation to bring it into line with the demands of the constitution.

Reading in: where the Court adds something to a statute to make it conform to the constitution.

Regulatory offences: offences that regulate risky behaviour that may cause harm but do not ordinarily involve truly criminal or morally reprehensible behaviour.

Rule of law: the ideal of the supremacy of law in the social order. There are three aspects to the rule of law: no one can be punished except for breach of a duly enacted law; everyone, from the highest official to the ordinary citizen, is subject to the ordinary law of the land; the courts have ultimate responsibility for the protection of right and respect for the legal order.

Search and seizure: state activity that invades a reasonable expectation of privacy.

Severance: where the court excises a discreet and identifiable measure of the challenged law without altering the overall structure or operation of the law in which it is contained.

Reference: the government may refer directly to the court questions of law or fact concerning the interpretation of the constitution, or the constitutionality of any legislation. A reference is an exception to the usual two-party, adversarial system.

Standing: the requirement that an individual must show a specific legal right or interest before bringing an action to challenge the constitutional validity of a law.

Stare decisis: the principle by which decisions of a higher court are binding on and must be followed by lower courts.

Stay of proceedings: a disposition where the court does not allow a prosecution to proceed because of objectionable police or prosecutorial conduct or a violation of the accused's rights.

Superior court: the highest level of trial court in each province. The judges of the superior courts are appointed by the federal government. The superior courts have exercise over a broad jurisdiction in both civil and criminal cases and have the authority to apply both federal and provincial laws.

Temporary suspension of invalidity: where the Court finds a law to be unconstitutional, but delays the implementation of its order of invalidity to afford Parliament or the legislature the opportunity to repair the constitutional deficiency.

Torts: non-contractual civil wrongs recognized at common law.

Under-inclusive law: a law that is found to be constitutionally defective in that it fails to extend its reach to those who have a constitutional claim to its protection.

CONSTITUTION ACT, 1982

SCHEDULE B
Constitution Act, 1982

PART I
CANADIAN CHARTER OF RIGHTS AND FREEDOMS

Whereas Canada is founded upon principles that recognize the supremacy of God and the rule of law:

Guarantee of Rights and Freedoms

Rights and freedoms in Canada

1. The *Canadian Charter of Rights and Freedoms* guarantees the rights and freedoms set out in it subject only to such reasonable limits prescribed by law as can be demonstrably justified in a free and democratic society.

Fundamental Freedoms

Fundamental freedoms

2. Everyone has the following fundamental freedoms:
   (*a*) freedom of conscience and religion;
   (*b*) freedom of thought, belief, opinion and expression, including freedom of the press and other media of communication;
   (*c*) freedom of peaceful assembly; and
   (*d*) freedom of association.

Democratic Rights

Democratic rights of citizens

3. Every citizen of Canada has the right to vote in an election of members of the House of Commons or of a legislative assembly and to be qualified for membership therein.

Maximum duration of legislative bodies

4. (1) No House of Commons and no legislative assembly shall continue for longer than five years from the date fixed for the return of the writs of a general election of its members.

Continuation in special circumstances

(2) In time of real or apprehended war, invasion or insurrection, a House of Commons may be continued by Parliament and a legisla-

tive assembly may be continued by the legislature beyond five years
if such continuation is not opposed by the votes of more than one-
third of the members of the House of Commons or the legislative
assembly, as the case may be.

Annual sitting of legislative bodies

5.   There shall be a sitting of Parliament and of each legislature at least
once every twelve months.

Mobility Rights

Mobility of citizens

6.   (1) Every citizen of Canada has the right to enter, remain in and
leave Canada.

Rights to move and gain livelihood

(2) Every citizen of Canada and every person who has the status of
a permanent resident of Canada has the right
(*a*) to move to and take up residence in any province; and
(*b*) to pursue the gaining of a livelihood in any province.

Limitation

(3) The rights specified in subsection (2) are subject to
(*a*) any laws or practices of general application in force in a province other than those that discriminate among persons primarily on
the basis of province of present or previous residence; and
(*b*) any laws providing for reasonable residency requirements as a
qualification for the receipt of publicly provided social services.

Affirmative action programs

(4) Subsections (2) and (3) do not preclude any law, program or
activity that has as its object the amelioration in a province of conditions of individuals in that province who are socially or economically disadvantaged if the rate of employment in that province is
below the rate of employment in Canada.

Legal Rights

Life, liberty and security of person

7.   Everyone has the right to life, liberty and security of the person and
the right not to be deprived thereof except in accordance with the
principles of fundamental justice.

Search or seizure

8. Everyone has the right to be secure against unreasonable search or seizure.

Detention or imprisonment

9. Everyone has the right not to be arbitrarily detained or imprisoned.

Arrest or detention

10. Everyone has the right on arrest or detention
    (*a*) to be informed promptly of the reasons therefor;
    (*b*) to retain and instruct counsel without delay and to be informed of that right; and
    (*c*) to have the validity of the detention determined by way of *habeas corpus* and to be released if the detention is not lawful.

Proceedings in criminal and penal matters

11. Any person charged with an offence has the right
    (*a*) to be informed without unreasonable delay of the specific offence;
    (*b*) to be tried within a reasonable time;
    (*c*) not to be compelled to be a witness in proceedings against that person in respect of the offence;
    (*d*) to be presumed innocent until proven guilty according to law in a fair and public hearing by an independent and impartial tribunal;
    (*e*) not to be denied reasonable bail without just cause;
    (*f*) except in the case of an offence under military law tried before a military tribunal, to the benefit of trial by jury where the maximum punishment for the offence is imprisonment for five years or a more severe punishment;
    (*g*) not to be found guilty on account of any act or omission unless, at the time of the act or omission, it constituted an offence under Canadian or international law or was criminal according to the general principles of law recognized by the community of nations;
    (*h*) if finally acquitted of the offence, not to be tried for it again and, if finally found guilty and punished for the offence, not to be tried or punished for it again; and
    (*i*) if found guilty of the offence and if the punishment for the offence has been varied between the time of commission and the time of sentencing, to the benefit of the lesser punishment.

Treatment or punishment

12. Everyone has the right not to be subjected to any cruel and unusual treatment or punishment.

Self-crimination

13. A witness who testifies in any proceedings has the right not to have any incriminating evidence so given used to incriminate that witness in any other proceedings, except in a prosecution for perjury or for the giving of contradictory evidence.

Interpreter

14. A party or witness in any proceedings who does not understand or speak the language in which the proceedings are conducted or who is deaf has the right to the assistance of an interpreter.

Equality Rights

Equality before and under law and equal protection and benefit of law

15. (1) Every individual is equal before and under the law and has the right to the equal protection and equal benefit of the law without discrimination and, in particular, without discrimination based on race, national or ethnic origin, colour, religion, sex, age or mental or physical disability.

Affirmative action programs

(2) Subsection (1) does not preclude any law, program or activity that has as its object the amelioration of conditions of disadvantaged individuals or groups including those that are disadvantaged because of race, national or ethnic origin, colour, religion, sex, age or mental or physical disability.

Official Languages of Canada

Official languages of Canada

16. (1) English and French are the official languages of Canada and have equality of status and equal rights and privileges as to their use in all institutions of the Parliament and government of Canada.

Official languages of New Brunswick

(2) English and French are the official languages of New Brunswick and have equality of status and equal rights and privileges as to their use in all institutions of the legislature and government of New Brunswick.

Advancement of status and use

(3) Nothing in this Charter limits the authority of Parliament or a legislature to advance the equality of status or use of English and French.

English and French linguistic communities in New Brunswick

16.1 (1) The English linguistic community and the French linguistic community in New Brunswick have equality of status and equal rights and privileges, including the right to distinct educational institutions and such distinct cultural institutions as are necessary for the preservation and promotion of those communities.

Role of the legislature and government of New Brunswick

(2) The role of the legislature and government of New Brunswick to preserve and promote the status, rights and privileges referred to in subsection (1) is affirmed.

Proceedings of Parliament

17. (1) Everyone has the right to use English or French in any debates and other proceedings of Parliament.

Proceedings of New Brunswick legislature

(2) Everyone has the right to use English or French in any debates and other proceedings of the legislature of New Brunswick.

Parliamentary statutes and records

18. (1) The statutes, records and journals of Parliament shall be printed and published in English and French and both language versions are equally authoritative.

New Brunswick statutes and records

(2) The statutes, records and journals of the legislature of New Brunswick shall be printed and published in English and French and both language versions are equally authoritative.

Proceedings in courts established by Parliament

19. (1) Either English or French may be used by any person in, or in any pleading in or process issuing from, any court established by Parliament.

Proceedings in New Brunswick courts

(2) Either English or French may be used by any person in, or in any pleading in or process issuing from, any court of New Brunswick.

Communications by public with federal institutions

20. (1) Any member of the public in Canada has the right to communicate with, and to receive available services from, any head or central office of an institution of the Parliament or government of Canada in English or French, and has the same right with respect to any other office of any such institution where

(*a*) there is a significant demand for communications with and services from that office in such language; or

(*b*) due to the nature of the office, it is reasonable that communications with and services from that office be available in both English and French.

Communications by public with New Brunswick institutions

(2) Any member of the public in New Brunswick has the right to communicate with, and to receive available services from, any office of an institution of the legislature or government of New Brunswick in English or French.

Continuation of existing constitutional provisions

21. Nothing in sections 16 to 20 abrogates or derogates from any right, privilege or obligation with respect to the English and French languages, or either of them, that exists or is continued by virtue of any other provision of the Constitution of Canada.

Rights and privileges preserved

22. Nothing in sections 16 to 20 abrogates or derogates from any legal or customary right or privilege acquired or enjoyed either before or after the coming into force of this Charter with respect to any language that is not English or French.

Minority Language Educational Rights

Language of instruction

23. (1) Citizens of Canada

(*a*) whose first language learned and still understood is that of the English or French linguistic minority population of the province in which they reside, or

(*b*) who have received their primary school instruction in Canada in English or French and reside in a province where the language in which they received that instruction is the language of the English or French linguistic minority population of the province, have the right to have their children receive primary and secondary school instruction in that language in that province.

Continuity of language instruction

(2) Citizens of Canada of whom any child has received or is receiving primary or secondary school instruction in English or French in

Canada, have the right to have all their children receive primary and secondary school instruction in the same language.

Application where numbers warrant

(3) The right of citizens of Canada under subsections (1) and (2) to have their children receive primary and secondary school instruction in the language of the English or French linguistic minority population of a province

(*a*) applies wherever in the province the number of children of citizens who have such a right is sufficient to warrant the provision to them out of public funds of minority language instruction; and

(*b*) includes, where the number of those children so warrants, the right to have them receive that instruction in minority language educational facilities provided out of public funds.

Enforcement

Enforcement of guaranteed rights and freedoms

24. (1) Anyone whose rights or freedoms, as guaranteed by this Charter, have been infringed or denied may apply to a court of competent jurisdiction to obtain such remedy as the court considers appropriate and just in the circumstances.

Exclusion of evidence bringing administration of justice into disrepute

(2) Where, in proceedings under subsection (1), a court concludes that evidence was obtained in a manner that infringed or denied any rights or freedoms guaranteed by this Charter, the evidence shall be excluded if it is established that, having regard to all the circumstances, the admission of it in the proceedings would bring the administration of justice into disrepute.

General

Aboriginal rights and freedoms not affected by Charter

25. The guarantee in this Charter of certain rights and freedoms shall not be construed so as to abrogate or derogate from any aboriginal, treaty or other rights or freedoms that pertain to the aboriginal peoples of Canada including

(*a*) any rights or freedoms that have been recognized by the Royal Proclamation of October 7, 1763; and

(*b*) any rights or freedoms that now exist by way of land claims agreements or may be so acquired.

Other rights and freedoms not affected by Charter

26. The guarantee in this Charter of certain rights and freedoms shall not be construed as denying the existence of any other rights or freedoms that exist in Canada.

Multicultural heritage

27. This Charter shall be interpreted in a manner consistent with the preservation and enhancement of the multicultural heritage of Canadians.

Rights guaranteed equally to both sexes

28. Notwithstanding anything in this Charter, the rights and freedoms referred to in it are guaranteed equally to male and female persons.

Rights respecting certain schools preserved

29. Nothing in this Charter abrogates or derogates from any rights or privileges guaranteed by or under the Constitution of Canada in respect of denominational, separate or dissentient schools.

Application to territories and territorial authorities

30. A reference in this Charter to a Province or to the legislative assembly or legislature of a province shall be deemed to include a reference to the Yukon Territory and the Northwest Territories, or to the appropriate legislative authority thereof, as the case may be.

Legislative powers not extended

31. Nothing in this Charter extends the legislative powers of any body or authority.

Application of Charter

Application of Charter

32. (1) This Charter applies
    (*a*) to the Parliament and government of Canada in respect of all matters within the authority of Parliament including all matters relating to the Yukon Territory and Northwest Territories; and
    (*b*) to the legislature and government of each province in respect of all matters within the authority of the legislature of each province.

Exception

(2) Notwithstanding subsection (1), section 15 shall not have effect until three years after this section comes into force.

Exception where express declaration

33. (1) Parliament or the legislature of a province may expressly declare in an Act of Parliament or of the legislature, as the case may be, that the Act or a provision thereof shall operate notwithstanding a provision included in section 2 or sections 7 to 15 of this Charter.

Operation of exception

(2) An Act or a provision of an Act in respect of which a declaration made under this section is in effect shall have such operation as it would have but for the provision of this Charter referred to in the declaration.

Five year limitation

(3) A declaration made under subsection (1) shall cease to have effect five years after it comes into force or on such earlier date as may be specified in the declaration.

Re-enactment

(4) Parliament or the legislature of a province may re-enact a declaration made under subsection (1).

Five year limitation

(5) Subsection (3) applies in respect of a re-enactment made under subsection (4).

Citation

Citation

34. This Part may be cited as the *Canadian Charter of Rights and Freedoms.*

PART VII
GENERAL

Primacy of Constitution of Canada

52. (1) The Constitution of Canada is the supreme law of Canada, and any law that is inconsistent with the provisions of the Constitution is, to the extent of the inconsistency, of no force or effect.

TABLE OF CASES

INDEX

ABOUT THE AUTHORS

Robert Sharpe was formerly a professor at the Faculty of Law, University of Toronto, where he wrote and taught in the areas of constitutional law, remedies, civil procedure, and criminal law. From 1990 to 1995 he served as Dean of the Faculty. He has appeared as counsel in a number of *Charter* cases in courts at all levels, including the Supreme Court of Canada. From 1988 to 1990, he served as the Supreme Court's Executive Legal Officer. Robert Sharpe was elected a Fellow of the Royal Society of Canada in 1991. He was appointed to the Ontario Court of Justice (General Division) in 1995.

Katherine Swinton taught and wrote extensively in the areas of Canadian constitutional law, federalism and public policy, and employment discrimination law as a professor at Osgoode Hall Law School, York University, and the Faculty of Law, University of Toronto. Prior to commencing her teaching career, she was a law clerk to the Honourable Mr. Justice R.G.B. Dickson at the Supreme Court of Canada. She has been an adviser to both federal and provincial governments on issues of constitutional law and federalism, and has been a labour arbitrator in both the public and private sectors. In 1997 she was appointed to the Ontario Court of Justice (General Division).